Pioneering Places of British Aviation

Pioneering Places of British Aviation

The Early Years of Powered Flight in the UK

Bruce Hales-Dutton

AIR WORLD

First published in Great Britain in 2020 by
Air World
An imprint of
Pen & Sword Books Ltd
Yorkshire – Philadelphia

ISBN 978 1 52675 0 150

A CIP catalogue record for this book is
available from the British Library.

Typeset by Mac Style
Printed and bound in England by TJ International Ltd,
Padstow, Cornwall

Pen & Sword Books Limited incorporates the imprints of Atlas,
Archaeology, Aviation, Discovery, Family History, Fiction, History,
Maritime, Military, Military Classics, Politics, Select, Transport, True
Crime, Air World, Frontline Publishing, Leo Cooper, Remember When,
Seaforth Publishing, The Praetorian Press, Wharncliffe Local History,
Wharncliffe Transport, Wharncliffe True Crime and White Owl.

For a complete list of Pen & Sword titles please contact

PEN & SWORD BOOKS LIMITED
47 Church Street, Barnsley, South Yorkshire, S70 2AS, England
E-mail: enquiries@pen-and-sword.co.uk
Website: www.pen-and-sword.co.uk

Or
PEN AND SWORD BOOKS
1950 Lawrence Rd, Havertown, PA 19083, USA
E-mail: Uspen-and-sword@casematepublishers.com
Website: www.penandswordbooks.com

Contents

Introduction

Those magnificent men in their flying machines,
They go up, tiddly up, up,
They go down, tiddly down, down.

The 1965 20th Century Fox movie *Those Magnificent Men in Their Flying Machines* was noteworthy for its use of replicas of period aircraft to recreate an early twentieth century airfield. In the film the airfield is called 'Brookley' but is clearly intended to represent Brooklands in Surrey which combined a banked motor racing track with facilities for pioneer aviators to test their aircraft.

In the film, Brookley acts as the starting point for the first London to Paris air race for which a newspaper magnate is offering a winner's purse of £10,000. He is persuaded to do this after hearing the shocking news that the first aeroplane flight in England was made only a couple of years earlier.

Britain did indeed enter the air age well behind the USA. And when the nation finally celebrated its first powered aeroplane flight it was actually achieved by an American. France was also ahead of Britain, although Europe was struggling to catch up with the Wright brothers.

But over the next few years intrepid – and wealthy – young men sought to make up for lost time. By 1911, according to one observer, flying fever was gripping Britain. In those innocent days of peace, aviation was seen primarily as a recreational activity or even a sport.

Indeed, in June 1911 the journal *Flight* was reporting that grandstands were being built for spectators at Shoreham airfield near Worthing, which was to be a waypoint in the real Paris–London–Paris air race. John Moore-Brabazon's 1909 flight with a pig stuffed into a waste paper basket lashed to his aircraft and his proclamation that pigs can fly was typical of the light-hearted approach to aviation.

But all this activity stimulated further interest and airfields were established up and down the country. Most were short-lived and soon fell into disuse, but a few remain in operation over a century later.

Only a handful can claim to have had a significant influence on the development of British aviation. Typical are Brooklands and Eastchurch on the Isle of Sheppey in Kent. Both claim to be the home of British aviation, even though it was Farnborough in Hampshire which was the site of Samuel Cody's first flight in 1908. A claim has also been made for Hendon, west of London, to be recognised as aviation's cradle; and what about Battersea which, for a brief while, could claim to be the centre of British aircraft manufacture?

Brooklands is probably better known for the spectacular banked track which justifies its boast to be the world's first purpose-built motor racing circuit. This is indisputable, yet by 1911 more spectators were watching the aeroplanes than the cars. Indeed, it could be argued that motor racing was essentially a sideshow compared with the manufacture of aircraft which took place on the site for over six decades. Nearly 19,000 machines, ranging from Sopwith Camels to Vickers VC10s, were assembled there.

The entrepreneurial Short Brothers reached an agreement with the Wright Brothers to build under licence six replicas of the American pioneers' *Flyer* at Eastchurch. The Aero Club moved there in search of ideal flying conditions and its members later trained the Navy's first aviators. Meanwhile, Larkhill on Salisbury Plain was established as Britain's first military airfield.

It is those pioneering places which form the subject of this book. It also attempts to unravel the claims and counter-claims to determine which of them can really call itself the birthplace of British aviation. Of course, this is also a story about people. It was, after all, the exploits of the intrepid pioneer aviators which brought fame and distinction to the places from which they operated.

And of course, class comes into it too. In 1910 *Flight* suggested the reason why French aviators were more successful than their British counterparts was that they were 'largely of the mechanic class' and therefore more likely to master 'the practical side of flight than our own amateurs'. A case of gentlemen versus players, perhaps. It was certainly true, though, that many of Britain's aviation pioneers came from the aristocracy, like Moore-Brabazon and the Hon Charles Rolls.

Generally this is a story of powered flight by heavier-than-air craft – aeroplanes in other words – although balloons and airships certainly merit more than a passing mention. It would, after all, be unforgivable to omit the exploits of Ernest Willows, if only because there is a Wetherspoons pub in Cardiff named after him.

The story opens a century before sustained and powered flight became a reality. It links places as distinct and as distant as the grounds of a stately home in North Yorkshire and the town of Chard in Somerset where Caley, Stringfellow and Henson developed the ideas that would make manned flight a reality.

That would not happen until the early years of the twentieth century, and within less than two decades aviation was playing a key role in in the First World War. During an incredibly short period the aeroplane had moved from curiosity to potent weapon of war which was also about to begin a revolution in civil transport.

Bruce Hales-Dutton
West Malling
December 2018

Summary of Key Locations and Events

Brompton Hall, Brompton-By-Sawdon, Scarborough, North Yorkshire – study of flight and aerodynamics, early experiments with models aeroplanes, 1796–1857.

Chard, South Somerset – early experiments with model aeroplanes, 1842–1848.

Bexleyheath, London Borough of Bexley – experiments by Hiram Maxim 1889/94.

Eynsford, (Upper Auston Lodge), Sevenoaks, Kent – gliding experiments by Percy Pilcher 1896/97.

Battersea, London Borough of Wandsworth – balloon flights, construction of balloons from 1906, manufacture of aeroplanes from 1908.

Lea Marshes, London Borough of Hackney – experiments by A V Roe culminating in his being recognised as the first Briton to flying in a British-built aeroplane 1908/09.

Farnborough, Borough of Rushmoor, Hampshire – Army Balloon Factory, part of the Army School of Ballooning, re-located from Aldershot 1904/06; Cody's experiments with man-lifting kites; early experiments with powered aircraft leading to first sustained flight by Cody of man-carrying aeroplane in England, 1908; site of Royal Aircraft Factory which became Royal Aircraft Establishment, 1918.

Brooklands, Borough of Elmbridge, Surrey – early experiments by A V Roe and others from 1908, flying contests, flying training and manufacturer of aircraft by Sopwith, Martinsyde and Vickers (later British Aircraft Corporation, British Aerospace and BAe Systems).

Eastchurch, Isle of Sheppey, Kent – main flying ground of Royal Aero Club from 1909/10, site of first powered aeroplane flight by a Briton (Moore–Brabazon), first circular flight of one mile (also Moore-Brabazon), site of flying instruction for RN personnel, site of Royal Naval Air Station, later RAF Eastchurch.

Doncaster, South Yorkshire, site of first flying meeting in Britain, 1909.

Blackpool, (Squires Gate), Lancashire, site of first officially-sanctioned flying meeting in Britain, 1909.

Lanark racecourse, South Lanarkshire, site of first flying meeting in Scotland 1910.

Hendon, London Borough of Barnet – promoted by Claude Grahame-White as site of first London aerodrome; site of first Aerial Derby in 1912 and numerous flying meetings and contests; closed as RAF station 1987; site of RAF Museum.

Larkhill, Durrington, Wiltshire – site of Britain's first military airfield, 1909, site of military aircraft trials, 1912; closed 1914.

Chapter 1

The Flying Coachman

In considering the places where the early aviators were active in furthering the development of British aviation you can start pretty much where you like.

In the very earliest days a tall building would do. But those determined to emulate the birds by strapping on a pair of wings, flapping vigorously and jumping, found there was more to it than that. When, in the nineteenth century, careful scientific analysis offered the first glimmerings of understanding the principles underlying sustained and controllable mechanical flight, it became clear that experiments could be conducted more or less anywhere, from the stairwell of a mansion to a disused laceworks.

For thousands of years humankind had dreamed of emulating the birds. Most who attempted to do this are, inevitably, unknown but in the ninth century AD King Bladud was one of those who tried with the aid of a pair of home-made wings. His name is known because he was also the son of King Lear immortalised by Shakespeare. His attempt to fly by jumping off a high building and flapping his wings ended with a heavy landing in the Temple of Apollo in the city of Trinavantum, better known today as London.

This set the fashion for the next 2,000 years. In two millennia of death and injury the most original excuse for failure might have come from John Damian who thought he could fly to France from Scotland. Watched by King James IV and his entourage, he stepped clear of the wreckage to declare that the reason for his fall to earth was that he had used for his wings the feathers of chickens instead of eagles!

It was a Yorkshire baronet who effectively brought years of tower-jumping to an end. In any case, by the beginning of the nineteenth century flight had been possible for fifty years. Man-carrying balloons had become well-established, although they relied too much on the wind to be regarded as a serious means of transportation. Meanwhile a few visionaries were coming to the realisation that the mechanics of sustained and navigable flight were rather more complex and subtle than wing-flapping.

Among them is Sir George Caley, the Yorkshire baronet who conducted most of his experiments at his ancestral home of Brompton Hall in the village of Brompton-by-Sawdon, eight miles west of Scarborough. In the twenty-first century it is a special school for boys between the ages of 8 and 16, which, according to Ofsted, caters for 'pupils who have struggled previously in other schools and have had to cope with difficulties in their home lives'.

It is perhaps appropriate that Brompton Hall should have become an educational establishment. Two centuries earlier this dignified sandstone mansion was inherited by Caley, who was not quite 19 when, in 1799, he became the sixth baronet. He was a man of wide interests in the fields of science and engineering and one who has since been hailed as a genius.

Among the products of Caley's restless brain was the design for an artificial hand, a device he patented as the 'universal railway' but which would be recognised today as the caterpillar tractor, and forms of internal combustion engines powered by gunpowder and hot air. He co-founded the British Association for the Advancement of Science and founded the Polytechnic Institution which later became the Regent Street Polytechnic and is now part of the University of Westminster.

If these achievements were not enough, Caley is better known for his scientific investigation of the underlying principles and forces of flight and for being the first to develop an understanding of them. This is why he has been called the father of the aeroplane even though his name is scarcely known outside aviation circles.

Caley was born in December 1773 at Scarborough, although the precise location of this event seems to be unknown. A blue plaque puts it at Paradise House close to the old Parish Church of St Mary's which is also the last resting place of novelist Anne Brontë. Caley, however, spent most of his life at Brompton Hall, often working with a local mechanic called Thomas Vick in a hexagonal stone building set into the wall surrounding the hall beside what is today the Pickering road. Testing of his aeroplanes was often conducted opposite at Brompton Dale.

This may have been the location of what were probably the first ever manned flights by a heavier-than-air aircraft. The first, in 1849, involved a boat-shaped glider suspended from a triplane wing which carried a 10-year-old boy. His identity is not known for certain and nor is that of the occupant of the second, larger machine. It seems most likely, however, that in the days when servants knew their place that it was one of Caley's employees, most likely his coachman because he is recorded as pleading with his employer: 'Please, Sir George, I wish to give notice. I was hired to drive, not fly!'

Throughout his life Caley published his ideas in a series of papers and magazine articles but generally they remained obscure and known only within a limited circle. Yet although the full extent of his contribution did not become apparent until the mid-twentieth century with the discovery of key documents, the Wright brothers were certainly aware of Caley and his work. In 1909 Wilbur Wright was quoted as saying,

> About 100 years ago an Englishman, Sir George Cayley, carried the science of flying to a point which it had never reached before and which it scarcely reached again during the last century.

Caley began his aeronautical studies in 1796, and in 1799, the last year of the century which had seen the invention of the hot-air balloon and the ascent of the first aviators, he produced illustrations which clearly depicted the forces that apply to flight. In 1804, a year before the Battle of Trafalgar, Caley was sketching out a model glider of strikingly modern appearance, and as early as 1809 he was setting out what today are recognised as the scientific bases of aerodynamics. And all this before railways and the steam locomotive had been invented.

Caley had built his first aerial device in 1796. It was essentially a model helicopter which represented an improved Chinese flying top but it proved that considerable lift and, consequently, thrust could be obtained from an efficient airscrew. As described in a paper dated 1809, it involved two corks mounted at either end of a shaft with four feathers projecting from them like propeller blades. The device was powered by a bow and string which were used to store energy as the bow was tightened. An interesting point about this toy is that, while it served as Cayley's practical introduction to flight, he largely avoided use of the propeller throughout his subsequent aeroplane experiments.

The shy, chubby country squire also set out to understand the forces that kept birds so effortlessly in the air. Caley was convinced that these forces could be harnessed to mechanical flight and so realise his vision of mass air travel across, as he so eloquently put it, 'the uninterrupted navigable ocean that comes to the threshold of every man's door'.

By the age of 26, Caley had divined the physical basis of flight, correctly identifying the fundamental force of lift that had baffled previous generations of experimenters and would-be aviators. Caley saw that the birds he studied achieved their lift from wings which were cambered with convex curves from front to rear. He discovered that a cambered wing's lifting power was produced by the passage of air flowing over it.

He then took what has come to be regarded as the first step towards the invention of the aeroplane when he engraved an illustration of his ideas on one face of a small silver disc. The key feature is that the propulsion and lifting systems were completely separated. Hitherto, flight had been attempted, unsuccessfully, by the use of flapping wings in a supposed emulation of bird flight. In Cayley's concept the lifting wing was a stationary low-aspect-ratio sail, its flexible surface cambered taut by the surrounding air pressure field. The separate propulsion system was a pilot-operated flapper arrangement which owed much to the past. A cruciform rudder was provided, presumably to enable the machine to be steered like a boat.

On the obverse Caley inscribed a simple diagram to illustrate the forces of lift and drag. What he failed to do – but what would come later – was to identify the true principal reason for lift by means of the creation of low-pressure 'suction' caused by the increased speed of the air rushing over the curved upper surface. Caley located the centre of this elusive force and established the equally crucial importance of the centre of the opposing force of gravity.

Having noticed how gliding birds held their wings in a shallow V to correct lateral rolling, Caley also realised the importance of the feature known as dihedral. When the birds rolled one way, he noticed that their lower wings generated more lift than the upper ones, swinging them back on to an even keel. He observed, too, that birds' wings were slightly tilted above the horizontal.

To simulate flight Caley built a rotating arm machine. It measured the variations in the force of the lift generated by airflow passing over a wing with its leading edge raised to face the flow, as the birds did, at different angles. Applied to aircraft wings, this would become known as the angle of attack.

Caley mounted his machine on a tripod, setting it at the top of the sweep of the grand baronial stairs at Brompton Hall. The arm was rotated by a chord pulled by a weight which he dangled above the entrance hall. To one side of the arm he attached a flat wing surface exactly a foot square, balancing it on the other with small ounce weights from the Brompton Hall kitchen scales. As the arm rotated, Caley raised the angle of the wing in three-degree increments. As it rose it produced more lift and supported progressively heavier weights.

But the lift only increased up to a point. When the wing was raised too far, its lifting power quite suddenly diminished. Caley had stumbled across the aerodynamic process that follows when an aircraft wing is raised too far – around 12 degrees – the airflow over the top surface breaks up, lift is lost and the wing stalls.

In a major intellectual leap Caley was able to design an aeroplane which, for the first time, would have separate systems for lift, propulsion and control. In the process he produced the cambered aeroplane wing. He also analysed the basis of mechanical flight – to make a surface support a given weight by the application of power to overcome the resistance of air.

Then in 1804 Cayley built the first practical glider. It was little more than a kite with a cruciform tail, but it established the relative positions of wing and tail units as on modern aircraft: and it flew. Five years later, having identified these physical forces, Caley began building gliders to test his theories. He launched them across a shallow valley on his estate.

Later he built and flew a pair of man-carrying craft whose flights would seal his place as a giant of aeronautical invention.

These were the world's first full-sized aeroplanes. They had cambered wings beneath which the pilots sat in a boat-shaped fuselage mounted on three wheels. An adjustable tail unit could be trimmed on the ground, while a separate rudder and elevator were pilot-operated. The only vital control missing was any form of aileron to correct rolling movement. Such devices were not to arrive for another half-century.

In 1816 and 1817 Caley turned his attention to lighter-than-air craft which transformed the familiar balloon into a more sophisticated device that could be steered: an airship, in other words. He proposed a streamlined craft with a tapered envelope built around a semi-rigid structure using separate gas bags to limit loss of lifting gas due to damage. Thrust was to be provided by flappers or propellers. He would return to these ideas in 1843 with a craft powered by a steam engine.

At that stage he seems to have regarded hydrogen-filled airships as more suitable for long-distance air travel. He emphasised the need for streamlining the envelope but like other designers he was prevented from advancing further by lack of a suitable engine. He did, however, indicate the next step in the human conquest of the air – development of a steerable, mechanically-propelled airship.

After 1818 Caley seems to have turned to other fields in which to exercise his inventive talents. He was, for example, concerned about safety on the railways and devoted much of his time to devising ways of making rail travel safer. Cayley's silence on the aeroplane continued until details of Henson's design for his 'Aerial Steam Carriage' emerged in 1843. This renewed Cayley's interest and involvement in the aeroplane. By now he was 70 years old yet, even at that advanced age, he had still much to contribute.

The first of Caley's machines, which also featured hand-pumped flappers protruding from the sides like dragonfly wings to provide forward propulsion, was flown in 1849 with a 10-year old boy as its 'pilot'. Another four years later Caley's petrified coachman flew several hundred yards across the valley. It is not clear to what extent the unfortunate man was in control of the device.

In a paper dated 1843 Caley published a description of what in later years would be termed a convertiplane. The lifting surfaces were four circular planform wings superimposed in pairs, each surface being slightly cambered, Caley said, 'like a very flat umbrella'. To provide lateral stability they were set at a marked angle of dihedral. For ascent or descent, these surfaces would have opened up into eight-bladed rotors, each pair on a common shaft, the latter being driven in contra-rotation by the fuselage-mounted engine. It would also have driven the rear propellers to provide forward motion.

There were no further manned flights, but Caley's aerodynamic work had taken the development of mechanical flight further than it had travelled in the whole course of human history to that point. Yet when he died in 1857 aged 84, *The Times* obituary made no mention of these achievements. Even though Caley had published some of his findings during his lifetime, it was to be another seventy years before his genius was to be fully revealed when his private papers were made public.

Although a description of his man-carrying gliders, illustrated with clear sketches, had appeared in a technical magazine in 1852, it seemed to have largely gone unnoticed. In 1960, aviation historian Charles Gibbs-Smith stumbled upon it. 'Here was the modern aeroplane – except for its engine and ailerons – and nobody noticed,' Gibbs-Smith observed. The following year more material, Caley's historically-significant notebooks, were published.

In 1842 a young inventor called Samuel Henson moved the development of the aeroplane a stage further using as his basis Caley's theories and his own experiments with model gliders. Henson, the son of a Nottingham lace maker, had moved to Chard where he was initially employed as a machinist in the local lacemaking industry, but he soon set up in business on his own.

From 1840 Henson began experiments with model gliders, corresponding with another enthusiast, John Stringfellow, about engine designs. In 1842 Henson submitted a patent application for what he called his Aerial Steam Carriage, which was effectively a steam-powered airliner. Henson and Stringfellow built a 20ft model which they attempted to fly, but without success, at Barlow Down. This can be seen in the Science Museum in South Kensington.

It looks crude by modern standards yet its design is more like that of a modern aeroplane than many which later flew successfully. However, Henson had let his imagination run free by issuing pictures of the aircraft in flight over London, France and even the Pyramids and then getting a Bill passed in Parliament to authorise the establishment of an Aerial Steam Transit company to operate world-wide air services. The whole thing was greeted with ridicule, and when his model failed to work Henson lost heart and in 1847 emigrated to the USA.

Stringfellow, however, carried on alone. He had been born in Sheffield and became a precision engineer specialising in the production of carriages and bobbins for the lace-making industry in Nottingham. To avoid the attentions of the Luddite movement, Stringfellow moved his business to Chard where, together with Henson, he began a study of bird flight.

In 1848 he built another model based on the Aerial Steam Carriage but with many improvements. Smaller than the earlier model, it had a wooden frame covered in silk. The wingspan was 10ft with a chord of 2ft at its widest part, tapering to a point at the tip with a rigid leading edge and a slightly curved upper surface.

The model was powered by a tiny steam engine designed and built by Stringfellow. It was located in a gondola below the wings and fired by a spirit lamp. It had a cylinder diameter of 0.75in and a stroke of 2in. Complete with water and fuel, the engine weighed 6.75lbs and drove two large propellers which rotated in opposite directions to give the machine lateral stability.

It was successfully flown inside a disused lace mill in Chard, and launched from an inclined supporting wire several yards long which ensured that the machine started flying at a reasonable speed and in the right direction. It flew a distance of 40 feet.

Writing in 1892, Stringfellow's son, also called John, recalled: 'The steam was successfully got up after a slight mishap; the machine started down the wire and, upon reaching the point of self-detachment, gradually rose until it reached the further end of the room, striking a hole in the canvas placed to stop it.'

It was the first-ever flight of a powered aeroplane. It later covered 120 feet in the open air. But nobody seemed keen to finance construction of a full-size machine, so John Stringfellow followed his friend and collaborator Samuel Henson to America. He did, however, return home to exhibit a model triplane at the first aeronautical exhibition staged by the Aeronautical Society of Great Britain (which had been formed two years earlier) at the Crystal Palace in 1868. The model was demonstrated to the Prince of Wales and the Duke of Sutherland. Flown from a wire, it was reported to have reached a speed of 20 mph. John Stringfellow died in 1883.

In the 1980s the BBC recreated the flight of Stringfellow's model inside a disused lace mill in Chard using a replica powered by a small modern petrol engine. Stringfellow's achievements have prompted the town of Chard to call itself the birthplace of powered flight. The museum and heritage centre at Godworthy House in the High Street has a section devoted to stringfellow and his achievements.

In 1866 a marine engineer who had studied the problem of human flight presented a perceptive and influential academic paper to the first meeting of the Aeronautical Society. Entitled *Aerial Locomotion*, Frank Wenham's paper was published in the Society's journal and reprinted in widely distributed aeronautical publications in the 1890s, including Octave Chanute's *Progress in Flying Machines* in the United States.

It introduced the idea of superposed wings in a flying machine, a concept that Wenham had tested in 1858 with a multi-wing glider, although it did not actually fly. In 1866 he patented the design, which became the basis for biplanes, triplanes and multiplanes that took to the air as gliders in the 1890s, and as aeroplanes in the early decades of the twentieth century. Superimposed wings increased the lifting area and avoided the structural problems of excessive wing length.

In 1866 Wenham produced a model with so many wings that it resembled a Venetian blind. Several further developments were sufficiently successful for Wenham to build a machine able to support a man. He tested it one evening hoping for calm conditions, but was taken by surprise when: 'A sudden gust caught up the experimenter, who was carried some distance from the ground.'

In 1871 Wenham and instrument maker John Browning designed and constructed what was probably the world's first wind tunnel. Their experiments showed that high aspect ratio wings – long and narrow – had a better lift-to-drag ratio than short stubby ones with the same lifting area. Writing about his work, Wenham may have been the first scientist to use the word 'aeroplane'. In any case, he had confirmed many of Caley's beliefs and laid down almost every basic principle upon which the theory and practice of aviation are founded.

Like Wenham, Horatio Phillips was attracted to the idea of multiple wings. Phillips is credited with advancing the aerofoil principle which established the basis for the design of subsequent aircraft wings. Working in his suburban villa in Streatham, south-west London, he too devised a wind tunnel in which he studied a wide variety of aerofoil shapes for generating lift. The tunnel's gas flow was provided by steam rather than air.

In around 1870 Phillips rented a railway arch at Battersea to use as a workshop and it was here that he built his first full-sized machine. Like many other pioneers, he was attracted by the idea of vertical lift and his first design was for a helicopter-type vehicle. Driven by a steam engine working at a pressure of 1,500 lbs per square inch, it featured a pair of contra-rotating propellers with cast steel blades, which were later replaced by pine wood screws 20 feet in diameter. The machine was taken for trials to nearby Battersea Fields where it failed to lift its own weight off the ground.

Phillips had now run out of money so he reverted to building models, which were tested at Norwood using a steam-powered catapult device to launch them. Further research led to his all-important patents of 1894 and 1891 for what he called the 'Phillips Dipping Entry Wing'. Indeed, Phillips' main contribution to aeronautical science was that he demonstrated the truth of Cayley's idea that giving the upper surface of a wing greater curvature than the lower accelerates the upper airflow, reducing pressure above the wing and so creating lift.

Phillips later built a series of machines with up to twenty superimposed wings in a frame. Inevitably they were known as 'Venetian blinds', but Phillips claimed that one of them actually flew. These aerofoil shapes were initially tried on a model powered by a 6 hp steam engine driving a twin-bladed pusher propeller. When tested on a circular track at Harrow, it reached a speed of 40 mph, and the two back wheels, which took most of the weight, actually rose off the ground.

In 1904 Phillips constructed a full-sized machine with twenty narrow aerofoil-profile wings in a single frame with a wingspan of 17ft 9in and mounted on a three-wheeled frame with a tail supported by a central boom. It had a four-cylinder, water-cooled 22 hp petrol engine built by Phillips himself. Mounted at the front, it drove a two-bladed propeller. It proved longitudinally unstable when tested at a farm at Mitcham, but was claimed to have managed a 50ft 'hop'. A replica appears in the opening sequences of the 1965 film *Those Magnificent Men in their Flying Machines*.

It was discarded in favour of a bigger machine which had four 'sustainer frames' mounted one behind the other each and having fifty blades. Its frame was made of spruce, ash and steel tubing and was powered by the engine removed from the previous model. Phillips claimed that this aircraft actually flew for around 500ft when tested at Norbury in 1907.

This claim was disputed although Charles Gibbs-Smith certainly accepted it. Writing in *Flight* in 1959, he said: 'In view of Phillips' previous achievements and his reputation and the fact that he never claimed to have made proper flights, it is difficult – if not impossible – not to accept his 500ft "hop" in 1907 as a fact.' But south London aviation historian Patrick Loobey believes that, as the only evidence to sustain Phillips' claim was his own statement, it was 'hardly an acceptable basis for an official "first"'.

In 1894 Sir Hiram Maxim built a four-ton steel-tube aircraft which was bigger than a Second World War Lancaster bomber. Yet it was not built to fly but to test some of Maxim's theories. An American-born inventor who was best known as the creator of the Maxim machine gun, he also held patents on numerous mechanical devices as varied as a mousetrap, hair curling irons and steam pumps. He also claimed to have invented the light bulb.

Maxim moved from the United States to the United Kingdom at the age of 41 and became a naturalised British subject 1899. He was knighted in 1901. After moving to England he settled in a large house in West Norwood, south London where he developed his design for an automatic firearm which operated by storing the recoil energy released by one shot to prepare the gun for its next. He ran announcements in the local press warning that he would be experimenting with the gun in his garden and that neighbours should keep their windows open to avoid the danger of broken glass.

In 1897 the Vickers Corporation formed Vickers, Son & Maxim, although Maxim resigned from the board in 1911 on his 71st birthday. The development of Maxim's design became the standard British machine gun for many years with variants used extensively by both sides during the First World War. The Vickers gun, however, became the standard armament mounted by British aircraft.

Maxim's father had conceived a helicopter powered by two contra-rotating rotors but was unable to find a powerful enough engine. Hiram Maxim first sketched out plans for a helicopter in 1872, but when he built his first 'flying machine' he chose to use fixed wings. Before starting design work, he carried out a series of experiments on aerofoil sections and propellers, initially using a wind tunnel and later a whirling arm test rig.

His attempts at flying a powered aircraft were less successful than his machine gun. Construction had started in 1889 of a 40-foot-long craft with a 110-foot wingspan that weighed 3.5 tons. It was powered by two lightweight naphtha-fired 360-horsepower steam engines driving two 17-foot-diameter laminated pine propellers.

Conceived as a test rig, the machine ran on an 1,800 foot length of rail track which Maxim laid for the purpose at his home, Baldwyn's Park Mansion, Bexley. The initial intention was to prevent the machine from lifting off by using heavy cast-iron wheels, but after initial trials, Maxim concluded that this would not suffice. The machine was fitted with four wheeled outriggers which were restrained by wooden rails 13 feet outside the central track.

During test runs in 1894, all the outriggers were engaged, showing that the machine had developed enough lift to take off, but in so doing, it pulled up the track; the tethered 'flight' was aborted in time to prevent disaster. Maxim subsequently abandoned it but put his experience to work on fairground rides.

Among Maxim's helpers was a young man called Percy Sinclair Pilcher. In 1896-97, seven years before the Wright Brothers' first manned flight in a powered aircraft, Pilcher was experimenting with his *Gull* and *Hawk* gliders at Upper Austin Lodge, Eynsford near Sevenoaks. The site had previously been used by Maxim as a range for testing automatic and quick-firing guns. The purpose-built hangar that housed Maxim's massive biplane had been relocated to this site in 1894, after the local authority insisted on its removal from Baldwyn's Park.

Pilcher had been greatly influenced by the work of two German brothers, Otto and Gustave Liliental, which is considered to have been the most significant in this field before the Wright brothers. Otto made over 2,000 flights in a series of what would now be called hang gliders to demonstrate that unpowered human flight was possible and that control of an aerial device while aloft was within reach. Otto died in August 1896 following the in-flight collapse of his glider. It was considered a distinct blow to progress in aeronautical development.

In the late summer of 1896, using Hiram Maxim's hangar as a base, Pilcher regularly flew his *Hawk* glider from both sides of the hill known as the 'Knob', achieving glides of up to 300 yards. On 20 June 1897 Pilcher gave his first public demonstration to a party of scientists and others. A thin 600-yard fishing line was passed through tackle on the opposite side of the West valley. Towed by three boys, man and machine rose to a height of about 70 ft before the line broke. Pilcher descended gracefully into the valley, having achieved a glide of between 150 and 250 yards.

What is believed to be the first recorded instance of a woman flying in a heavier- than-air aircraft occurred on the same day when Dorothy Rose Pilcher, Percy's cousin, made a short towed glide in the *Hawk*. She flew down the hill and collided with a man operating a cinematograph camera. Both camera and operator escaped serious damage, as did Dorothy.

Pilcher later designed and built a triplane fitted with an engine, but his trailblazing work was unfortunately terminated when, during a demonstration at Stanford Hall near Rugby on 30 September 1899, he crashed. Percy was fatally injured and died on 2 October aged 32. A monument to Pilcher was unveiled at Eynsford on 17 June 2006. The granite inscription plate set in a slab of Kentish ragstone reads:

PERCY SINCLAIR PILCHER
1866-1899

The British aviation pioneer who conducted extensive trials with full size hang gliders of his own design and construction from 1895 – 1899. He made successful towed flights in his *Hawk* glider from this site during 1896–1897.

The triplane was never flown. Had Pilcher survived this tragic accident, he might have become the first person to fly a powered aeroplane. Nevertheless, he made a valuable contribution to aviation's early development.

By the turn of the century many of the necessary ingredients of powered flight were in place. The major deficiency, however, was the lack of a suitable power source, but the invention of the internal combustion engine removed even this difficulty. The stage was now set for the Wright brothers to assemble all the building blocks of aviation that had been painstakingly fashioned at Brompton Hall, in Chard, in London, in Eynsford and elsewhere to realise the dream of millennia.

The scene therefore changes from the attractive Kentish village of Eynsford in the Darenth Valley, whose charms were captured in the paintings of Samuel Palmer, to the dusty wind-blown sand dunes of Kill Devil Hills, North Carolina. At aviation's first and most celebrated pioneering place on 17 December 1903, Orville and Wilbur Wright flew the world's first practical aeroplane. In fact, it was little more than a series of hops, but to paraphrase a later pioneer, it represented one of the biggest technological leaps humankind had ever taken.

In their workshop at Dayton, Ohio, the two brothers had come up with a machine which not only incorporated the three-axis control system that was to become universal but also a 12 hp petrol engine which they designed and built themselves. This powered efficient propellers which were geared down relative to engine revolutions to provide optimum thrust. Over the next few years the two sons of a Methodist bishop refined their invention to the point where they could undertake complex manoeuvres and stay aloft for over thirty minutes at a time.

European inventors had also been struggling with the problems of powered flight but with less success. Many of the machines that resulted from their efforts looked cumbersome compared with the relative simplicity of the Wrights' latest *Flyer*. Most also looked unlikely to justify their creators' hopes. Indeed, the best they could achieve was to underline the Wrights' superiority. Orville and Wilbur were at least five years ahead. They had progressed to flying apparently effortless circles and even figures of eight several hundred feet in the sky.

Yet European inventors could have achieved what the Wrights had done, if, that is, they had applied the same levels of disciplined reasoning, observation and mechanical skills combined with intelligent analysis of the work of pioneers like Caley, Stringfellow, Wenham, Phillips, Liliental, Pilcher and others.

Chapter 2

Brothers and Balloons at Battersea

There are few clues amid the elegant riverside apartments, smart shops and fashionable restaurants of twenty-first century Battersea to indicate the key role this area of south-west London played in the development of British aviation in its earliest years.

A new road has been named Sopwith Way and there is a discreet blue plaque on the arches beneath the London to Brighton railway lines. But that hardly seems sufficient acknowledgement that, for a brief while in the early twentieth century, Battersea was Britain's aviation capital. In the pioneering days before the First World War factories based here turned out around 30 balloons and at least 50 aeroplanes.

It started, as did manned aviation itself, with balloons. While the theorists of heavier-than-air flight argued earnestly among themselves, the balloon enthusiasts got on with the business of getting aloft.

For centuries humankind had dreamed of flying like the birds but attempts to do so had all ended in failure and often serious injury if not death. It was not until the second half of the nineteenth century that the dream became reality sparked by an idea which led to the invention of the balloon.

In 1766 the notion that hydrogen could provide lift came from Henry Cavendish. He saw that hydrogen had negative weight as it is lighter than air, and that this property could cause a vessel filled with the gas to rise. The idea was taken a step further in 1782 by Joseph Michel Montgolfier from Annonay, near Lyons in France. Using a silk bag filled with hot air, which is less dense than air at room temperature, he was able to make the bag rise and fly for ten minutes.

Many stories, doubtless fanciful, have been told to explain the way in which Joseph Montgolfier and his brother Étienne discovered that hot air rises, and how they concluded that if contained in an envelope of sufficient size it would have enough 'lift' to raise passengers into the air.

The choice of paper for the envelope of their first balloon must have seemed natural to the brothers, who were paper-makers by trade. The balloon, which was fairly rigid, stood over a pit containing wool and straw which, when ignited, filled the balloon's envelope with hot air. On 25 April 1783 the first successful Montgolfier balloon took to the air at Annonay. It is reported to have risen to a height of about 1,000 ft and to have travelled about 3,000 ft before falling to the ground as the air in the envelope cooled.

The brothers gave a public demonstration, again at Annonay, on 4 June using a newly-constructed balloon which rose to an altitude of about 6,000 ft. This success resulted in a summons to Paris to enable King Louis XVI to see the Montgolfiers' invention for himself. A balloon of about 42 ft in diameter was constructed especially for the event and a basket hung beneath it was intended to carry the world's first aerial voyagers: a rooster, a duck and a sheep.

The balloon was launched at the Court of Versailles on 19 September, climbing to about 1,800 ft before the eyes of the astonished King Louis, Queen Marie Antoinette and their court. It landed about two miles away. The three occupants seemed little the worse for their adventure, although the rooster might have been trampled on by the sheep.

For the next stage of their experiments – the carriage of human passengers – the Montgolfiers created a magnificent new balloon 49 ft in diameter. Elaborately decorated in a blue-and-gold colour scheme, it displayed the royal cipher in those pre-revolutionary days, signs of the zodiac, eagles and smiling suns. Around its open neck was attached a wicker gallery capable of accommodating one or two men.

In this vehicle, on 15 October, 26-year-old scientist Francois Pilâtre de Rozier made a tethered flight to a height 85 ft, remaining airborne for about 4½ minutes. Just over a month later, on 21 November 1783, de Rozier and his passenger, the Marquis d'Alandes, became the first men in the world to be carried in free flight by a balloon. They rose from the garden of the Chateau La Muette in the Bois de Boulogne, Paris, and were airborne for 25 minutes before managing to land about 5 miles away from their departure point. The air in the balloon was kept hot by a fire burning on a grill below the envelope to which straw was added as required.

Later that year, Jacques Charles reverted to the idea of using hydrogen gas to fill a balloon which he and Noel Roberts flew for 27 miles in December.

In 1785 Pilâtre de Rozier was killed while attempting to cross the English Channel. He had hedged his bets by using a hydrogen balloon connected to a hot air balloon but both envelopes exploded after thirty minutes' flying, casting the intrepid de Rozier into the sea below. Yet the channel was conquered shortly afterwards by Jean-Pierre Blanchard and Dr John Jefferies.

The first manned balloon ascent in the British Isles had been made the previous August by James Tytler who flew for ten minutes at a height of 350 ft. The following month a dashing Italian called Vincent Lunardi ascended from Moorfields, London, to make the first flight in England, while in June 1785 Letitia Sage became the first British woman aeronaut in one of Lunardi's balloons. The same year, a balloonist called Arnold went up from St Georges Fields, London, but came down in the River Thames, while Major John Money took off from Norwich, in an attempt to raise money for the Norfolk and Norwich Hospital. He passed over Lowestoft at 1800 hrs and came down in the North Sea about eighteen miles from the shore and was rescued by a revenue cutter about five hours later.

Ballooning continued to be a popular pastime into the nineteenth century and beyond but sightings of balloons in their natural element remained comparatively rare. So it was that one day in 1893 in Derby two boys, one 18, the other 10, goggled in amazement as a balloon sailed past their house. 'Breathlessly, we scrambled up through the skylight on to the roof of our house in Friar Gate, from whence we trained a telescope on to the balloon and watched every movement,' the younger of the two boys, wrote later. He went on:

We could see the aeronaut moving about in the basket or car and occasionally throwing out a small quantity of sand to preserve the equilibrium of his vessel. How grand it must be to float in space, we thought. This man had a world to himself – what a tremendous field of adventure waited on him who possessed such a balloon. The imagination of Jules Verne could not improve upon it.

That day in Derby would turn out to be a highly significant one for British aviation. From then on Oswald Short and his older brother Eustace could think of little else beyond the theory of ballooning and the construction of the craft. Their ambition was to build one themselves.

The brothers came from a family of colliery engineers originally domiciled in Northumberland. But in the 1870s Samuel Short moved to Derbyshire when he married a farmer's daughter called Emma Robinson. He became chief engineer at an iron works at Stanton-by-Dale midway between Derby and Nottingham. Altogether, the couple had four children, three boys and a girl.

Horace, the oldest, was born in 1872. During infancy he suffered a head injury which led to meningitis and left him with an abnormally large head. This left him with a wide mental horizon, a quick wit and a sharp tongue. Ernest arrived in 1873, then Albert Eustace, always known as Eustace, in 1875, and Oswald, initially called 'the kid' by Horace, followed in 1883. The family moved to Friar Gate, Derby, where Samuel died in 1895.

Following their father's death, Eustace was despatched to track down Horace, then satisfying his urge to travel, in an attempt to persuade him to return home. Eustace's travelling costs had been raised by public subscription after a local newspaper published a letter from Horace describing his adventures. Horace appears to have been unaware of his father's passing and of the reduced family circumstances that followed. In later years Oswald recalled that they had lived in poverty and that his mother could no longer afford Eustace's school fees.

Pending his return home, Horace gave Eustace £500 to sustain the family and some of the cash was used by him and Oswald to start a coal and coke business at New Malden in South London. This enabled the brothers to pursue their ballooning obsession to greater effect and with greater vigour. They bought their first balloon in 1897 having paid £30 for the grandly named *Queen of the West*. It was, however, somewhat past its prime and attempts to inflate it fully were thwarted by its propensity to leak gas. Even so, the brothers used the balloon – 'black, brittle and rotten' according to their great, great niece Elizabeth Walker – to start another enterprise, giving displays at public events. Nevertheless, the brothers became expert pilots and moved on to designing and building their own craft, first at Hove in Sussex and then in London.

The brothers also started offering balloon rides to the public, the first ascent being from London's Crystal Palace. It was followed by another at a fete at Teddington, Middlesex. This time they were accompanied by two passengers one of whom was Horace. It was to be his first and last time in a balloon. 'It was a rough flight with the balloon dragging on landing,' wrote Elizabeth Walker. They ended up in the village of Otford near Sevenoaks, forty miles away. Horace climbed out of the basket convinced that balloons were useless and dangerous and that his brothers were completely mad.

Yet the *Queen of the West* was still in use in 1900 when Eustace made an ascent to mark the opening of Aldrington Recreation Ground, Hove, but without passengers. The *Sussex Daily News* reported: 'Would-be passengers could not accompany the aeronaut owing to the balloon not being fully inflated. In fact, the quantity of gas was hardly sufficient to carry one person.'

The balloon limped as far as the Old Shoreham Road before collapsing. For the watching Horace, this was no doubt further proof that his attitude towards balloons was the right one. But then he fell 20 ft from a wooden balcony when the handrail gave way, breaking both his arms.

The same year Eustace and Oswald were able to see at first-hand how ballooning was developing overseas. Oswald recalled: 'We were in Paris at the International Exhibition. My brother Horace was demonstrating his loudspeaker from the top of the Eiffel Tower. I was studying French balloons.' Horace had patented his Auxetophone sound amplification device in 1898, and while he deafened passers-by, Oswald made sketches of the balloons' constructional details and components.

The brothers were particularly attracted to the French designs because they featured spherical envelopes rather than the pear-shaped ones favoured by the leading British constructor of the time, the Spencer Brothers, even though this made them prone to uncontrolled spinning when airborne. The firm of C.G. Spencer had been founded by a ballooning dynasty active in the second half of the nineteenth century (see box on page 26).

Horace, meanwhile, had set up business in Hove and he allowed Eustace and Oswald to use a loft in his building to construct their first balloon, which was completed in the early summer of 1901. Its envelope had a capacity of 38,000 cubic feet of gas and made its first flight on 22 June from St Ann's Well Gardens with Eustace in command.

The *Brighton Gazette* reported: 'The balloon, keeping in the lower air current, was carried eastward and not far inland. Sailing along gallantly over an hour and a half, the balloon was carefully brought to *terra firma* at Willingdon near Eastbourne about half past seven.' The newspaper helpfully noted: 'It may be added that the grounds of St Ann's Well are open all day, so visitors may witness the interesting process of inflating the balloon.'

It was at about this time that Eustace and Oswald decided to promote their services to 'secretaries and proprietors of fetes, galas, flower shows, pleasure gardens, exhibitions, etc.' Their round-robin letter stated,

> As aeronauts of long and practical experience both in England and abroad, we beg to draw your attention to what is undoubtedly one of the greatest attractions that can be added to a programme, viz a Balloon Ascent [sic]. Balloon Ascents are always exciting and always draw large numbers of spectators in addition to the number who would otherwise attend.

When Horace closed his Hove laboratory in 1903 Eustace and Oswald moved their operations to a rented mews carriage shed off Tottenham Court Road in London. In 1905 an advertisement in *The Times* set them on the road to becoming aircraft manufacturers for it sought contractors to supply three balloons to the Indian government for use as reconnaissance vehicles. The brothers applied and got the business.

By 1904 their exploits were achieving national newspaper coverage. The *Daily Mirror* of 26 September published a picture of an ascent –

'witnessed by scores of *Mirror* readers' – from Crystal Palace of a Shorts-built balloon which was claimed to be the biggest in the world at that time.

The brothers were also creating a good impression for the quality of their products. Colonel James Templer, superintendent of the Army Balloon factory at Farnborough, was so impressed by the high standard of workmanship that he recommended the brothers to the Hon Charles Rolls. He commissioned them to build a 78,500 cu ft craft for the first Gordon Bennett race in 1906. Rolls called it *Britannia*.

It was this contract which was to lead the Short brothers to move again. They rented two archways – numbers 75 and 81 – in the viaduct near Battersea Park Station.

At this time Charles Rolls was negotiating with the London Coal and Coke Company to use its gas works alongside the railway as a site for inflating and launching balloons. Between the gas holders and the viaduct was an area of grassland – later to become known as 'The Field' – from which the Short brothers launched their balloons. They also secured the agreement of the coal and coke company to demolish the wall between The Field and the viaduct.

In 1967 Oswald wrote that 'the ground was lined on one side by three gasometers, the tallest of which was 97ft high. We could never get more than 250ft away from that gasometer. North westerly winds, generally quite strong, were necessary to cross the English Channel. Fortunately, we never had accidents involving loss of life or injury.'

The brothers' reputation was enhanced by Rolls' second place in the Gordon Bennett race, which he achieved with a flight from Paris to Norfolk in 26 hours. They were also appointed official aeronautical engineers to the Aero Club and this resulted in orders from many well-known individuals such as Warwick Wright, Leslie Bucknall, T.O.M. Sopwith and John Moore-Brabazon. Other customers included the Hon Mrs Assheton Harbord, the club's only female member and a notable aeronaut, who made four cross-channel flights and won an award for a 78-mile trip in 1909.

Moore-Brabazon was a successful racing driver in the early years of motoring and had followed his great friend Charles Rolls into ballooning.

He made his first ascent with London wine merchant Hedges Butler, who was one of the founders of the Aero Club. 'He had the most astonishing lack of fear and a wonderful imagination,' Moore-Brabazon wrote later. 'His astonishing confidence was very inspiring to the beginner. The first time I went up with him his daughter was with us and also a General Colville, who was quite well-known at the time.'

The trip ended spectacularly. When Butler threw out a grapnel to anchor the craft as it came down, it failed to hold. 'The result,' Moore-Brabazon remembered, 'was that we started to bump across England and I assure you we went over a mile – crash, bang, crash bang – in that manner. As Butler weighed a good 17 stones and for the most part he was on top of me, that particular part of the trip wasn't the greatest fun.'

The future cabinet minister's second trip was no less eventful. This time he went up from Crystal Palace with one of the Spencers. Moore-Brabazon said it was Charles Spencer but it was more likely to have been Percival – 'complete with beard and yachting cap with a balloon on the front'. A third passenger was Professor Alfred Huntingdon, the formidable professor of metallurgy at London University's King's College. It was clear, however, that the balloon would lift only two occupants. Huntingdon said he had some ballooning experience and proposed that the two of them should go up without Spencer. The balloon drifted over London's East End where it came down so low that the basket knocked the chimney pots off a house. It eventually came down south of the Thames. 'It was all very enjoyable,' Moore-Brabazon said.

Prof Huntingdon was a founder member of the Aero Club and took part in its first race in July 1906 in his balloon, *Zenith*. He also competed in the first Gordon Bennett race.

In his autobiography, written half a century later, Moore-Brabazon recalled how he and Rolls had become discontented with the Spencer brothers' products and had 'discovered two delightful young brothers named Short, who were doing ballooning shows, and we asked them if… they would make us a balloon.'

This was the first craft built by the brothers in their new premises. The new owners named it *Venus*. 'We made many very satisfactory flights in it,' Moore-Brabazon recalled, adding that it was the first spherical balloon to be made in England.

Moore-Brabazon was now hooked on ballooning and continued to fly during his time as a Cambridge undergraduate. On one occasion he told his tutor that his late return was due to landing in his balloon 'in some outlandish place in the south of England'. The tutor thought this 'the most original and outrageous excuse that he had ever had put up to him or had to put up with.'

With his wife Hilda, Moore-Brabazon made frequent trips in the *Venus*. He recalled that one of the most useful accessories for an early twentieth century balloonist was an ABC railway guide. He explained: 'You could draw a line on the map showing more or less where you were going and arrange to come down in a place where there was a reasonable train to come back in.'

He also recalled the Aero Club's first race, from Ranelagh, in which he competed with Hilda. A thunderstorm was approaching as they ascended and, when there was a 'really frightening flash in front of us,' they decided to come down. They landed in a field which was later used by Wimbledon Tennis Club. The storm arrived just as they landed, and the aeronauts, together with the crowd which had assembled to watch, sheltered underneath the now deflated envelope. The race turned out to be something of a fiasco, but one competitor at least managed to reach Hastings.

Moore-Brabazon made several trips with his friend Phil Paddon, who was also Sopwith's partner in his motor business and co-owner of the balloon *Padsop*. In an attempt to win a contest for the longest balloon flight in England, the aeronauts were forced to land when it started to rain heavily. In their second attempt they got as far as the Midlands where they spent the night, before pressing on in the morning to reach Yorkshire. 'It was all great fun,' Moore-Brabazon wrote later, 'but I myself had always thought of ballooning as training for what was soon to come – and that was actual flying.'

Meanwhile, the Shorts continued to enhance their reputation with the Aero Club. Members were given the opportunity to store their balloons in their Battersea premises alongside the club's own craft, *Aero Club IV*, which could be hired for two guineas (£2 10p). Balloons could be inflated and made ready for flight in just ninety minutes thanks to a special device installed by Shorts and the gas company's engineers. A telephone call to 788 Battersea was all that was required.

Despite the growing interest in heavier-than-air craft the Short brothers continued to be active balloon manufacturers, giving rise to the claim that the Battersea arches were Britain's first aircraft factory. Balloon manufacture was certainly a major aspect of the brothers' activities by November 1908 when *The Airship* reported that they had conducted 155 balloon ascents in the first ten months of the year. There had been 483 aeronauts and nearly 7 million cubic feet of gas were used. The field continued to be used for balloon ascents until the outbreak of the First World War.

In May 1910 the Aerial League of the British Empire conducted an exercise to test the possibility of Boy Scouts collecting messages from balloons. The league had been founded the year before to raise the UK's awareness of emerging aeronautical developments. Despatches were dropped from a pair of balloons which had ascended from Battersea. They were piloted by Charles Rolls and Major Baden Baden-Powell, president of the Aeronautical Society and younger brother of the founder of the scouting movement. The messages had to be retrieved and taken to the Aerial League's headquarters. The organisation is now known as the Air League but no details of its further involvement with the Battersea balloonists are recorded.

During the First World War Shorts' Battersea works were busy servicing and repairing captive balloons used by a military unit based at Roehampton. 'Many calls were received for the supply of replacement ropework and valve gear and a special delivery service was operated between Battersea and Roehampton for this purpose,' wrote local aviation historian Patrick Loobey.

But change in emphasis from balloons to aeroplanes had been in prospect several years earlier. In 1908, on hearing reports from Aero Club members who had seen the Wright brothers' demonstrations of their aircraft in France, Oswald Short reportedly said to Eustace, 'This is the finish of ballooning: we must begin building aeroplanes at once.'

THE SPENCERS

Until the arrival of the Short Brothers, the firm of C.G. Spencer and Sons of 56a Highbury Grove, Holloway, North London, enjoyed a virtual monopoly in the manufacture of balloons. It started with Charles Green (1785-1864), regarded as Britain's foremost balloonist of his era, and his long-time associate Edward Spencer (1799-1849).

Green, the son of an East End fruiterer, had joined his father's business when he left school. He made his first ascent in 1821 and by the time of his retirement had made over 600 ascents, carried 700 people aloft and reached a height of 21,000ft. Among his epic flights was one made in 1836 which took him and two passengers as far as Weilburg in Germany, a distance of nearly 500 miles. This set him thinking about the possibility of trans-Atlantic balloon flights. But novelist Edgar Allen Poe jumped the gun when wrote about it in the *New York Sun* in 1844 under the headline 'The Atlantic Crossed in Three Days!' It was completely fictional although based on a book about Green's flight. Two days later the newspaper published a retraction of what was perhaps an example of Victorian fake news.

Among Green's other significant contributions to ballooning was the discovery that coal gas, which was available in large quantities following its introduction to light the streets of London in 1813, was a good substitute for the more expensive hydrogen.

Spencer, a solicitor, became Green's friend and trusted assistant. Together the pair made 27 ascents, with Spencer making 40 solo flights. The birth of Spencer's son Charles Green Spencer in 1837 represented the start of a ballooning dynasty which continued well into the twentieth century. Charles fathered six professional balloonist sons, Percival, Arthur, Stanley, Henry, Sidney and Herbert, all of whom were involved with the family firm. A daughter, Juliana, also became a balloonist.

By the turn of the century the firm was advertising itself as 'manufacturers of aeronautical apparatus of every description,' and specifically, 'balloons, airships and flying machines'. Later, it was offering 'Salvus' parachutes with their promise of 'the certainty of escape for aviators'. In 1901 one of the company's kites was used by Guglielmo Marconi to aid his trans-Atlantic wireless demonstration.

Percival Spencer was said to have made over 1,000 ascents. In 1909, *Flight* published a letter from him in which he claimed to have flown the English Channel eight times between 1898 and 1906, the last three from 'Wandsworth Gas Works'. He died in 1913.

Stanley, meanwhile, was experimenting with airships. Influenced by the success of Brazilian aviator Alberto Santos Dumont, who flew an airship around the Eiffel Tower, he used money from a sponsorship deal with a baby food manufacturer to fund his first craft. It was built at Crystal Palace in south London and made its first flight in 1902.

Its 75ft envelope, containing 20,000 cu ft of hydrogen, was emblazoned with his sponsor's name. Slung beneath the envelope was an open framework of bamboo poles on which was mounted a 3.5 hp Simms petrol engine driving a propeller in the nose of the gondola. The pilot sat at the back.

In September 1902 Spencer took his creation on a flight over London during which he tossed rubber balls from the craft to show what a military bomb-carrying airship could achieve. Despite the sensation it caused, the airship suffered from poor steering and the planned circumnavigation of St Paul's Cathedral could not be completed.

Spencer's sponsor, Mellins, refused to pay the full fee for the space on the airship's envelope and Spencer sued for the outstanding £500. An employee testified that he and a ground crew had towed the balloon around the polo ground at Crystal Palace to give a favourable impression of its manoeuvrability. The jury found against Spencer but ruled he should keep the £1,000 already paid.

During the First World War C.G. Spencer and Sons continued as a contractor to the War Office and Admiralty. In the difficult post-war trading conditions, Herbert attempted to revive the family firm and in 1926 the Welsh aeronaut Ernest Willows was killed in an accident while flying a Spencer-built craft.

Born in Cardiff in 1886, Willows had been the first person in the UK to hold an airship pilot certificate awarded by the Aero Club. He had built his first airship in 1905 and flew it from East Moors, Cardiff. His second craft, powered by a 35 hp JAP engine, flew from Cardiff to London's Crystal Palace in August 1910. Willows III, christened the *City of Cardiff*, had the same JAP engine and was used by Willows to cross the channel and fly on to Paris.

Willows IV was powered by a 35 hp Anzani engine mounted above a small well-streamlined car. It was sold to the Admiralty in 1912 and the proceeds of the sale were used to establish a balloon school at Hendon. Willows V, completed in 1913, was a four-seater and was employed in giving joy rides over London. During the war Willows built barrage balloons for the government. He died in a crash at Hoo Park near Bedford together with two passengers and is remembered today by a Wetherspoons pub, the Ernest Willows, in City Road, Roath, Cardiff. There is also a Willows High School in Willows Avenue, Cardiff.

The graves of Edward Spencer and his son Charles are both in Highgate Cemetery while Percival Spencer was buried at Islington.

Chapter 3

Buckskins and Bamboo

F arnborough in Hampshire has been associated with aviation for as long as anyone can remember.

For decades the airfield to the south of the town was the location of a government aeronautical research establishment and now, privately operated, it remains a prominent business aviation airport. It still hosts the famous air show with which the town's name has become synonymous the world over.

But all of Farnborough's many distinctions are dwarfed by its status as the site of Britain's first officially-recognised powered aeroplane flight. There are other contenders for this honour, but it belongs indisputably to Farnborough.

In the late 1890s an area of heathland between Aldershot and Farnborough had been selected to be the centre of British military aviation, such as it was in those days. As Aldershot was considered the home of the British army it was not surprising that it should have been chosen, especially as it was predominantly flat.

At the end of the nineteenth century, aviation meant balloons. Indeed the lighter-than-air craft, for all its limitations as a navigable flying machine, had come of age. Hundreds of people had made ascents, lengthy journeys across continents had been successfully undertaken and aeronauts had reached nearly six miles above the earth. In addition, important scientific discoveries about the layers of atmosphere encircling and protecting the planet had been made.

Balloons had also demonstrated their value in more serious situations. Both sides in the American Civil War had routinely used them for battlefield reconnaissance, while in France they carried mail and despatches over the ring of steel the Prussian army had clamped around Paris in 1870. In fact, in four months there had been over 60 flights into and out of the besieged city and more than 100 passengers had been carried in what was undoubtedly the balloon's finest hour to date.

The Royal Engineers had first become interested in the use of balloons in 1862 following reports of the use by Union and Confederate forces of tethered observation craft. A year later a series of experimental flights followed using a hired coal-gas balloon operated by Henry Coxwell, who in 1862 had accompanied meteorologist James Glaisher on his record-setting – and near-fatal – ascent to 29,000ft without oxygen.

These experimental flights further demonstrated the military potential of airborne observation but, at a time of prolonged peace, the army decided it could not justify the expense of balloons and the necessary supporting infrastructure. Even so, research, albeit sporadic, continued into the most efficient way of filling the envelopes of balloons by producing hydrogen, which was superior to coal-gas.

In 1878, Captain James Templer, a serving officer and accomplished free-balloonist, was instructed to design and build a craft for service use. It was to be constructed by the Royal Engineers at Woolwich Arsenal in south-east London and £150 was allocated to cover the cost. The resulting craft, named *Pioneer*, was designed to use hydrogen to provide lift, which meant that the capacity of its envelope could be just 10,000 cu ft, making it easily portable and a more elusive target for enemy fire. The envelope was made of varnished cambric, and the whole craft, complete with basket and ancillaries, cost just £71.

Pioneer made its first ascent on 23 August, after which it was used for instructing Royal Engineers personnel in the techniques of ballooning. This led to the unit concerned being known unofficially as the School of Ballooning. The following year an equipment store was established at the corps' Woolwich depot. Meanwhile, experiments continued to determine the equipment needed to produce hydrogen from the chemical action of hydrochloric acid on zinc.

By the end of 1879 Templer's unit mustered five balloons and was able to make a successful contribution to the army's Aldershot manoeuvres of 1880 and 1882. In 1882 the store and the school were moved to the more spacious School of Military Engineering at Chatham in Kent.

Further experiments led to the adoption of 'goldbeater's skin' – derived from the intestines of cattle and normally used in the production of gold leaf – as the best material for the construction of balloon envelopes. But the material was produced in small strips, requiring much work to sew them together to form an envelope that was strong, light and impervious to hydrogen. The qualities of goldbeater's skin were amply demonstrated in the craft known as the *Heron* to such effect that all subsequent British army balloons and airships would use it.

The army's 1890 summer manoeuvres reinforced the value of aerial reconnaissance and the following year a special section of the Royal Engineers was formed to operate balloons in the field. This left the school to concentrate on instruction and development, and there was a new equipment store which had now become a fully-fledged balloon factory relocated to Aldershot. The section now had a total complement of three officers and thirty-three men. It was Britain's first military aviation unit.

The move was completed by the relocation of the school to a new site near Aldershot Wharf to the south of Basingstoke Canal in 1892 near what is today the Airborne Forces Museum. A large shed was erected in 1892 for the production and housing of balloons. But the site was soon found to be too cramped for the construction and testing of balloons and this started a lengthy search throughout southern England for a suitable location.

In the end it was decided to move the Balloon School to a new site at South Farnborough on the eastern edge of what was then known as Farnborough Common. The area was indeed just that, common land leading westward from the area of what is now the A325 road and the Swan public house to Laffan's Plain a mile and a half away. In the winter of 1904/05 the Balloon Factory moved into what is now the north-eastern edge of the present airfield. The balloon shed, gasholder and hydrogen production plant were dismantled and moved to the site. The move was finally completed in 1906.

Meanwhile, by 1901, Templer, now established as superintendent of the Balloon Factory, had been turning his attention to the development of navigable balloons or dirigibles following a visit to a French government research establishment. He was given permission to conduct his own experiments and he started work on a craft with a 50,000 cu ft envelope. A halving of the factory's budget meant that it was not completed until 1904; with five layers of goldbeater's skin it was found to be too heavy and work started on one with three skins. This was to be *Nulli Secundus*, British Army Airship No 1.

The army had also been experimenting with man-lifting kites for aerial observation, having recognised that such craft had certain advantages over balloons as they took less time to prepare for flight and were not as vulnerable to ground fire. In 1894 a kite section had been added to the balloon school using equipment designed by Baden F.S. Baden-Powell, younger brother of the founder of the scout movement.

In the early 1890s Baden-Powell was a captain in the army when he designed a hexagonal-shaped kite intended for battlefield reconnaissance. On 27 June 1894 one of his kites lifted a man 50 ft off the ground at Pirbright Common and by the end of the year ascents of 100 ft and more had become routine. But the craft were found to be unstable in gusty conditions and the experiments were terminated.

It was at this point that a charismatic American showman arrived on the scene claiming to have designed kites that were superior to anything else available. Samuel Franklin Cody made other claims too. In fact, he wove an intricately crafted web of stories about his early life in America that were to prove virtually impossible to disentangle.

He falsely claimed kinship with the legendary Buffalo Bill Cody; he actually called himself Cody, although his real name was Franklin Cowdery. He claimed to have been born in Texas when he was really from Iowa. In short, he was what some people would have called a fraud. Yet for a brief while this extravagantly-moustachioed con-man in buckskins and a big hat was the doyen of British aviators and carried the hopes of the nation on his shoulders. There was, of course, another side to Frank Cody: he was hard-working, imaginative, clever, dogged and very brave.

The source of Cody's initial interest in kites is, like much else in his early life, obscure. He liked to attribute it to a Chinese cook who taught him to fly kites while pounding the cattle trails of the American West. But it is more likely that it stemmed from his friendship with Auguste Gaudron, a balloonist Cody met while performing at Alexandra Palace. Gaudron would later fly from London to Moscow with two other balloonists to establish a British distance record.

Cody's interest evolved into the creation of kites capable of flying to high altitudes and of carrying a man. Leon and Vivian, the two sons of his partner Lela – Cody's domestic life was just as complicated as the rest of it – also became interested, and the three of them competed to make ever-larger kites capable of flying at ever-increasing heights.

Financed by his wild west shows, Cody developed the double-cell box kite developed by UK-domiciled Australian, Lawrence Hargrave. By adding wings to either side, Cody's modifications provided increased lifting power, but the real breakthrough came with his idea of multiple kites flown on a single line. This system could carry several men in a gondola attached to the kite at the end of the train. It could reach several thousand feet. Patented in 1901, his design became known as the Cody kite.

Cody's first formal approach to the government was made by letter in October 1901. 'I believe I possess certain secrets which would be of use to the government in the way of kite flying,' he wrote. He went on to explain how his man-lifting kite system would be 'practical and useful in times of war'. He claimed he could go up or down at will in a variety of weather conditions and that his system could be operated by eight men: 'five to manipulate the windlass, one officer, one signalman and one aeronaut'. Not one to hide his light under a bushel, Cody claimed that he had achieved more success in this field 'than any other living man'.

Cody's approach had been made at a difficult time for the army, which was heavily engaged in the second Boer War. Balloons had already played an important role in several key actions in South Africa but had also revealed their operational limitations. They took a long time to inflate, were bulky to transport and were virtually useless in even moderate winds. Baden-Powell's kites had proved even less successful.

Even so, the War Office took a while to respond to Cody. By the time it had despatched a holding reply in early December he had already staged two public demonstrations of his man-lifting kite system, at Wanstead in east London, and at Bury St Edmonds.

A crowd of 500 had gathered to watch the Suffolk demonstration. On his first ascent Cody zoomed up 300 ft in a basket beneath the carrier kite, fifth and biggest in the train, strung from a one-inch thick steel cable suspended from the pilot kite. On his second ascent a squall sent the whole train spiralling to earth with Cody ending up in a tree. But for this 'friendly tree', reported a local newspaper, Cody might well have been telling the story of his ascent 'in another world'.

The army continued to drag its feet in responding to Cody who turned in frustration to the navy. The Senior Service was deeply impressed and Cody won a growing circle of admirers including the Director of Naval Intelligence and a future First Sea Lord, Prince Louis of Battenberg. But when he was asked to name a price for his patent and for his services to the navy Cody overplayed his hand. The service considered his demands excessive and promptly lost interest. This coincided with the War Office's notification that the man-lifting kites were 'not considered suitable for army purposes'.

Cody's response was to embark on another round of demonstrations. In the most spectacular, in November 1903, Cody crossed the English Channel in a lightweight boat towed by one of his kites. It took him thirteen hours to cross from Calais to Dover by a meandering route which took him as far north as Ramsgate, skirting the notorious Goodwin Sands. It showed, the *Daily Mail* concluded, that 'there are some possibilities in the use of kites.'

By the following year a shift of opinion within the army towards Cody and his kites was becoming apparent. He was now in correspondence with Lieutenant Colonel John Capper, the new superintendent of the Balloon Factory, who arranged for him to participate in a series of tests. Capper was impressed and reported positively to his superiors. 'I cannot speak too strongly as to the excellence of these kites as regards their design and ability to perform what Mr Cody claims for them.'

Capper recommended that Cody be engaged as kite-flying instructor to the Balloon Section. He duly started on 1 February 1905 and his full-time appointment was confirmed the following August. He was given honorary officer status as the equivalent of a lieutenant. His salary was £1,000 a year and, such was their expertise, that Leon and Vivian were also employed.

Cody was soon busy with other projects, including *Nulli Secundus* for which he had designed the engine installation together with wings and control surfaces, making many of the parts himself. Cody joined Capper for the dirigible's planned circumnavigation of St Paul's Cathedral, which ended prematurely at Crystal Palace, rather than the triumphal return to Farnborough that had been planned. Nevertheless, the flight received wide publicity and the newspapers all carried illustrations of the vessel passing the dome of St Paul's. Capper and Cody were lionised for their achievement.

The next stage was the development of a powered heavier-than-air-machine. Despite initial scepticism of the Wrights' claims, the War Office had responded to the brothers' overtures by appointing Capper to conduct negotiations for the purchase of rights to the *Flyer*. But the Balloon Factory superintendent was hedging his bets, clearly hoping for a British solution which would be superior to the Wright brothers'.

In 1906 Captain James Dunne had arrived at Farnborough to construct the aircraft he had designed. This machine, known as the D1, was a biplane with swept-back wings and no tail. Capper clearly expected great things from Dunne's machine. On completion it was taken to Blair Atholl in Scotland so that tests could be carried out in secrecy. It was first tested as a glider and later, after it was damaged in a crash, it was fitted with two 12 hp Buchet engines. It crashed again.

Alliott Verdon Roe was another contender for the honour of being the first man in Britain to fly a powered aeroplane, but Cody enjoyed several advantages. He had the resources of the Balloon Factory behind him as well as the knowledge gained from developing his kites and *Nulli Secundus*. He had already modified one of his kites to use petrol power with a 12 hp Buchet engine. It was flown on a long wire suspended between two 100ft poles. Later it was flown unmanned on Cove Common. This is generally recognised as the first powered flight at Farnborough.

Cody began construction of British Army Aeroplane No 1 in late 1907. It was similar in concept to the Wrights' *Flyer* but bigger as it was designed from the outset to carry two people. A three-bay biplane with horizontal control surfaces mounted in front of the wings and a rudder behind. It was fabricated mainly of bamboo and larch held together by tensioned piano wire.

As originally constructed it had a short square-section wire-braced wood frame with the engine mounted in front of the leading edge of the lower wing and the pilot's seat behind it. A pair of 'V' struts at the front carried two spoked wheels on an axle with another mounted at the back. Further small wheels were mounted on the leading edges of the lower wingtips. The wings themselves had wooden spars at the leading and trailing edges and it was possible to alter the camber when on the ground using tensioned wires between the spars.

The wings were connected by streamlined interplane struts, some wind-tunnel experiments on strut sections having been carried out at Farnborough. Lateral control was to be achieved using a pair of small ailerons mounted above the leading edge of the lower wing. The forward-mounted elevator was installed on three sets of bamboo booms attached to sockets on the leading edge of the wings, the lower members inclined steeply upwards so that the surfaces were just below the level of the upper wing. They could be operated to act as elevators as well as assisting in the aircraft's lateral control.

A single rectangular rudder was mounted between two booms, the upper edge being attached to the centre of the rear spar and the lower to the rear of the fuselage. A large canvas triangle was stretched between the trailing edge of the upper wing and the end of the upper tail boom. A small fixed vertical surface was also mounted above the upper wing. Some of the Farnborough wives were recruited as seamstresses to produce the fabric wing covering.

The engine drove a pair of tractor propellers using a belt. It was started by a vertically-mounted wheel fixed to the crankshaft. Twin radiators were vertically mounted in a 'V' configuration. The original intention had been to use a 50 hp Panhard-Levassor engine but it proved unreliable on the test bench. Lacking funding for a replacement, Cody had to wait until August 1908 when the 50 hp Antoinette engine from the *Nulli Secundus* became available.

In September the aircraft was ready for what would now be called taxying trials. It was during this period that it briefly left the ground. The area was thick with reporters and *The Times* had a correspondent based there. Cody told him that the 80-yard hop had been 'only a jump'. The machine was then returned to the workshop for the first of a long series of modifications. These involved removing the small ailerons, adding a front wheel and shifting the radiators outboard from their central position to the forward interplane struts. Changes were also made to the booms supporting the elevator. In this form, the aircraft was presented to the press at Farnborough on 13 October.

After further ground trials and more 'jumps', Cody finally judged conditions suitable on the 16th for an attempt to fly the aircraft. With a Union flag bravely flying from the strut between the upper and lower tail booms of his machine, Cody finally achieved his ambition. 'In less than 100 yards,' *The Times* reported,

> he had reached an altitude of between 30 ft and 40 ft so that the spectators on the southern boundary of the common saw the aeroplane flying above the roof of the balloon shed. Shaping a course that led to Cove Common, Mr Cody kept the aeroplane about 30 ft from the ground and he travelled across the greensward for a quarter of a mile.

But twenty-seven seconds later, Cody found himself heading for a clump of birch trees. He managed to avoid them but his left wing-tip struck the ground hard, wheeling the machine round into more trees and bringing it to a halt. It had been airborne for 1,390 ft. Cody emerged from the wreckage unscathed but the machine was badly damaged. 'I'm sorry that the accident happened,' he told *The Times*, 'but I have accomplished what I have aimed at: I have constructed a machine which can fly.'

The following day's newspapers carried extensive reports of Cody's triumph. Postcards showing him and his damaged machine sold in thousands. Later, the Aeronautical Society acclaimed him when he addressed its members on the details of his flight.

The rest of the year was spent in repairing the aircraft and making major modifications to it. The gap between the wings was increased from 8 ft to 9 ft, the booms carrying both sets of control surfaces were lengthened, and provision for lateral control was made by installing a wing-warping system and fitting differentially-moving surfaces at each end of the elevator. The radiators were moved to the aft interplane struts, the triangle of canvas that had stretched between the trailing edge of the upper wing and the top of the rudder was removed, and the small vertical stabiliser was shifted from above the top wing to a position between the centre booms supporting the elevator and linked to the rudder control. New larger propellers were fitted. Overall, it was bigger than before.

On 6 January 1909 this work was completed to enable testing to continue. Streamers were attached to the struts so that the airflow could be observed. After further ground trials, the ailerons were moved to the middle of the aft interplane struts and the radiators were shifted forwards slightly to adjust the aircraft's trim. Cody flew the aircraft again in this configuration on 20 January when he covered about 1,200 ft and reached a height of 25 ft. Again, though, he crashed after a turn but was unhurt. By now Colonel Capper was becoming frustrated with the continual crashes. He even suggested that Wilbur Wright be invited to take over the test flying because 'we shall have a good many smashes before Mr Cody has learned to manipulate the controls.'

The aircraft was returned to the factory again for more alterations and repairs. The ailerons were discarded and a pair of horizontal stabilisers fitted in front of the rudder. After a further flight on 18 February the aircraft landed with no worse damage than a burst tyre and a broken rigging wire. More flights followed on 22 February after which the rear stabilisers were removed and the ailerons repositioned. They were now located on short outriggers trailing from the forward interplane struts. The front rudder was moved to a position above the elevator.

Despite the fact that Cody's aircraft could now be considered a success, few people in positions of influence seemed to be aware of it. In February 1909 the report by a sub-committee of the Committee for Imperial Defence appointed to examine the significance of aerial navigation to Britain's defences recommended that all government-funded heavier-than-air experimentation should stop. It called for such development to be left to the private sector.

Amazingly, in his evidence to the sub-committee the previous December after Cody's flight, Colonel Capper made no reference to it. According to Cody's biographer Peter Reese, the result was that the committee 'had scant appreciation of the Balloon Factory's most creditable achievements despite its strictly limited funding and – criminally – no knowledge of Cody's triumphal first flight'. This seems incredible given the widespread publicity given to Cody's achievements.

On 24 February the War Office terminated Cody's employment, and James Dunne's as well. Secretary State for War Haldane dismissed both men, as well as the Wright brothers, as 'clever empiricists'. The sub-committee considered Dunne's machine to have no practical value. Instead, funding was to be confined to supporting the construction of airships. Official support for anything else was limited to tolerating some aviation activities on government-owned land.

This meant that if Cody wished to develop his aircraft further he would have to do so at his own expense and not as an employee of the Balloon Factory. His contract was not renewed that September as scheduled, but he was allowed to keep the aircraft – now officially declared surplus to requirements – and to continue to use Laffan's Plain for flight testing. The army was left with just a set of drawings of Army Aeroplane No 1. It was labelled 'top secret' and may have been the earliest full set of technical drawings for an aeroplane.

Cody was back in the air at Farnborough on 14 May 1909, when he flew for over a mile between Laffan's Plain and Danger Hill. Later the same day, he attempted to repeat the performance at the request of the Prince of Wales who was observing army manoeuvres at Aldershot. On take-off his machine was caught by a gust of wind as it turned to avoid a group of troops on the ground and Cody was forced to land. The aircraft sustained damage to its tail. Even so, the Prince pronounced himself satisfied, later telling Cody of his pleasure at seeing a British aeroplane actually able to fly.

Cody made further adjustments to the machine, discarding the twin rudders and moving the radiators to position them ahead of the front interplane struts, while the tailwheel was replaced by a substantial skid. In mid-July Cody flew the aircraft again. This time he managed to complete a circular flight of four miles, after which he decided to fit a 60 hp ENV Type F engine. He swapped the positions of pilot and engine so that the pilot's seat was now directly in front of the wing leading edge with the engine above. The position of the ailerons was adjusted. The outriggers were removed so that the ailerons were directly mounted on the forward interplane struts. Apart from minor adjustments, these modifications put the aircraft into its final form.

It was flown for three miles on 11 August. Cody was initially startled by the experience provided by the new seating position, recording,

> I find my new position in front of the engine has a much more sensational effect on the nerves than the old position, in fact until last night I never knew I had any nerves. I think, however, I shall get over this slight timidity after a few runs.

The aircraft was now performing well and after several further flights on 13 August Cody considered it safe enough to take a passenger. That honour fell to Capper. In view of their somewhat strained relationship Cody couldn't resist giving the colonel a bit of a scare by taking his hands and feet off the controls and letting the machine fly itself for a while. Capper's reaction is not recorded.

Later that day Cody took Lela, her hair wrapped in a heavy scarf and her skirts bound tightly with tape, for a three-mile flight, making her the first woman to fly in an aeroplane in Britain. She admitted to being apprehensive but later told reporters of her 'glorious sense of exhilaration'.

On 8 September Cody flew for over an hour. He covered around forty miles, landing only when he ran out of fuel. Although Cody was still able to use Farnborough's facilities, that did not extend to the use of military transport to tow his machine to Laffan's Plain. On one occasion he had to recruit a local coal merchant and his horse to do the job. 'Mr Cody's Aeroplane Towed by a Coal Cart,' chortled the press.

He also flew the aircraft at the Doncaster aviation meeting in October 1909. Although he did not win any of the prizes on offer, Cody made use of his appearance to publicly take British citizenship on 28 October. He also entered the *Daily Mail* contest for the first British aircraft to make a circular flight of over a mile. But as the Doncaster meeting had not been sanctioned by the Royal Aero Club, none of the flights made there could be officially ratified, and the prize eventually went to John Moore-Brabazon.

In January Cody was hoping to win the £1,000 prize offered by Sir William Hartley for a flight between Manchester and Liverpool which had to be made before 26 January. Although he took the aircraft to Aintree, his attempt was thwarted by fog. After this Cody concentrated his efforts on the new biplane he was building to compete for the Michelin Trophy which would be awarded to the aviator who, by the end of 1910, had flown the longest distance around a pre-determined circuit.

Cody's victory against the likes of Sopwith and Alex Ogilvie represented his first major competitive flying success. It brought him a £500 cash prize plus a huge bronze Pegasus trophy. It was a hard-won triumph. Cody flew around a 2.5-mile circuit at Farnborough in the face of increasingly high winds and plummeting temperatures which caused his engine air intakes to ice up. By the time he called it quits he had been in the air for 4hr 47min and covered just over 185 miles, 35 more than Sopwith.

As Peter Reese observed: 'Throughout the flight, made in sub-zero temperatures, Cody was completely unprotected and he landed with his beard, moustache and clothing covered in ice. In a rare demonstration of skill and endurance, he set a new all-British record for both duration and distance.'

Cody's was the first British machine home in the Circuit of Great Britain race in July 1911. But he was only fourth overall in the race to complete a circuit from Brooklands to Edinburgh and back with compulsory stops *en route*. It was another test of endurance for Cody as he battled against bad weather and accident damage. The race organisers extended the event by two days to enable him to make the finish.

His popularity with the public soared, particularly after a further Michelin Trophy victory later that year. But his biggest test was still to come. Cody planned to enter the military aeroplane trials at Larkhill during the summer of 1912 to select the most suitable machine for the newly-created Royal Flying Corps. Clearly the recommendations of the 1908 sub-committee had been forgotten and the War Office had again changed its mind about the military value of aeroplanes.

Cody was up against competitors from Britain and abroad but three weeks before the competition two of his entries crashed and were virtually destroyed and he was obliged to create a new one from the wreckage. He managed to find a suitable engine to power it, a 120 hp Austro-Daimler, but although powerful Cody's bamboo and wood machine was obsolete compared with some of the other entries. Yet it was judged the winner. This time he pocketed £5,000 and laid plans to start his own aeronautical company.

Another Michelin Trophy win followed but while practising in a new machine for a race around the coastline of Britain, Cody crashed. He had been making a series of short flights from Farnborough and on 7 August 1913, while preparing to land, his machine appeared to fold up. It plummeted into a copse of oak trees and Cody and his passenger, cricketer W.H. Evans, were killed instantly.

Samuel Franklin Cody, aka Cowdery, was interred in Aldershot Military Cemetery. He was the first civilian to be accorded such an honour. Every member of the newly-formed Royal Flying Corps volunteered to participate and every battalion of every regiment stationed at Aldershot was represented. In a hand-written telegram of sympathy sent to Lela, the King spoke of Cody's 'dogged determination and dauntless courage'.

Cody is not forgotten at Farnborough, the scene of his greatest triumph. There is a monument there known as Cody's Tree. It is actually an aluminium replica of the tree to which the aviator tethered his aircraft. The plaque beneath it reads:

S F Cody measured the thrust of his first aeroplane in 1908-9 by tying it to this tree. Near-by he made his first tests with his powered aeroplane on 16 May 1908 and his flight of 1,390 ft on 16 October 1908 was the first powered and sustained flight in Great Britain.

There is a replica of British Army Aeroplane No 1 in the museum of the Farnborough Air Sciences Trust.

SAMUEL FRANKLIN CODY

For all his falsifying of his life before his arrival in Britain, for all his baseless claims of kinship with Indian fighter and sharp-shooter 'Buffalo Bill' Cody, the fact remains that the man who called himself Samuel Francis Cody was the first to make a sustained flight in a powered aeroplane in Britain. At the time, Samuel Franklin Cowdery was still an American citizen. He did become a naturalised British subject but not for another couple of years.

He was a flamboyant but enigmatic character who had created a false persona to further his show business career before he became recognised as an accomplished pilot. Why he felt he needed to do this is unclear. What is probably true is that his antecedents arrived in America with the Pilgrim Fathers and that during his early life he became an outstandingly talented horseman. He seems to have participated in some of the legendary cattle drives from Texas, being good enough at his job to become a trail boss.

Changing tastes and the coming of the railroad rendered such marathon 1,000-plus mile drives irrelevant, but Cody was one of those who sought to maintain the glamour of the Wild West – even as it was being tamed – by recreating on stage its wildest days. As well as his ability with horses, Cody was also a crack shot.

In 1890 Cody left the USA to bring the excitement of the Wild West to British and European audiences with his new wife Maude Lee. However, Maude returned home when Cody became infatuated with a married woman, Elizabeth King, fifteen years his senior. He and Lela, as she became known, never married which caused the couple some difficulty in Victorian Britain, but she took Cody's name and he virtually adopted her four children. All participated in the Wild West shows which evolved into the melodramatic and bloodthirsty *Klondike Nugget*.

It was during this period that Cody developed and improved his kites, working with Lela's sons, Vivian and Leon. He was granted a patent in 1902 and in 1903 offered his system of man-carrying kites to the War Office for use for observation craft. He was later employed full-time by the War Office as chief kite instructor, although he seems to have worked on other projects such as the dirigible *Nulli Secundus*.

Much of this work was conducted in secrecy and, partly as a consequence of this and partly due to internal politics, Cody's achievements as the inventor of Britain's first aeroplane took time to achieve public recognition. Although no longer working for the War Office, Cody was allowed to continue his flying activities at Farnborough, the place whose name will forever be linked with his.

When he died in a crash in 1913 there was an outpouring of public grief. He was given a full military funeral and a crowd of 100,000 gathered to watch the cortège pass by. Cody and Lela had only one child together. Their son, Frank, joined the Royal Flying Corps and was killed in action in France in 1917.

Cody had been hurt by the initial lack of recognition for his epoch-making flight. He remarked bitterly to the London *Evening Standard* in 1909, 'I have been subjected to a great deal of ridicule and derision – laughed at, scoffed at, and been generally made a butt. Now it's my turn.' A friend recalled his complicated relationship with the military: 'The authorities countenanced him if they did not encourage him, but even they, I fancy, did not regard him very seriously. But Cody had genius, and to genius he added craftsmanship, a good deal of practical business ability, and an unconquerable determination to go through with what he took in hand.'

BADEN BADEN-POWELL

Baden Fletcher Smyth Baden-Powell was the youngest brother of Robert Baden Powell founder of the scouting movement.

He saw his first balloon ascent in 1880. It was an event that sparked a life-long involvement with aviation. He made a point of getting to know some of the balloonists and joined the Aeronautical Society and in 1886 was elected a member of its council, a role he was to fill for over fifty years. He was president between 1902 and 1909 and also a Fellow of the Royal Geographical Society. Baden-Powell served during the second Boer War in South Africa. When his older brother was in command of Mafeking during the siege he was a major in the relief column.

He was one of the first to see the value of aviation in a military context. He built his first balloons and aeroplanes together with his sister Agnes. In 1897 he made a small ornithopter glider which was not successful. In 1904 he experimented with conventional gliders from a chute over water at the Crystal Palace, assisted by John Moore-Brabazon. In 1908 he went to France, just before the first powered flight was achieved in England, to fly with Wilbur Wright. Baden-Powell's powered quadruplane was designed and built during 1909, appearing at the Dagenham flying-ground in the same year, but it did not fly.

A single-seat pusher monoplane, known as *The Midge*, was designed by Baden-Powell and built by Handley Page at Barking in 1909. It was exhibited at the Olympia Aero Show of 1909 and again at the Stanley Show of 1910, but there is no record that it ever flew. At the 1910 Olympia Air Show he successfully demonstrated his own semi-rigid airship and a clockwork aeronautical camera. Between 1910 and 1911 he developed another variant of his quadruplane.

He was elected an Honorary Fellow of the Royal Society in 1919, a position he retained until he died in 1937.

Chapter 4

Nearly But Not Quite

O n the face of it there would appear to be little to connect a mansion in the Surrey countryside with an Italian motor race and one of Britain's most important aircraft manufacturing sites.

There is a link, though, and it's provided by one man, a man who until then had probably not held down a job and was regarded as something of a playboy. Hugh Fortescue Locke King had been heir to a sizable estate and was also an enthusiastic motorist. But above all he was the man whose patriotism achieved a world first for Britain and created a valuable national asset.

Locke King's father, Peter, had inherited substantial agricultural estates near Weybridge, Surrey, and through a series of shrewd purchases had considerably expanded the estate. But as is sometimes the way of it, the inheritance assiduously built up by a prudent parent passed to a child who used it as the basis for an extravagant lifestyle. That seems to have happened when Peter Locke King died in 1885. His estate was valued at £500,000, which probably equates to around £200 million in twenty-first century terms.

It enabled Hugh and his wife Ethel, daughter of the Governor of New Zealand, to live well and spend freely. And not always wisely. A hotel venture in Egypt failed and Hugh lost money. By the early years of the twentieth century he had become an enthusiastic motorist and in September 1905 he went to northern Italy to watch the 500 km *Coppa Florio* motor race at Brescia, a town which would later become the start and finish point of the *Mille Miglia* race around Italy.

Hugh watched the Italian driver Carlo Raggio win the race in an Italian-built Itala. In fact, all the competitors were driving French, German or Italian cars. Why, Hugh wondered, were there no British machines in the field? The answer, he was told, was that the British were unable to build suitable cars because there was nowhere in the country where they could be raced or tested at speed. The European practice of closing public roads for the purpose was illegal in the UK.

Hugh realised that Britain was in urgent need of a purpose-built track on which cars could travel at sustained high speeds. The following year he met interested parties including Lord Northcliffe, proprietor of the *Daily Mail*, the secretary of the Automobile Club and the two leading British racing drivers of the day, S.F. Edge and Charles Jarrott, to seek their opinions.

The result was that Hugh decided to build a permanent track which would enable manufacturers to test and improve cars and also be the venue for races. To him its location was obvious. Later he would say: 'The site was not far to seek. When a few who were consulted saw the place, they owned that nature seemed to have formed it for the purpose.'

One of his first acts was to enlist the help of Lieutenant Colonel (later Sir) Henry Loft Holden of the Royal Engineers. Holden was superintendent of the Royal Gun and Carriage Factories at Woolwich Arsenal, a past chairman of the Automobile Club and inventor of a four-cylinder motor cycle engine. It was Holden who pointed out that if cars were to travel at the speeds anticipated it was essential for the curves to be banked. He drew up plans for a 2.25-mile oval track accordingly.

It turned out to be a huge undertaking which consumed money at such a ferocious rate that it nearly beggared Hugh, but the world's first purpose-built motor racing track was completed the following year. It would be named after the mansion originally built by Peter Locke King: Brooklands.

Brooklands was creating strong impressions even before its completion. Locke King had originally budgeted £22,000 for the project but once civil engineers were engaged to undertake the necessary work that figure rapidly swelled to over £60,000, probably around £30 million in twenty-first century money. During construction thirty acres of woodland were felled, 350,000 cubic yards of earth moved and 200,000 tons of concrete laid to form the track surface.

The workforce grew from an initial 500 to around 2,000, many of them Irish labourers. They were paid 6d (2.5p) an hour for work which was mostly done by hand. Construction materials arrived almost continuously, brought to the site by rail. Eight miles of track were laid within the site and linked to the London & South Western Railway line which ran past the site. Additional construction muscle was provided by two light locomotives, seventy-eight wagons, ten steam grabs and a host of horses.

Work proceeded rapidly. It was intended that the race track would be lapped in an anti-clockwise direction at speeds up to 120 mph. The northern banking, also known as the Home or Members' banking, was set at a mean radius of 1,000 feet and had a maximum height of 28 feet 8 inches. The southern banking, also known as the Byfleet banking, had a mean radius of 1,550 feet and a maximum height of 21ft 10in. A bridge had to be constructed to take the track over the River Wey.

The project did not end with the track itself. A separate contractor was engaged to build a clubhouse and offices beside the Finishing Straight with an adjoining paddock containing 75 spaces for competitors' cars. The main public enclosure provided seating for 5,000 with tiers of seats, covered grandstands and elevated terraces. It was laid out on the hill between the Members' Banking and the Finishing Straight. For spectators arriving by train there was a footpath from Weybridge station to the track via a tunnel running under the track. There was a separate enclosure for members of the Brooklands Automobile Racing Club (BARC) which would organise most of the activities that would be held at the track.

The BARC established an office at Carlton House in London's Regent Street. As it had been intended that racing at Brooklands would be run on similar lines to horse racing, the club's committee included many notable racehorse owners, including the Duke of Beaufort and the Duke of Westminster. Lord Lonsdale was appointed club president. The clerk of the course was also titled. Ernst, Baron de Rodakowski, was an Austrian who had settled in England following his marriage to Ethel Locke King's god-daughter. He had been involved in the Brooklands project from the beginning and would become a familiar figure at the track supervising activities while immaculately turned out in smart peaked cap and spats.

It had originally been intended to have the track ready for use by June 1907, and although the engineers had expected it to slip until October the circuit was ready by the original date. Curiously, though, the identity of the person who completed the first lap of the track is not entirely clear. While it is widely accepted that it was Ethel Locke King, there is a suggestion that she was beaten to the honour by an 11-year-old local boy riding a tricycle!

Brooklands would soon achieve national and even international prominence, but not just because of its association with motor racing. Pioneer aviators were encouraged to fly from the site and the flying contests would be watched by thousands of spectators. Flying schools were established and sheds erected for the assembly of aircraft. By 1914 three manufacturers whose output would have a major impact on Britain's participation in the First World War had established factories at or near Brooklands.

The first-ever race meeting at Brooklands was run on 6 July 1907, but aviators, or rather would-be aviators, were showing an interest in the venue even before the track was completed. A Frenchman named Bellamy appeared at the track in December 1906 with a bizarre-looking biplane largely made of bamboo and powered by a 35 hp engine. He claimed to have been a successful aviator in France and wanted to be the first to fly in Britain.

Locke King seems to have taken to Bellamy because he loaned him £100 to meet his expenses. He also ordered a stretch of land parallel to the railway line to be rolled flat to serve as a runway while the machine itself was housed in a huge tent. An attempt to taxi it ended in failure and Bellamy departed the area leaving a string of debts.

It is possible, though, that this fiasco prompted the Brooklands management to consider using the area in the centre of the track as a flying ground. In fact, shortly after its formation, the BARC offered a £2,500 prize to the first aviator to fly a complete circuit of the track before the end of 1907. This, it should be borne in mind, was well before the first officially-recognised powered flight in Britain.

One of those attracted by this offer was Alliott Verdon Roe. By 1907 the 29-year-old marine engineer-turned motor industry draughtsman was turning his attention from models to full-sized powered aircraft. He built his first biplane at his brother's house in Putney but before transporting it to Brooklands, where he hoped to fly it, he had a meeting with Rodakowski. It seems that the pair did not hit it off too well. Avro later described him as a belligerent character who was sceptical about the possibility of flight but reluctantly agreed to his building a shed at Brooklands to house his machine.

The shed, which Roe constructed at his own expense, was 40ft long and 20ft wide. It was just big enough to house his biplane but only if it was pushed in sideways. The machine itself, which Roe called the Avroplane, was largely made of bamboo and ash. It was copiously braced with a cat's cradle of wires. The mainplanes spanned 36ft (top) and 30ft (lower) and both had a chord of 5ft 4in. They were mounted at the rear of the 'fuselage' which comprised wire-braced struts. Additional bracing for the wing was provided by several king posts. Mounted about 8ft ahead of the main planes was a 24ft span steering plane.

The engine was mounted behind the pilot and drove a pusher propeller. The propeller was made of steel tubing and 'magnalium', a metal said to be slightly lighter and stronger than aluminium. The blades were detachable and there could be four or two of them. Their pitch could be altered. The whole thing was mounted on four small pneumatic-tyred wheels with helical-spring suspension.

A lack of engine power was to hamper Roe in his attempts to become airborne. Even at full throttle his first engine, a twin-cylinder unit made by J.A. Prestwich, generated just 9 hp, barely enough to propel the aircraft forwards. In fact, at his first attempt, Roe found himself rolling down the banking and onto the Finishing Straight.

But John Moore-Brabazon, who was to be Roe's biggest rival for the honour of being the first Briton to fly, was in worse trouble. He had also established himself at Brooklands in a shed next to Roe's with a powered glider built by the Short brothers. It cost £25 and was the first heavier-than-air machine to be built by the brothers who had hitherto specialised in balloons. It was powered by a 16/18 hp Buchet engine driving a four-bladed propeller.

Brabazon soon discovered that his machine was too flimsy even to taxi on the rough concrete track surface. He had clearly found Brooklands unsatisfactory because he decided to pursue his flying experiments elsewhere. Accordingly he left for Paris to fly Voisin machines. In his autobiography he condemned Brooklands as 'wholly unsuitable for aviation experiments because it consisted of the track alone with spiked railings to the side.' He added that both he and Roe were not welcome there.

Roe, however, continued his activities at Brooklands despite constant harassment by clerk of the course, Rodakowski, who seems to have disapproved of Roe's lifestyle. According to his grandson, Eric Verdon Roe, Alliot was living in the shed, sleeping in a large wooden box and existing on a diet of tinned fish and prunes for which, according to Eric, he maintained a taste for the rest of his life.

In June 1908 Roe replaced the JAP engine with a 24 hp Antoinette and had the biplane towed up and down the track with himself at the controls. Very early on the morning of 8 June Roe claimed to have seen light between his wheels and the track surface. 'He thought he'd flown about 75 yards,' Eric told a gathering of Brooklands Trust Members in June 2018. 'He said it flew and I believe him,' Eric insisted. Yet Roe was never able to prove this claim. According to Eric, witnesses did come forward later to support his story, but the documentation was lost and consequently the claim was never officially recognised. The biplane, however, was wrecked when helpers dropped it while it was being lifted onto the track. Its successor, a triplane, was also wrecked when it crashed in the centre of the track.

Rodakowski's patience finally ran out. In July he served Roe with notice to quit. After his departure Roe poured out his heart to readers of *The Autocar*. In a long letter published in August 1908 he claimed that had he been allowed to remain at Brooklands 'there was every chance of my succeeding'. He had, he insisted, not left because his machine was a failure. Rather, he wrote, it was 'making rapid progress and [I] have gathered knowledge which I hope will prove valuable in the near future'.

He explained that following the arrival of the Antoinette engine in May,

fresh difficulties arose as I was only allowed to use the track between 9 and 10 in the morning and I was not allowed to make a section of the railings detachable which would save lifting the machine over some

7ft gateposts – a difficult and risky task for eight men. However, I managed under great difficulties to get six trials and was making rapid progress since receiving the 18-24 hp engine up to 17 July on which day I left. It was during the end of May Mr Rodakowski regretted I should have to move my aeroplane and shed as they required the site for a refreshment room. I overcame this difficulty by lending my shed for a refreshment room on race days. Even this was not sufficient as I was not allowed to leave my aeroplane in the corner of the paddock where it would have been in no one's way; instead it had to be lifted…into a field.

On the first occasion it was a gusty day and, in getting down a bank, the wind proved too much, the machine falling on the edge of the bank breaking some of the ribs. Further damage was caused owing to the men catching hold of the wrong parts when trying to move it. One can easily imagine how utterly disconcerting this was. I do not mind breaking my machine in a trial but to do so under these unnecessary conditions is quite different.

As Mr Rodakowski witnessed the incident, I did not expect the machine would have to go over again. Consequently, on the next occasion I said I did not wish to have it taken over the rails as I feared still further damage. At this, in threatening tones, he imperatively insisted that my aeroplane should be removed in half an hour's time and, consequently on 4 July, I had a fortnight's notice to remove my shed and my aeroplane.

Roe was a prolific correspondent and adept at self-publicity. Similar letters appeared in *Motor* and *The Automotor Journal*. Interestingly, he made no claims to have flown his machine freely and under its own power. Indeed, on the eve of his enforced departure from Brooklands, on 16 July, he wrote to Major Baden Baden-Powell to say he was planning to form a company to acquire land in London for aviation experiments. He invited Baden-Powell to become a director of the proposed company. Explaining his difficulties with Rodakowski, he admitted 'secretly' making part of the railings detachable. He added: '[I] have made my trials in the early hours of the morning.'

But in this handwritten letter, which is now in the archives of the Royal Aeronautical Society, Roe added a statement which has been the focus of much controversy. He wrote: 'I have made several towing flights rising 6ft or so towed by motor cars and have *nearly* [author's italics] left the ground with present engine & next time out should see something interesting.'

Over the next two decades claims were made on Roe's behalf in newspaper articles, books and Avro company publicity material that he had in fact made the first flight by a British subject in Britain in a British machine. Matters came to a head in 1928 when the British aviation establishment decided to hold a banquet to honour Roe's achievement. *The Times*' aeronautical correspondent claimed that at Brooklands on 8 June 1908 Roe had made 'a free flight of some 60 yrd at a height of about 2ft from the ground'.

Among those to protest was John Moore-Brabazon who declined to attend the banquet at the Savoy hotel even though its purpose had been amended to honouring Roe's achievements in less specific terms. But the controversy continued to rage, and later in 1928 the Royal Aero Club instituted a formal inquiry chaired by Lord Gorell, a former air minister, to reach a definitive view of who was actually the first to fly in Britain.

Roe produced two witness statements which were obtained by him and his brother, Humphrey, in 1912. But the inquiry clearly found this testimony and other evidence produced by Roe as failing to substantiate his claim to have made a free flight conforming with the Royal Aero Club's definition. It upheld Moore-Brabazon's claim in respect of the flights he made at Eastchurch on the Isle of Sheppey in 1909.

Nevertheless, when inviting guests to attend a garden party at Brooklands in June 1988, the museum's trustees said the purpose was to honour Roe and to 'commemorate the 80th anniversary of the first flight by an Englishman in a British designed and built aeroplane'. A replica of Roe's biplane, built by museum volunteers, went on display together with a replica of Roe's shed. Both are still there.

Historian and author Philip Jarrett maintains that the belief that Roe had been the first was at least partly based on a misreading of his letter to Baden-Powell. For decades, Jarrett says, the phrase 'nearly left the ground' had been read as 'already left the ground.' Despite Roe's scrawl it is difficult to understand how this misreading could have occurred.

Jarrett points out that the matter may have been an early example of what is now known as 'spin'. He says: 'In later years, as the founder and head of a major British aircraft company, Roe had the benefit of his own public relations department and it was hardly surprising that the press releases and publicity issuing from it down the decades made frequent reference to the founder's foremost pioneering achievements.'

When Roe was given notice to quite Brooklands, the clerk of the course had also demanded that he sell his shed to the management for £15. At that stage it was an offer he could hardly refuse. Roe therefore returned to Putney to seek another suitable site in London for his activities. He found one at Lea Marshes near Walthamstow where, in July 1909, flying his rebuilt triplane he became acknowledged as the first Englishman to fly an all-British aeroplane in Britain.

With Roe, who according to his grandson 'crashed more than most other early aviators', off the premises there seems to have been a lull in aerial activity at Brooklands. Elsewhere, however, Samuel Cody made the first officially-recognised aeroplane flight in Britain in October, and the following July Louis Blériot piloted the first aeroplane across the English Channel to reawaken the British public's awareness of aviation and its possibilities.

Blériot's success encouraged the BARC to rediscover its enthusiasm for aviation. Rodakowski left, and his successor, Major Frederick Lindsay Lloyd, took a rather different view of aviation. The real stimulus, however, came from George Holt Thomas. He was not only the proprietor of *The Graphic* newspaper but also the British agent for Henry Farman's successful biplane. He had arranged for an example to be present at the Blackpool Aviation meeting in October 1909 where it was flown alternately by Farman himself and Louis Paulhan.

When Holt Thomas suggested to Locke King that the Farman should be flown at Brooklands, the ground within the track at the Byfleet end was cleared and a shed erected to house the aircraft. A meeting was organised at the Surrey speed-bowl over three days in October at which the Farman was demonstrated by Louis Paulhan. Watched by a crowd estimated at

20,000, the French aviator reached a height of 720ft. A few days later he made a 96-mile flight which broke the British distance record.

Yet despite the big attendance the Brooklands meeting was not a financial success: Holt Thomas's ten per cent share of the gate money yielded just £18. But even this could not dampen the BARC's enthusiasm. By autumn the ground at the Byfleet Banking end was complete with several rows of aircraft sheds erected. A 'flying village' was being created with three rows of wooden huts erected near the aeroplane sheds.

The original sheds were draughty buildings and in winter most of the occupants treated themselves to buckets of coal to keep themselves from freezing. Although many of the aviators had ample private means, others were strapped for cash, spending every spare penny on their machines. Each morning they were up early before the wind rose to try to coax their machines into the still air. In the early days a brief straight flight was an achievement and a circuit of the track an occasion to celebrate.

Progress was being made, however, and in May 1910 six machines were in the air over Brooklands simultaneously. The same month, Claude Grahame-White carried two passengers for 8 miles in his Henry Farman. It was represented as a major achievement.

Aero engines were still unreliable, however, and there were further hazards for aviators to contend with at Brooklands, particularly during the summer. Former *Times* aviation correspondent and historian E. Colston Shepherd wrote during the 1950s of the

> further trouble caused by the dense clouds of dust (until the grass began to grow in the autumn) by the slipstream from the bare sandy earth. Often a pilot would try to take off, taxying slowly but hopefully across the ground with his engine giving only a fraction of the power necessary for him to succeed. But in this experimental stage there was one great advantage – owners could do just what they liked to their aeroplanes in efforts to improve performance and airframes did not have to comply with any particular standards of design, construction or maintenance.

In the early days of aviation there was no industry regulator to approve the design of each type and no airworthiness regulations to observe. Nor were there any real restrictions on the way a pilot could fly. Claude Grahame-White created something of a sensation by flying his Farman biplane from Brooklands to Woking to answer a summons for a motoring offence. After the magistrates had risen, one of the them, who had been impressed by the aviator's arrival at the court, invited him home for tea.

In November 1909 leases had been offered to Brooklands tenants at annual rents of £100 a year or £10 per month. By the following May, #17 sheds were ready to accommodate 22 aircraft with the tenants offered unlimited use of the flying ground. Such was the growth in enthusiasm for aviation that by the end of 1910 eight flying schools had been established. By the beginning of the following year around fifty students had qualified for a pilot's certificate awarded by the Royal Aero Club (see box). There was also an unofficial qualification. It was said that no pilot was fully qualified until he had crashed into the sewage farm located alongside the flying ground and been decontaminated. One of Roe's triplanes, used for tuition at the A.V. Roe Flying School, was said to have spent more time in the sewage farm than in the air!

But one aviator decided to teach himself to fly. Having treated himself to a £5 flight offered by the school established by Gustav Blondeau and Hilda Hewlett – she was the first female pilot to gain a pilot certificate – he was so enthusiastic that he spent £630 on an Avis Monoplane. It was delivered to Brooklands in October and he immediately made a couple of short hops in it. This was how one of the best-known names in British aviation began his flying career: the aspiring aviator's name was T.O.M. Sopwith, better known as Tommy.

Sopwith's early career was punctuated by crashes, and the Avis, essentially a copy of the successful Blériot, was replaced by a Howard Wright pusher biplane based on a Farman design. Still flying without instruction, Sopwith used the machine to gain his pilot certificate. This raised his confidence to the point where he felt able to compete for the British Empire Michelin Cup. By 31 December he had covered over 150 miles in 4hr 7min at Brooklands, but he was beaten to the £500 prize by Samuel Cody flying from Farnborough later the same day.

THE ROYAL AERO CLUB

Originally formed as a gentlemen's club which aimed to promote aviation as a sport, the Aero Club – the royal prefix was granted in February 1910 – was to take on a key regulatory role during aviation's pioneering phase.

From 1910 it was responsible for issuing pilot certificates internationally recognised by the Fédération Aéronautique Internationale of which the club was the UK representative.

It was founded in 1901 by Frank Hedges Butler, the first Briton to own a car, his daughter Vera, and the Hon Charles Rolls. Initially concerned with ballooning, the club embraced heavier-than-air machines after taking a close interest in the Wright brothers' demonstrations in France in 1908.

The club's original premises, which it retained until 1961, were in London's Piccadilly, but in early 1909 it established its first flying ground at Shellbeach on the Isle of Sheppey with a nearby farmhouse, Mussell Manor (now Muswell Manor), as the clubhouse.

Among the first occupants were the Short brothers, Eustace and Oswald, who had previously made balloons for Aero Club members and were appointed the club's official engineers. Later joined by elder brother Horace, they turned to aeroplanes when they acquired a licence to build copies of the Wright brothers' *Flyer* and set up Britain's first aeroplane factory on the Isle of Sheppey. In 1910 the club moved its flying ground to nearby Eastchurch.

Because of a lack of pilot training facilities, most of the early military and naval pilots were trained by members of the club and many became members. By the end of the First World War, more than 6,300 military pilots had gained pilot certificates issued by the club.

The Royal Aero Club continues to be the national governing and coordinating body of aviation sport and recreational flying with its secretariat co-located with the British Gliding Association at its Leicester premises.

The first ten pilot certificates issued by the Royal Aero Club were awarded to:

1. J.T.C. Moore-Brabazon, 8 March 1910
2. Hon C.S. Rolls, 8 March 1910
3. Alfred Rawlinson, 5 April 1910
4. Cecil Stanley Grace, 12 April 1910
5. George Bertram Cockburn, 26 April 1910
6. Claude Grahame-White, 26 April 1910
7. A. Ogilvie, 24 May 1910
8. A.M. Singer, 31 May 1910
9. L.D.L. Gibbs, 7 June 1910
10. S.F. Cody, 14 June 1910.

T.O.M. SOPWITH

Thomas Octave Murdoch Sopwith was born in London in 1888, the only son of a well-to-do civil engineer and his wife. Initially interested in motor cycles, the young Sopwith entered the motor trade, selling cars from premises in London's Piccadilly. He made his first balloon ascent with Charles Rolls in June 1906 and subsequently bought his own balloon from the Short brothers.

In 1910 Sopwith won a £4,000 prize for making the longest flight from a point in England to anywhere on mainland Europe. He flew 169 miles in 3hr 40 min and used the prize money to establish a flying school at Brooklands in 1912. The following year he founded the Sopwith Aviation Company at Kingston-upon-Thames, although all its aircraft were flown at Brooklands.

In fact Sopwith established three factories in Kingston, transforming a small town on the southern outskirts of London into the source of most of Britain's First World War fighter aircraft and the heart of the military aircraft industry for years afterwards. Over nine decades Sopwith and its successor firm is thought to have employed 40,000 people in Kingston.

In addition to the Tabloid, a variant of which won the 1913 Schneider Trophy, Sopwith turned out a variety of successful designs including the Pup, One-and-a-Half Strutter, Dolphin and Snipe. His factories made a major contribution to the nation's war effort by producing over 18,000 machines, and the 5,700 Camel fighters included in this total helped make the post-Armistice Royal Air Force the world's most powerful air arm.

But despite, or perhaps because of, its wartime success, the company was faced with punitive taxes. The decision was taken in 1920 to liquidate it and start a new company. In this enterprise Sopwith was joined by Harry Hawker, Fred Sigrist and Bill Eyre, each of whom contributed £5,000. To avoid any possibility of claims against the new company in respect of wartime contracts undertaken by the previous one they chose to call it H.G. Hawker Engineering.

Later the company became Hawker Aircraft Limited and in 1935 it merged with Sir W.G. Armstrong Whitworth Aircraft and AV Roe & Company – Avro. Sopwith – he was knighted in 1953 – remained chairman of the Hawker-Siddeley Group until he retired in 1963 at the age of 75.

In 1977 the group became part of nationalised British Aerospace. Privatised in the 1980s, BAe Systems remains one of the world's leading defence companies. Thomas Sopwith died in 1989 at the age of 101.

Chapter 5

Success by Inches

At first glance it doesn't look much like the place where great deeds were done, much less the launch pad of a new industry using the most advanced technology.

The bridge itself looks more like something from the Victorian era and, indeed, it was originally built by the Great Eastern Railway Company in the 1880s. It is a steel truss design built on brick piers with brick arches either side. Today it carries the railway line between London's Liverpool Street station and Chingford over the River Lea, also known as Lee. Nearly two million people pass over the Clapton Junction Viaduct every year.

The arches are open now but in the early years of the last century they were probably enclosed with timber screens and doors. Alliott Verdon Roe assembled his No 1 Triplane in these arches before making the first all-British powered flight in July 1909. Blue plaques attached to the brickwork of the viaduct commemorate this achievement.

Having been evicted from Brooklands, scene of his initial experiments, the determined, never-say-die Roe looked around for another suitable site in the London area. He applied for permission to use Wormwood Scrubs and Wimbledon Common but the authorities refused. He had applied for permission to use Farnborough alongside Samuel Cody but the War Office's lofty reply noted that it was 'not disposed to provide facilities for amateur experimenters of aeroplanes…they were a waste of time'.

'With grim determination,' wrote aviation historian Graham Smith, 'Roe cycled around the outskirts of London looking at every available stretch of open land.' Eventually he settled on Lea Marshes (now Walthamstow Marshes, then in Essex, now in London). In 1909 the area was considered to be waste ground but in the twenty-first century it has been transformed into a complex of nature reserves and recreational facilities. It offers a wide array of bio-diversity and is bounded on its eastern side by the River Lea which rises near Luton and twists and turns its way for forty-two miles through Hertfordshire and North London to meet the Thames at Bow Creek.

In July 1908 Roe decided to re-think his ideas about flight and this prompted him to turn from biplanes to a triplane design on the assumption that such a configuration would combine a significant increase in wing area with a reduction in span. This would make the machine easier to handle on the ground compared with the cumbersome biplane which had given him so much trouble at Brooklands. It would also permit wings of much higher aspect ratio and bring superior flying properties.

The triplane also incorporated his latest ideas on the control of aircraft in flight. He had realised that the control system developed for his biplane was not suitable and that a better means was required. The following January he filed a patent for a novel control system applied to a tandem triplane arrangement. It was accepted in November with the grant of British patent No 750 for a system of control which allowed twisting of the structure without slackening the bracing, straining the planes laterally or causing undue stress on the machine.

The main wings provided pitch control by varying incidence. This was achieved by fore and aft movements of the pilot's control lever. Side-to-side movement of the lever warped the centre wing, while the upper and lower planes were warped in unison by the rear wing struts acting as push rods. The rear triplane unit acted simply as a fixed lifting surface. Roe followed Wilbur Wright's advice by adding a rudder behind the tail planes; this was intended to operate in conjunction with the wing warping.

Roe planned to climb and descend by altering the angle of incidence of the mainplanes. The tail-planes were not moveable. Lateral control would be achieved by twisting the trailing edges of the wings in conjunction with the side-to-side movement of the rudder. He would control the machine using a single 'handle-bar': moving it up and down altered the incidence of the wings, while rocking it from side to side twisted the planes and turned the rudder.

A.V. Roe's first triplane (known as the Roe I) was a two-bay machine. The main planes spanned 20ft with a chord of 3ft 7in. The outer sections could be folded upwards to facilitate ground handling. The tail surfaces comprised a single-bay triplane unit spanning 10ft and represented a lifting rather than a stabilising surface, contributing around a third of the machine's total lifting area. The chord was similar to the mainplanes.

Most of the airframe was constructed of deal but with oak and ash used in the parts of the wings subject to the greatest stresses. The fuselage was a triangular section wire-braced structure. The wing ribs were made from two narrow strips of deal fastened together to provide the desired measure of curvature. The middle wing and tail-plane were mounted on the upper longerons with the lower planes of both main and tail-plane suspended beneath the lower longeron. The rudder was not hinged but made flexible enough to turn in the desired direction.

The engine was mounted below the leading edge of the wing, with a belt to transmit the drive to the propeller driveshaft via a wheel mounted in a rectangular cut-out in the middle wing. Both fuselage and wings were covered with cotton-oiled paper backed with muslin. The covering's yellow colour has given rise to the erroneous belief that Roe used brown paper to save money. The undercarriage comprised a pair of bicycle-type wheels in bicycle-type forks suspended from a structure attached to the bottom longeron at the front. There was a smaller wire-spoked wheel at the rear.

Roe had built the aircraft to be as light as possible to offset the low power of its engine but viewed without its covering 'flimsy' seems a more apt description. He had planned to use a four-cylinder in-line engine being developed by J.A. Prestwich but it failed during bench-testing. Roe therefore had to fall back on the puny 6 hp JAP from his previous aircraft. Triplane No 1 is preserved at the Science Museum in London, while the Museum of Science and Industry in Manchester displays a full-scale replica made in 1952 by apprentices to show the aircraft as it appeared at the 1909 Blackpool Aviation Meeting. Although Roe had a customer for another triplane a dispute meant the order was never fulfilled.

Roe designed and built his aeroplanes in the stables adjoining the house of his brother, Dr Spencer Verdon Roe, at 47 West Hill, Putney in south-west London. The house is no longer standing but Wandsworth Council has erected a commemorative (green) plaque on a gate post at the entrance to a housing estate on the south side of West Hill. The plaque records that Roe, 'aircraft pioneer and designer, experimented in stables on this site'.

The triplane was dismantled and transported across London to the new flying ground where Roe had rented two arches under the viaduct from the Great Eastern Railway. At the same time, he applied to Walthamstow Council for permission to board up the arches to transform them into a workshop and hangar.

In February 1909 Roe wrote to Major Baden-Powell to report progress. He said he expected the machine to be ready in two months' time and that he hoped the 6 hp engine would be powerful enough to make flight possible. The aircraft had been designed to use a 35 hp unit but, Roe told Baden-Powell, 'I am not a believer in large HP.' He also expected the railway arches to be ready 'in 15 days' time' but he was not then planning to be in residence for long. 'I expect we shall have to seek a larger and more private spot for experimenting on, however I expect the arch place will be handy for erecting aeroplanes,' he wrote. It is possible that this was encouraged by hopes of renting land at Dagenham but it turned out to be unsuitable for flying because there were too many ditches.

In early May the journal *Motor* was able to report that Roe was active 'in the marshes that border the River Lea…and that test trials are being made daily'. Roe told Baden-Powell that this area was 'excellent' apart from hazards like a row of posts. In fact, there were further obstacles for Roe to contend with. Fifteen years later one of his helpers, R.L. Howard-Flanders, revealed that the Lea Marshes were 'far from ideal', with fences and posts in place for containing and tethering animals. Crashes were frequent. 'Every hop meant a crash,' Howard-Flanders noted.

Roe and Prestwich were briefly in partnership, and the engine manufacturer contributed £100 to his efforts but when it was dissolved Roe entered into a similar arrangement with his older brother. Henceforth Humphrey would become responsible for finance and organisation while Alliott concentrated on designing and building the machines. The triplane was named *The Bullseye* after the brand of braces manufactured in Manchester by Humphrey's company, Everard & Co. The firm also made the rubber webbing which supported the pilot's seat and fuel tank.

By early May, Alliott was able to tell Baden-Powell that despite the JAP engine's low power he had been 'able to get some very interesting results'. On one occasion, he wrote, 'I managed to get 6in off the ground, but this was hardly a fair flight as I was running against a head wind of only about 14 mph.'

At the end of the month a new JAP engine was delivered and beginning on 5 June a series of brief flights of around 50 ft was made. Roe experimented with different reduction ratios between the engine and propeller and also with varying pitch settings for the propeller blades which could be adjusted between flights. In a letter to *Flight* published on 26 June Roe gave the journal's readers an insight into handling the triplane. On his first two flights, he wrote,

> the machine heeled over and broke the left tips of the lowest plane on both occasions. I thought this was due to the torque of propeller but am glad to say it was my bad steering and should the machine lurch over a slight twist of planes brings it back instantly; but running against winds of 12 mph or less the machine practically balances itself. It can be steered entirely by twisting main-planes in conjunction with rear vertical rudder when running along the ground and the front or back of machine can be raised first according to the angle of main planes. I usually run along with main-planes at a slight angle; this allows machine to gain speed, and the tail to rise. On increasing the angle of main-planes to about 10 degrees the front comes off the ground but owing to insufficient thrust it soon comes down again. While it is up it is quite obvious how quickly the machine answers to the steering.

He also explained that the reasoning behind the triplane's lightweight construction was to produce a machine 'that will rise at low speed and once off the ground the angle of planes can be reduced and speed increased'. He added: 'I am of the opinion that if the main planes can be twisted it will be more easily controlled than a heavy one with rigid planes and my experiences seem to bear this out.'

During June and July, Roe made several modifications to the triplane. Wing tip skids were fitted and removed, the pilot's seat was moved forward and the lower undercarriage forks were replaced. The drive belt was replaced by a chain, the vertical tail surfaces were removed and both the engine and pilot's seat were moved forwards. A new propeller was installed and the fuel tank relocated behind the engine.

When Roe attempted his flights the procedure was for the team to assemble at 0400 or 0500 hrs to wheel the machine from its hangar under the viaduct to the narrow towpath beside the river. This process was complicated by the need to pass through a small gate. Once the flying ground was reached it usually took fifteen minutes to start the engine. When Roe was ready he called 'let go'. One of the team pedalled his bicycle behind the machine as it gathered speed with a fire extinguisher ready to put out the fires which not infrequently broke out. The other helpers grabbed tools and pieces of timber to repair 'the inevitable smash'. What was left of the machine was then partially dismantled and taken back to the 'very damp and dark railway arches to prepare for the next crash,' according to Howard-Flanders.

These difficulties were watched by a sceptical crowd which gathered to jeer at the efforts to get this flimsy contraption into the air. Roe's activities were less popular with the local constabulary which wanted to stop them on the grounds that they were endangering the public. On 3 July *Flight* published a letter from Roe lamenting the lack of suitable flying grounds in Britain compared with France. Wimbledon, Hackney Marshes and Wormwood Scrubs were 'practically deserted 23 out of 24 hours'. Yet 'the chief aeroplane builders' required practical steps to be taken for 'aeroplanists' to use them. 'It is for the nation's good we should keep abreast of the times,' Roe added.

Nevertheless, on 13 July Roe achieved the flight which has come to be recognised as the first by an all-British aeroplane when he covered 100 ft. Two days later he repeated the feat and the *Daily Mail* carried a picture of the aircraft in flight. On the 23rd he made several longer hops. *Flight* reported that his machine was 6 ft to 10 ft off the ground and that on three occasions it flew for 300 yards.

Flight praised Roe for managing to fly with such low engine power: 'The fact that he has succeeded thus far is very encouraging.' *Motor* was also impressed by Roe's achievements with a machine of such small dimensions, light weight and modest engine power. 'Success,' the journal observed, 'has come by inches and slowly.' It also reported that Roe had fitted magneto ignition and a supplementary ignition system to his 10 hp JAP engine. He had also altered the propeller 'time after time' and had settled on an 8ft diameter four-bladed unit. The flights made on 23 July were, *Motor* observed,

> perfectly clean and straightforward, the machine gathering way quickly after being released and lifting clear of the ground in less than 100 yards. The first flight was at about 4ft from the ground and each subsequent flight was at a higher level, the last showing about 8ft or 10ft of daylight between the lowermost plane and the grass sward.

Motor also reported that Roe was not happy with his latest flying ground. 'It is unfortunate,' the journal observed, 'that the Walthamstow authorities have threatened him with proceedings if he uses the marshes…for flying experiments.' The journal also noted that Roe had applied to London County Council for permission to use the adjacent Hackney Marshes early in the mornings.

Roe's flying ground straddled two local authority areas: Walthamstow and Leyton. At first he had been using the grass area close to the railway arches but after a week he was warned off by a council official. This meant that Roe and his team of helpers had to manhandle the triplane the quarter-mile to Leyton Marsh. But they were no more welcome there than they had been at Walthamstow and Roe was warned off again.

There were further official rebuffs to follow. Leyton council informed him that permission to use the area would not be forthcoming and the LCC denied him the use of Hackney Marshes. Similarly, the War Office had rejected his application to use Laffan's Plain and Salisbury Plain.

Yet the world was changing and with it official attitudes towards aviation. On 25 July, two days after Roe's success, Louis Blériot had flown the English Channel. The ability of a French airman in a French-built aircraft to cross twenty or so miles of sea was in stark contrast with the best that a Briton in a British machine could manage: 300 yards at a maximum of just 10 feet. Court proceedings pending against Roe were quietly dropped. Under the circumstances, as he noted later, it would have been 'ironical to say the least' if he had been hauled through the courts. In any case, Roe remained determined to continue his efforts, especially as he felt he was on the brink of real success.

Throughout August he made further flights, many culminating in minor mishaps. Each repair, however, brought an opportunity to improve the machine, and alterations were continually being made. By October Roe had had enough of Leyton Marshes. Apart from the official harassment, the area was not suitable for longer flights and the turns that Roe believed he and his triplane were now capable of achieving. He started a further search for a suitable flying ground but was, meanwhile, laying plans to attend the first Blackpool Aviation Week from 18 to 24 October.

At this time he was working on a second triplane. Broadly similar to the first, it was powered by a new four-cylinder air-cooled JAP engine, rated at 20 hp but probably capable of delivering little more than 14 hp. It also had a larger, cylindrical fuel tank mounted ahead of the pilot, a skid in place of the tail wheel and a tapered fuselage.

Both machines were taken to Blackpool but little was achieved at a meeting dominated by foreign aviators and aircraft. To make matters worse the weather for the last few days was unsuitable for flying. Roe decided to concentrate on the older aircraft but the only result of his efforts to fly, rather than make a few hops, were broken struts. The engine seemed reluctant to run at full power for longer than a minute or two and the damp atmosphere slackened the wing covering, impairing its efficiency.

In fact Triplane No 1 was not to fly again. Between 1910 and 1914 it was displayed at a couple of public exhibitions before going into long-term storage. In 1925 it went to the Science Museum. Meanwhile there was a further disappointment for Roe. The *Daily Mail* £1,000 prize offered to the first Briton in a British-built machine to fly a circular mile had been won by John Moore-Brabazon in a Short biplane.

In early November Roe took his new machine to Wembley Park to renew his flying activities in what he hoped would be a more suitable and less hostile location. In fact, as *Flight* reported, 'the ground is being cleared and many trees and bushes have been removed.' Roe was joined at Wembley Park by a French aviator with a monoplane powered by a 36 hp Anzani engine. 'The machine is beautifully made,' *Flight* observed.

The journal also reported that Roe had made several successful flights on 19 November 'in spite of the gusty wind'. But he was finally caught out when he was 20ft up. He 'struck the ground very heavily before he had time to recover, the machine being rather badly damaged but he hopes to be out again in a few days'. *Flight* also commented favourably on the steering system of Roe's machine, reporting that

> it seemed to work quite satisfactorily, for several times when making flight between the goal posts on the polo ground he was blown out of his course and promptly brought the machine back again.

Roe was clearly making progress. He was out again on 9 December and, according to *Flight's* correspondent, made 'a number of good steady flights the length of the ground, which was about 0.5 miles long. He flew from one end to the other, rising and falling at will, at times maintaining an altitude of from 20 to 30ft.' The control system worked 'very well for he had to dodge various obstacles'. The correspondent added,

> It is a pity he did not accomplish this, and previous flights when at Blackpool, since these would have gained for him both the All-British and British Aviator prizes amounting to £400.

Roe's confidence was growing. The Wembley Park authorities agreed to clear more trees and railings to enable him to make circular flights. 'Since he has fitted his new engine to his triplane much better results have been obtained and Mr Roe hopes to make flights every day now,' according to *Flight's* issue dated 25 December. It added helpfully: 'Notices will be exhibited at the Metropolitan Railway stations when flying is in progress.'

But the year ended on a less positive note. On Christmas Eve the triplane was damaged when it crashed while making a turn. According to *Flight,* Roe was attempting to turn sharply but 'as a result of some recent modifications in the steering arrangements, [he] found it impossible to rectify the tilting movement quickly enough and this caused the machine to fall, damaging one of the planes.' Before the accident Roe had made several flights of 400 to 500 yards.

The triplane's wings and undercarriage were badly damaged, although the engine was unharmed, as was the pilot who set to with his usual vigour to repair the damage. *Flight* published a picture of the triplane in flight before the crash. Other photographs show a smiling Roe surveying the damage. Such mishaps had become routine and the machine was soon repaired. By now Roe was running out of money. His brother Humphrey had helped buy the 20 hp JAP engine and, together with his father, had contributed over £400 to help Alliott. But 1910 was to bring major changes to his fortunes plus another change of location.

ALLIOTT VERDON-ROE

According to his grandson, Eric, the man who established one of the world's most respected aircraft manufacturing companies and which later built the immortal Lancaster bomber was 'well-known within the family for creating havoc and making a mess of everything'.

Edwin Alliott Verdon Roe – he never used his first Christian name and later hyphenated his surname – was born in Manchester in 1877 to a family which originated in Ireland. His father was a doctor. The younger Roe seems to have been a restless individual and this was apparent during his school days. 'He was not a good student,' says his grandson. 'He failed most of his exams, mainly because he wouldn't concentrate. He was also continually getting into scrapes and his younger brother Humphrey had to get him out of trouble.'

On leaving school Roe became a professional cyclist. He was obviously successful because he won a number of silver cups, which he later had melted down when he was in need of cash. He was to try several careers before turning to aviation.

He went to Canada where he trained as a civil engineer and on his return to Britain joined the Merchant Navy as an engineer officer. It was while watching sea birds soaring around his ship, the SS *Inchanga*, that he became intrigued by the possibilities of flight. This, according to Eric, prompted him to conduct experiments with gliders made of paper and cardboard which he launched from the stern of the ship.

Roe later became a draughtsman in the burgeoning motor industry but his experiments with gliders continued. Two of them won the first two prizes in a *Daily Mail* competition in 1906 but when the organisers decided that the overall quality of the entries was not what they had expected they halved the prize money awarded to Roe from £50 to £25. Later he applied for the post of secretary to the Aero Club. He was offered the job following an interview with the Hon Charles Rolls, but after just two days he left to work as a draughtsman for G.L.O. Davidson who claimed to have invented a steam-powered British 'airliner'.

Following his successful flights at Lea Marshes, Roe and his brother established A.V. Roe and Co (later known as Avro) at Brownsfield Mill, Great Ancoats Street, Manchester. Humphrey's contribution was chiefly financial and organisational. He acted as managing director until he joined the RFC in 1917. One of their first employees was Roy Chadwick, who worked on the Avro 504 which was to form the basis of the company's early success. In December 1914, 504s of the Royal Naval Air Service raided the German Zeppelin sheds at Friedrichshafen. The damage inflicted on the enemy was minimal but this was the first-ever strategic bombing raid in the history of air warfare.

The 504 went on to become a highly successful trainer; over 8,000 were built and it remained in RAF service until 1933. Chadwick went on to design many other well-known aircraft types such as the Anson. His re-design of the unsuccessful Manchester became the Lancaster which was to form the backbone of Bomber Command during the Second World War.

By that time, however, Roe had left the company following its acquisition in 1928 by J.D. Siddeley. Avro became part of the Armstrong Siddeley Development Company and was associated with Armstrong Whitworth. When Siddeley sold out to Hawker in 1935

Avro became part of the Hawker Siddeley Group. In 1963 the group merged with de Havilland and in 1977 became one of the constituents of British Aerospace, now BAe Systems.

In 1929 Roe acquired a controlling interest in S.E. Saunders and Co, an Isle of Wight-based firm of boat builders. Renamed Saunders-Roe, the company concentrated on the manufacture of flying boats, but after the Second World War it built aircraft as varied as the giant ten-engined Princess flying boat, of which just two were built, and the advanced SR53 rocket fighter which was later cancelled by the government.

A.V. Roe was knighted in 1929 and died in 1958. He was in his mid-70s when Eric was born but his grandson recalls him 'as a hoaxer and prankster who loved playing tricks'.

Chapter 6

Showing Off

It was hardly a triumph of organisation when Britain's first two aviation meetings were staged on conflicting dates. Yet people were so keen to see flying machines in action just a year after the country's first officially-recognised aeroplane flight that 360,000 spectators were claimed to have attended the events at towns eighty miles apart.

The clash of dates was made more controversial by the fact that the meeting staged at Doncaster in Yorkshire was not sanctioned by the aviation authorities yet it beat, by just three days, the officially-approved event at the popular Lancashire resort of Blackpool to the honour of being Britain's first-ever aviation gathering. Years later the *Yorkshire Post* called it a 'war of the roses spat' over which of the two was to ensure its place in history.

The Doncaster meeting opened on 15 October 1909 and closed on the 23rd, while the Blackpool event was staged from the 18th to the 26th. Despite the conflicting dates both events could boast the participation of the leading British and French aviators of the day. The key difference between them, however, was that while Blackpool was officially sanctioned by the Aero Club, Doncaster was not. As a result, the Doncaster participants were punished for attending the 'rogue' event despite warnings about the consequences of attending.

The organisers of the two events were clearly influenced by the success of the Rheims meeting in France. The first International Aviation Week, which opened on 22 August, used a rectangular six-mile course which was marked out on a large plain near the village of Bétheny, three miles from the city itself. Grandstands able to seat 5,000 spectators, public enclosures and aircraft sheds were erected together with a 600-seat restaurant.

The course was marked by tall pylons at each corner and a take-off area was designated in front of the sheds so that the contestants could become airborne before they joined the course. Special trains were laid on to bring the crowds of spectators in from Paris. Some thirty-eight aeroplanes were entered for the competitions to be held during the week, which included speed, distance and altitude contests. The most prestigious competition, however, was the first race for the Gordon Bennett International Aviation Cup. This was to be an annual competition in which pilots would represent their countries in a speed trial over 20 km.

Of the aircraft entered, six were Wright A biplanes, one was an American Curtiss-Herring machine flown by Glen Curtiss, and the rest were of French manufacture. Of the pilots only one, George Cockburn, was British. He had learned to fly in France, and was entered with a Farman biplane powered by a 50 hp Gnome engine. It seems that the man who was to later become the first chief inspector of accidents at the Air Ministry did not particularly distinguish himself at the meeting. 'At least he displayed practical ability as a pilot,' acknowledged historian Dallas Brett.

Anglo-French pilots put up outstanding performances by winning the biggest prizes at Rheims. Henry Farman took home a total of 63,000 francs while the Oxford-educated Hubert Latham won 42,000.

Farman was born in Paris, the son of a British journalist and his French wife, and he was a racing driver before taking to aviation. In October 1908 he made the first cross-country flight in Europe, flying the 27 km from Châlons to Rheims in 20 min to win a 50,000-franc prize. In 1909 he opened a flying school at Châlons-sur-Marne where his first pupil was George Cockburn. That year Farman started manufacturing machines of his own design having fallen out with Gabriel Voisin because the French manufacturer had sold as an original design an aircraft that had been built to Farman's specifications to John Moore-Brabazon.

Inevitably, perhaps, Hubert Latham was better-known for two failed attempts to fly the Channel than for his other exploits. The Paris-born son of an Englishman set a world speed record by covering 100 km in 1hr 28min 17sec at the controls of his 50 hp 8-cylinder Antoinette. Farman, though, flew the greater distance, 180 km which he covered in 3hr 4min 56sec. He set a world record by covering 100 km at an average speed of 67 kph.

Proof that Britain had not been entirely idle had come in March when the first British Aero Show opened at Olympia. It attracted eleven full-scale exhibits – seven pusher biplanes, two monoplanes and a pair of strange machines described as 'orthopters'.

If the aircraft on display were not considered wildly impressive, an exhibit of greater significance could be found among the aero-engines. Yet at the time the 7-cylinder Gnome attracted relatively little interest. Part of the reason was that it was a rotary engine. This meant that the cylinders were arranged around a central crankshaft like a conventional radial engine, but instead of having a fixed cylinder block with a rotating crankshaft, the entire cylinder block rotated around the stationary crankshaft. The propeller was bolted to the front of the crankcase.

The Gnome developed 50 hp and weighed just 165 lbs. It was compact and easy to install. A total of 8,000 Gnome rotaries was produced before the First World War. Farman was using one to achieve his distance record at Rheims four months later and this helped to focus attention on the engine and its advantages.

Inspired by the success of the Rheims meeting, the local authorities at Doncaster announced in September that the town would host its own aviation meeting, billed as the first in Britain. The organisers also had the support of the owner of Doncaster racecourse who allowed them to stage the meeting there. The local authority had guaranteed £5,000 towards the expenses and had contracted several flyers. Frantz Reichel, sporting editor the French newspaper *Le Figaro*, was appointed to handle the general arrangements, just as he had done at a recent meeting in Spa in Belgium.

But the organisers' announcement immediately caused controversy in British aviation circles. The Aero Club (with the support of the FAI) had already sanctioned a meeting in Blackpool but on dates which clashed with the Doncaster event. The committee of the Aero Club declared on 6 October that it could not sanction the Doncaster meeting. It stated that 'considering the scarcity of prominent aviators, it is palpable that such a proceeding is bound seriously to prejudice the success of both meetings, and if for no other reason should be banned.'

The Doncaster organisers insisted that there was no other possible date for their meeting because of the horse racing timetable. The French flyers who were contracted to fly there were unmoved: they had signed up to participate in good faith and the FAI had let them down. The Aero Club committee held another meeting on 12 October with representatives from Doncaster present. The club pointed out that Doncaster's claim that its meeting was being held under FAI and club regulations was 'not in accordance with the facts'. It warned that aviators who participated in the Doncaster meeting would be liable to disqualification from future competitions held under FAI rules in Britain and abroad.

Yet a dozen aviators defied the authorities and turned up to fly at Doncaster. The best-known were Léon Delagrange and Roger Sommer. But to further his ambition to win a prize offered by the *Daily Mail* for the first British pilot in a British aeroplane to fly a circular mile, Samuel Cody signed British naturalisation papers. As the crowd watched, the band played the *Star Spangled Banner* and *God Save the King*. But, as it happened, Cody crashed his machine on the first day of the meeting and made no significant flights.

The following flyers were entered for the Doncaster meeting: Samuel Cody (Cody), Léon Delagrange (Blériot XI), Hubert Le Bon (Blériot XI), Edward Mines (Mines), Léon Molon (Blériot XI), Georges Prévoteau (Blériot XI), Georges Saunier (Chauvière), Roger Sommer (Farman), John van der Burch (Blériot) and Walter Windham (Windham No 3).

The prizes on offer included the Doncaster Cup for the pilot flying the longest total distance, the Great Northern Cup for the greatest distance flown, the Doncaster Tradesmen's Cup for the longest time in the air, and the Chairman's Cup for the highest speed over two laps. Other cups were awarded for height, passenger-carrying, the best cross-country journey and the best flight by a British aviator. Cash prizes were also offered.

Only four pilots made significant flights during the meeting and the total distance flown was about 225 miles. An estimated 160,000 spectators attended, yet the meeting recorded a significant financial loss of £8,000 despite a Doncaster Corporation guarantee of £5,000 to cover expenses. Even before the meeting opened there were disagreements between the organisers about the distribution of surplus cash but in the end there was none. Press reports suggested that appearance money paid to the aviators totalled £11,600, of which Delagrange and his team (Le Blon, Molon and Prévoteau) received £6,000.

In November the Aero Club, obliged by the FAI, duly suspended the French flyers from taking part in any contests held under FAI rules until 1 January 1910. Cody, who had not actually taken part, managed to escape sanction. However, the Aero Club de France called for the disqualifications of Delagrange, Le Blon, Molon and Prévoteau to be reduced by a month to enable them to compete for the 1909 Michelin Cup which ended on 31 December. On the flyers' behalf it was claimed that they had signed contracts with the Doncaster organisers in August, two months before it was known that the meeting would not be sanctioned. The club argued that the aviators would have risked financial penalties for being in breach of their contracts had they not honoured their commitments.

Sommer, who had made the best flight of the meeting by covering 30 miles in 45 min, had subsequently sold his machine for £1,200. He announced that he planned to start building aircraft of his own design and was no longer concerned about the disqualification. After hearing the arguments, the British Aero Club lopped a month from the ban but the committee still felt that 'it would be desirable that these aviators should fully recognise the justice of the sentence pronounced upon them and to that end would be glad to receive from these three gentlemen a letter acknowledging this fact.' Molon did write such a letter, which was published in *Flight*.

This controversy, compounded by feelings that UK aviation was being regulated from London, led to the formation of a breakaway organisation of local aviation societies known as the Aeroplane Club of Great Britain and Ireland. It seems not to have lasted very long.

In the meantime, the Blackpool meeting was judged a great success. After the first day, when an estimated 100,000 spectators were claimed to have attended, Huntley Walker, chairman of the Lancashire Aero Club declared: 'The meeting is an enormous success. There can be no comparison between Blackpool and Doncaster and nothing finer was even seen at Rheims.'

Roger Walker, chairman of the Aero Club said: 'The aviators here are much more prepared than at Rheims. Blackpool Corporation and Lancashire Aero Club are to be congratulated on their admirable arrangements. In the present state of aviation, however, it is an absurdity to have two race meetings at the same time.' The *Manchester Guardian*'s special correspondent praised the 'herculean labours of organisation' which in just eight weeks had created the conditions for a successful meeting.

Manufacturers, quick to spot an opportunity, filled the newspaper's pages with aviation-themed advertisements. These included a call for 'aeroplanes for all' from William Arnold, of Chorlton-cum-Medlock, Manchester, who styled himself 'aeroplane and motor carriage builder'. 'There is no difficulty in having an aeroplane,' the advertisement claimed. It went on,

> They are not dear, they do not depreciate. They cost little for upkeep and they are the most fascinating playthings mankind has ever had. Indeed, you may say that mankind has been longing for them since he learned to walk erect. After waiting so long it is a source of considerable pleasure to us to be able to gratify that primitive desire. We can make aeroplanes guaranteed to fly.

It seems that despite his enthusiasm Mr Arnold's career as an aircraft manufacturer did not take off. His company began making car bodies in 1910 and between the two world wars they clothed luxury brands like Rolls-Royce and Bentley as well as buses. After the Second World War the company continued to build vehicle bodies but later concentrated on its agency for Morris and then Volkswagen cars. It was dissolved in 1985.

In a twenty-first century look-back at the 1909 meeting, *The Guardian* declared that it had placed Blackpool 'on the map as the home of aviation in the UK'. The newspaper recalled that the week opened with calm skies but that 'the weather tailed off at the end of the week as storm clouds gathered and flight became impossible.'

Even so, the 200,000 spectators at Squires Gate, which today is the site of Blackpool airport on the boundary between the resort and Lytham St Anne's, were said by the organisers to have consumed 36,000 bottles of beer, 1,000 hams and 500 cases of champagne.

There were a dozen aircraft present, including three Voisins, in the hands of Rougier, Fournier and Mortimer Singer, a lone Henry Farman with 50 hp Gnome, which was flown alternately by Louis Paulhan and its designer, two Blériots (for Leblanc and Parkinson), Hubert Latham's *Antoinette*, A.V. Roe's triplane, and several unspecified machines for Sanderson, Cleese, Neale and Fernandez.

Roe was the first to attempt a flight but his aircraft's puny JAP motor was not up to the task and he retired to the hangar to swap it for a more powerful unit. This enabled him to make a couple of short hops. The stars of the show were again Farman and Latham. Farman pocketed £2,400 in prize money, more than his three closest competitors put together. His premier achievement at the meeting was a flight of 47 miles in 1hr 32min 16sec at an average speed of 31 mph.

Latham, however, was the hero of the meeting. As the weather worsened and the wind speed rose, he completed two laps of the course in just over ten minutes despite winds gusting up to 38 mph. This exploit was believed to have been the first time a pilot had knowingly defied the elements and it established Latham's reputation as a skilled bad-weather pilot.

Among the spectators at the Blackpool meeting was a young mechanic from Belfast. While working for his brother's bicycle and car repair business, Harry Ferguson had become interested in the idea of powered flight. He was an enthusiastic follower of the Wright Brothers and their exploits and he also attended the Rheims meeting. On the strength of the notes he made at Blackpool and Rheims he managed to convince his brother, Joe, to start building a monoplane to his design. As a result, Harry Ferguson eventually became the first man to fly in Ireland and the first to build and fly his own aeroplane there. The venture led to Ferguson's invention of the modern agricultural tractor and the four-wheel drive system used by the Range Rovers and later constant four-wheel drive Land Rovers (see box on page 88).

Despite the controversy, the Blackpool and Doncaster meetings were repeated the following year. This time however, the two northern towns were joined by others as far apart as Wolverhampton, Folkestone, Bournemouth and Lanark, with their organisers all eager to cash in on the public enthusiasm for aviation.

This time the majority of the participating aircraft were British with a mixture of types including machines built by A.V. Roe, Blackburn, Bristol, Handley Page and Short. Most were monoplanes but among the biplanes exhibited was the Short machine with which Moore-Brabazon had won the *Daily Mail* Prize. Roe displayed his triplane design. Other manufacturers included Avis, Humber, Lane, Mann and Overton, Mulliner, Nicholson, Spencer Stirling, Star Twining and Warwick Wright. French influence continued to be strong: nearly all the monoplanes were copies of the Blériot, while some of the biplanes were inspired by Farman or Wright.

Britain was represented at the Nice meeting by A.W. Rawlinson and Charles Rolls, who achieved a 40-mile flight and was eventually placed fourth in the final order of merit. But the event of the year was probably the race to be the first to fly between London and Manchester. As far back as 1906 the *Daily Mail* had offered a £10,000 purse to the first pilot of any nationality to fly from a point within five miles of the newspaper's London office to one a similar distance from its Manchester office or vice-versa.

It was not, though, until 1910 that aeronautical technology and pilot ability had advanced to the point where such a flight was practical. But it was certainly worth waiting for: it came down to a contest between two men, probably the most accomplished airmen of the day, one British, one French.

Both were using French-built Henry Farman biplanes with 50 hp Gnome rotary engines. At first, Claude Grahame-White seemed to have stolen a march on Louis Paulhan because he was erecting his machine at Park Royal while his rival was at Hendon waiting for his to arrive. A crowd of journalists estimated at 300-strong watched the Briton take off at 0515 hrs on Saturday, 23 April. He headed for Wormwood Scrubs where Harold Perrin, secretary of the Royal Aero Club, was waiting at the top of a gasometer to officially flag him away.

Just over two hours later Grahame-White had reached his first planned stop at Rugby. He had averaged over 40 mph but it was cold and he needed time to thaw out with a cup of hot coffee. It was beginning to look as though he would claim the prize before Paulhan had even started but things began to go wrong for the Briton soon after he took off at 0825 hours for his next scheduled stop at Crewe. After just thirty miles however, he was forced to land in a field near Litchfield when his engine suffered valve trouble. A skid was damaged on landing and, while the repairs were being made, Grahame-White had lunch and slept for a few hours.

Towards evening a high wind sprang up, making further progress impossible. Time was getting short. He needed to reach his destination by 1715 hrs if he was to claim the prize, but he was forced to abandon the flight and contemplate taking his machine to Manchester to try again from there. But the next night his aeroplane, which had not been pegged down, was wrecked by the continuing high wind.

The machine was taken back to London for hurried repairs which were completed the following Wednesday. That same evening, however, Paulhan had taken off at 1721 hrs and headed for his official starting point at Hampstead Cemetery. He then followed the railway line north from Harrow: the railway sleepers had been painted white to help the aviators. Meanwhile, Grahame-White, exhausted by his efforts to get his machine ready, had gone to bed. He was woken with the news that Paulhan had started his attempt. Within ten minutes he was in the air, crossing the start line at 1829 hrs.

The Frenchman landed at Litchfield at 2010 hrs, while Grahame-White came down at Roade, 67 miles behind his rival. With the prize slipping away from him he then decided to throw caution to the winds and take off in the dark using car headlights to provide some illumination. His boldness nearly paid off. But just before 0400 hrs engine trouble forced him down again, this time at Polesworth, 107 miles from London. Three minutes later, Paulhan took off from Litchfield and completed his flight to Manchester without further drama to claim the *Daily Mail* prize.

When he heard the news, Grahame-White called for three cheers for Paulan, 'the finest aviator the world has ever seen'. *Flight* praised Grahame-White's 'plucky attempt' and both men were guests of honour at London's Savoy Hotel Hill where the *Daily Mail* hosted a celebratory lunch. Aviation had taken another major step forward.

There was some consolation for Grahame-White at the Wolverhampton meeting held at the Dunstall Park racecourse when he won the duration prize for flying a total of 1hr 15min during the week. Other awards were won by Charles Rolls, Cecil Grace, and George Cockburn. None of the continental stars were at Wolverhampton as they were busy at Rheims where Henry Farman raised the world's duration record to over 5 hours, covering 245 miles. At the same meeting Hubert Latham hoisted the European altitude record to 4,440ft.

Tragedy at the July Bournemouth meeting, however, cast a pall over the rest of the season. It started well enough with an entry comprising some of the most distinguished British and European aviators for a meeting that was held from 6 to 16 July at Southbourne, the most easterly part of the borough of Bournemouth. A specially laid-out aerodrome consisting of a mile of grassland between Tuckton and the Double Dykes near Hengistbury Head was used for the occasion. The area has since become a housing estate.

Among the twenty aviators entered were George Cockburn (Henry Farman), Samuel Cody (Cody), Captain Bertram Dickson (Henry Farman), Cecil Grace (Short), Alec Ogilvie (Short-Wright), John Moore-Brabazon (Short and Voisin), Leon Morane (Blériot) and Charles Rolls (Short-Wright). Rolls was among the prize winners on the opening day, winning the award for the slowest lap of the course with a time of 4 min 13 sec, at a speed of 25 mph. He then put in a quick lap at 40 mph.

On the second day the organisers had arranged a spot-landing competition but, according to aviation historian Dallas Brett, 'with almost incredible foolishness' they had placed the landing mark right under the shadow of the grandstand and immediately to windward of it. Rolls realised the only way to hit the mark was to approach and land into the wind. He made a trial run from behind the grandstand but realised too late that he was almost overshooting the mark. He put his aircraft into a dive but it was too steep. He pulled his control stick back too sharply and the tail booms broke away leaving the rest, together with the pilot, to fall to the ground. Although the drop was only 20 ft the damage to his skull was fatal. He was 33.

The popular Rolls was widely mourned, not least by his friend John Moore-Brabazon who had met him at Cambridge and acted as his mechanic when he went motor racing. 'He became my greatest friend,'

Brabazon wrote later. 'He was the strangest of men and one of the most likeable,' he recalled. 'He was tall and rather thin and his eyes stood out of their sockets rather more than was normal. He was rather fond of a Norfolk jacket and always wore a high stiff white collar....He didn't suffer fools gladly and his sense of humour was rather crude....Really Charlie Rolls' only fault – if it can be called that – was extreme parsimony. He simply hated spending money.'

Other accidents marred the Bournemouth meeting. Two days after Rolls' accident, Captain A. Rawlinson was badly injured when his Farman's undercarriage collapsed as he was landing. The following day J. Christiaens joined Rawlinson in hospital and later the Hon Alan Boyle suffered concussion when he wrecked his Avis monoplane. On a happier note, Morane was adjudged the overall winner on general merit. He lapped at 56 mph and climbed to 4,107 feet in 17 minutes.

The Blackpool meeting, now called a carnival, opened on 28 July and lasted three weeks. It also attracted a decent entry but not as good as it might have done had there not been another clash of dates, this time with a meeting at Lanark in Scotland. Grahame-White was there with his Henry Farman and was one of the stars of the show. Despite a wind gusting up to 30 mph, he flew several laps of the course, reaching a ground speed downwind of 70 mph. The Peruvian pilot Chavez flying a Blériot monoplane raised the European altitude record to 5,887ft.

Among the star turns at Blackpool was actor-turned-pilot Robert Loraine. He planned to fly from there to Anglesey but had to make a forced landing near Holyhead. The fabric covering his tail plane had become sodden with oil and was bellying upwards, making the clipped wing Farman tail heavy. He took off after repairs and returned to Blackpool after an absence of nearly four hours.

Later that year Loraine decided to attempt an aerial crossing of the Irish Sea. After a flight marked by an almost incredible series of difficulties, he was forced to ditch in Dublin Bay, leaving the intrepid aviator, who until then had accumulated just ten hours of solo flying, to swim the last 200 yards to the shore.

Roe had entered two triplanes for the Blackpool meeting and, together with spare parts, they were loaded into an open railway truck at Weybridge and covered by a tarpaulin. But during the journey to Preston, where the train was due to arrive the day before the meeting opened, the two machines were destroyed. The truck carrying them had been coupled immediately behind the locomotive and sparks from the engine had set fire to the machines and burned them out. 'I do not think I have ever been so stunned or disappointed in my life,' Roe wrote later.

But he was determined to have a presence at Blackpool. The Manchester workshop contained enough components for a new triplane to be assembled. By working night and day, Roe, Pixton and the rest of the workforce had completed a third version of the Roe III design by midnight on Saturday. Final assembly was completed at Blackpool where Roe took it for its first flight, making four laps of the circuit. But the new machine was not easy to handle, and this, combined with poor weather, ensured that Roe's participation in the meeting was punctuated by a series of accidents.

True to form, he crashed after four laps of the Blackpool course. After further repairs there was yet another crash. The organisers took pity on him and awarded him a special prize of £50 for his perseverance. The machine was later transported to the USA where Roe was due to take part in the Harvard-Boston Aero Meet. After a further series of mishaps, the machine was sold to the Harvard Aeronautical Society.

Like the first, the second Blackpool meeting made a financial loss, this time of around £20,000. The weather was bad throughout and in addition many spectators realised there was no need to pay to see the flying as there was a perfectly good view from the hills outside the airfield.

The Lanark meeting, held at the town's racecourse between 6 and 13 August 1910, also failed to make a profit. But that was not the only noteworthy feature of Scotland's first international aviation meeting which was said to have been one of the largest events organised in the country up to that time. It also meant that the racecourse, 25 miles from Glasgow and reputedly established in the Middle Ages during the reign of King William the Lion, was effectively transformed into an aerodrome with a smooth grass 1.75-mile circuit.

Not only was the land relatively flat but it already had facilities for the paying public, there were stables to act as aircraft hangars and the venue was accessible by both road and by rail. The Caledonian Railway Company constructed a new station near the main entrance and it was served by at least fourteen trains a day during the meeting. The participating aircraft arrived by rail. It was reported that nine miles of telephone cable were laid and a special post office employed thirty telegraph operators.

As the meeting was being staged soon after the tragic Bournemouth event, the organisers decided to impose restrictions on the participating aviators in the interests of safety: no aircraft was permitted to fly closer to the spectators than 300 yards. Yet they, like the Bournemouth organisers, seem not to have grasped the dangers of landing marks placed close to the grandstand. For the first time, aircraft were timed over a straight measured distance, allowing the first world records to be set for flights over one mile.

There were twenty-two entrants including Cody, Grace, Ogilvie and the American pilot Armstrong Drexel. Half were English and there were six British-built aircraft, although Blériots and Henry Farmans were also prominent. An attempt by McArdle in a Blériot to reach Edinburgh was thwarted by the weather, but 17-year-old Marcel Hanriot gave an exhibition of polished flying which delighted a crowd estimated at 50,000. Italian pilot Cattaneo broke the British distance and duration records in his Blériots by covering just over 140 miles in 3hr 11min.

Drexel set a new altitude record of 6,621 feet which beat the existing mark by 440ft, while James Bradley (Blériot) covered a kilometre at over 77 mph and a mile at 75 mph. He also covered five laps at over 58 mph, 2 mph faster than Cattaneo. At the other end of the speed scale, Ogilvie completed a lap in his Short-Wright at a ponderous 24 mph. Cattaneo took the prize for the aggregate distance flown during the meeting, covering a few yards short of 400 miles.

All told, an estimated 215,000 spectators attended the meeting, which *The Aero* magazine called 'the most successful yet held in Britain'. It may not have made a profit but its success persuaded Lanark Town Council the following May to grant a one-year lease to W.H. Ewen to establish a flying school on the site. The first Scot to hold a pilot's licence, Ewen had been taught to fly by Louis Blériot. He started his school using a French-built Deperdussin monoplane and also constructed several other aircraft on the site. But there appears to have been only sporadic flying at Lanark over the next two years and in October 1913 the council terminated Ewen's lease. It was to be nineteen years before Lanark saw further significant aviation activity when Air Alan Cobham's flying circus introduced its flying shows to the area. Ewen, meanwhile, was the first to fly across the Forth estuary and the first Scot to fly the English Channel. During the First World War he trained over 300 pilots for the Royal Flying Corps at Hendon.

The Folkestone meeting in late September was held at the town's racecourse. Only three pilots attended but one of them, Cecil Grace, gave a masterly exhibition of high-altitude flying in his record-setting Blériot. One of the participating pilots, G.A. Barnes, got into trouble with his Humber-Blériot and he jumped out from thirty feet, sustaining head injuries and a broken wrist. The second Doncaster meeting, which took place at the same time, was an all-French affair but marred by bad weather.

Over the next few months British aviators distinguished themselves in international competitions. Grahame-White won the prestigious Gordon-Bennett contest in the USA, which *Flight* described as a 'British Triumph' despite bemoaning the fact that it had been achieved with a French-built aircraft. 'This is not as it should be,' the journal observed, 'for at this stage in the development of the aeroplane some native genius should surely have come forward with designs at least equal to the best of the French machines.'

Samuel Cody won the British Empire Michelin Cup despite stiff competition from Ogilvie, who flew from Camber Sands near Rye, and Sopwith (Brooklands). In misty conditions at Laffan's Plain, Farnborough, Cody covered 185 miles in 4hr 47min to win the cup and a cash prize of £500. Sopwith, however, received ample compensation in December when he won the £4,000 Baron de Forest prize. The contest involved a cross-channel flight from Dover followed by an eastward flight to test pilot endurance and fuel tank capacity.

Also in the running were Claude Grahame-White (Bristol), Robert Loraine (Bristol), Frank McLean (Short) and Cecil Grace (Short-Farman). Sopwith, McLean and Grace started from Eastchurch.

Sopwith in his Howard Wright with ENV engine made a trouble-free Channel crossing and headed over France into Belgium. Three hours later he reached Thirimont, 169 miles as the crow flies from his starting point. It was good enough to win him the prize.

Cecil Grace left Eastchurch soon after Sopwith but the weather worsened and he joined some of the other contestants sitting it out at Swingate Downs, Dover. After one failed attempt to cross the Channel, Grace tried again. He was not to survive it.

THE HON CHARLES ROLLS

Racing driver, balloonist, pioneer aviator, co-founder of one of the world's most famous engineering companies, Charles Stewart Rolls was born in London in 1877, the third son of John Rolls, the first Baron and Lady Llangattock.

Charles Rolls developed an interest in engines at an early age and he attended Cambridge University where he gained a BA degree in applied science and later an MA in engineering. He was a keen cyclist but in 1896 bought his first car, a Peugeot Phaeton, and campaigned against the restrictions imposed on motor vehicles by the Locomotive Act, becoming a founder member of the Automobile Club of Great Britain.

Rolls competed in some of the earliest motor sport events and was the first British driver to race overseas. He participated in some of the notoriously dangerous city-to-city races on public roads which were later abandoned in favour of events on closed circuits. He was one of several personalities whose names were to become linked with major car manufacturers to start the 800-mile Paris–Madrid race in 1903. It was abandoned at Bordeaux because of a series of accidents, one which claimed the life of Marcel Renault.

Although Rolls worked for the London and North Western Railway at Crewe, it soon became clear that his talents lay more in salesmanship. In January 1903, helped by £6,600 provided by his father, he started one of Britain's first car dealerships. C.S. Rolls &

Co, based in Fulham, London, imported French Peugeot and Belgian Minerva cars.

The following year Rolls was introduced to the older Frederick Royce who was just beginning to build quality cars. Royce the artisan had little in common with Rolls the aristocrat yet they became friends and agreed that Royce would build cars and Rolls would sell them: Rolls-Royce was born. The first fruit of the partnership was the Rolls-Royce 10 hp car, which was unveiled at the Paris Salon in December. Two years later the two principals formalised their partnership by creating Rolls-Royce Limited, with Royce appointed technical managing director and Rolls providing financial backing and business acumen.

Rolls had, meanwhile, developed an interest in ballooning and in 1901 co-founded the Aero Club. In 1905, when he was at the New York motor show promoting Rolls-Royce cars, he was introduced to the Wright brothers. This meeting prompted Rolls to develop an interest in powered flight. In 1909 he bought the first of six aircraft built by the Short brothers under licence from the Wright brothers. He made more than 200 flights with this machine and on 2 June 1910 completed the first non-stop double crossing of the English Channel by aeroplane, returning after 95 minutes to a hero's welcome. Statues of Rolls at Dover and also Monmouth, location of Rolls' family home, commemorate this achievement. The same year Rolls received the Aero Club's pilot certificate No 2.

Rolls had tried hard but without success to interest the War Office in the potential of the Wrights' *Flyer*. He was the first to order one of the Short-built Wright aircraft in 1909 but was not flying this aircraft at Bournemouth. Instead he was at the controls of a French-built *Flyer* which had been modified against Wilbur Wright's advice. Rolls had added wheels and an auxiliary elevator in the tail. It was this second elevator which collapsed in a steep dive during a spot-landing competition at Bournemouth with disastrous consequences.

In its obituary of Rolls published on 13 July 1910, *The Times* noted: 'Mr. Rolls is the tenth airman who has met with a fatal accident in a motor-driven flying machine, and he is the first Englishman who has sacrificed his life in the cause of modern aviation.' His friend John Moore-Brabazon declared: 'This terrible disaster to aviation and also the loss of so dear a friend sickened me and my wife of aviation altogether and I never flew again until the war.'

A stained-glass window in Eastchurch parish church was dedicated as a memorial to Rolls by the Archbishop of Canterbury in 1926. Another window remembers Cecil Grace who was lost in an attempted cross-Channel flight in 1910.

HARRY FERGUSON

Born in 1884 in County Down, Northern Ireland, the son of a Scottish farmer, Harry Ferguson worked as a mechanic for J.B. Ferguson & Co, the bicycle and car repair business run by his brother Joe.

By November 1909 he had designed and built a two-seat monoplane. It featured a triangular cross-section fuselage and was powered by a Green engine, later replaced by a 35 hp JAP unit. To make its first flight, the aircraft had to be towed through the streets of Belfast to Hillsborough Great Park after its wings had been detached and with the tail resting on the back of a car.

The first attempt to get airborne failed due to a combination of bad weather and propeller trouble. But over the next few weeks Ferguson's monoplane made several hops, the first flight, of 130 yards, being achieved on 31 December.

Ferguson persisted with his experiments so that by 23 August 1910 he was able to take up the first female passenger to fly in Ireland. The lady concerned, Rita Marr, had travelled from Liverpool to make the flight. Later that year Ferguson made a flight along the beach at Newcastle to win a £100 prize offered by the town's sports committee for the first powered flight over a minimum distance of two miles. It took him several attempts, but eventually Ferguson flew for almost three miles along the foreshore at an altitude of between

50 and 150 ft. The achievement is commemorated by a simple stone memorial on Newcastle North Promenade.

Despite this success the Ferguson brothers fell out over the best way of developing the aviation side of the business and Harry quit to sell cars and tractors. It was during this period that he began developing his ideas for attaching implements to tractors to provide a more integrated and efficient system.

Following an arrangement with Henry Ford, which ended with a $9 million lawsuit, Ferguson turned to Sir John Black of the Standard Motor Co. The result was 21,000 of the soon-to-be-familiar grey-painted TE20 tractors being built between 1946 and 1947.

Ferguson continued to undertake research into four-wheel drive systems which resulted in the P99 Formula One car and Range Rover and later constant four-wheel-drive Land Rover vehicles. Ferguson died at his home in Gloucestershire following a barbiturate overdose. It was never determined whether or not this was accidental.

LORD NORTHCLIFFE

Alfred Harmsworth, the first Viscount Northcliffe of St Peters in the County of Kent, probably did more than any other to champion aviation's early development.

It was said that Northcliffe was obsessed with aviation. He went to the international aviation meeting at Rheims in 1909, met Wilbur Wright and appointed Harry Harper as the *Daily Mail*'s air correspondent. It was a world first for the newspaper Harmsworth had founded in 1896.

Through the cash prizes awarded by the *Daily Mail*, Northcliffe inspired the early aviators on to ever greater efforts. Among them was the £10,000 offered for the first flight from London to Manchester, the £1,000 for the first cross-channel flight and the £10,000 for the first non-stop crossing of the Atlantic.

Recipients of the *Mail's* largesse included such great names of pioneer aviation as Louis Paulhan, Louis Blériot, John Moore-Brabazon, Thomas Sopwith, John Alcock and Arthur Whitten Brown, and Amy Johnson. Between 1910 and 1930 the *Mail* handed out over £60,000 in prize money. Some of the losers also received consolation awards like the £5,000 which went to Harry Hawker and Kenneth Mackenzie Grieve for the gallant failure of their bid for the Atlantic prize in 1919.

Northcliffe was a visionary whose ideas were often ahead of his time. The *Mail's* announcement of a £10,000 prize for the first trans-Atlantic flight in 1913 was greeted with ridicule. It was, after all, made on 1 April. The general attitude was that if it wasn't an April Fool gag then it must be a circulation-boosting gimmick. The satirical magazine *Punch* offered a similar prize for the first flight to Mars.

But Northcliffe was not joking. He had been aware that France was still well ahead in the development of aeronautical technology – several of the *Mail's* awards had gone to French aviators in French-built machines – and now he was shocked by the huge sums being spent by Germany on military aviation.

Chapter 7

Underneath the Arches

O swald Short's first reaction when he heard reports of Wilbur Wright's flying displays in France was to tell his brother Eustace that it meant the end of ballooning: they should 'begin building aeroplanes at once.'

His next thought was, 'We must get Horace to join us.'

Despite his dislike of balloons, the oldest of the Short brothers did not, apparently, have the same aversion to heavier-than-air machines. Having sold the patents to his Auxetophone sound-amplifier to C.A. Parsons, Horace Short went to work for the Newcastle-based company on steam turbine design. Now Oswald's task was to persuade Horace to join him and Eustace in building aeroplanes.

As the notion of powered flight was much more appealing than steam turbines, Horace seems not to have needed much persuasion. In fact, Oswald was surprised by Horace's response: 'Yes, but you'd better be quick; I'll be with you in three days and if you aren't ready by then I'll start without you.'

He duly quit his job with Parsons and returned to London. In November 1908 the new partnership was registered at Battersea under the name Short Brothers. Each brother contributed £200. Horace was to be head of the firm and its chief designer. He would soon be responsible for a steady flow of designs. In fact, his ideas would lay the foundations for naval aircraft design in Britain.

The Shorts' first attempt at building aeroplanes had been a glider for John Moore-Brabazon in 1907. It was not a success. Oswald wrote much later: 'At that time neither Eustace nor I had given any thought to gliding or aeroplanes.' Indeed, contemporary photographs of the interior of the railway arches at Battersea used by the brothers show the relatively crude equipment and machinery available for building the early aircraft. These machines were produced entirely by hand and on a one-off basis for each individual customer.

Moore-Brabazon's new glider quickly acquired an engine. Into the ash and bamboo framework, Howard and Warwick Wright, who were neighbours of Eustace and Oswald at Battersea, fitted a 12 hp Buchet engine. The machine was then taken to Brooklands in the hope of winning the £250 prize for flying a complete circuit of the motor racing track. This it failed to do and the engine was removed.

Nevertheless, the Shorts received two orders for powered aircraft. The others came from Charles Rolls, who ordered a glider based on photographs of the Wright *Flyer* and the other from Francis McClean, a member of the Aero Club who later bought several more aircraft from the Short Brothers and also acted as an unofficial, unpaid test-pilot.

McClean's aircraft, designated the Short No 1 Biplane, was also similar to the Wright *Flyer* design but incorporated several of the Shorts' own ideas. In March 1909 it was exhibited, without its fabric covering, at the first British Aero Show at Olympia. Horace apparently drew up the designs in his mother's flat in Prince of Wales Mansions, Prince of Wales Road (later Drive), a stone's throw from the workshop in Battersea. The first was for a biplane with front elevators and rear-mounted rudder. A further machine was built for John Moore-Brabazon.

In August 1908 Wilbur Wright came to Europe to give demonstrations and passenger flights in the *Flyer* biplane at Hunaudières Racecourse near Le Mans, then at Camp d'Auvours and later at Pont-Long near Pau. Many aspiring British aviators went to France and went up with Wright. They included Charles Rolls, Francis McClean, Frank Hedges Butler, Major Baden Baden-Powell and Griffith Brewer. When Brewer told Rolls he was going to Auvours to see the *Flyer,* Rolls had just returned from watching Wright demonstrating the craft. 'We at once recognised the miracle that had taken place,' Brewer wrote later. 'From that moment we kept our balloons for pleasure races and accepted the idea of mechanical flight.'

At Auvours, Brewer approached the shed containing the *Flyer* and presented his card to a mechanic, asking him to pass it on to Wright. Later that evening the two men had dinner together in a nearby restaurant.

It seems they hit it off because Brewer not only got his flight but also became a lifelong friend of the Wrights, later using his expertise as a patent agent to help the brothers protect their invention in Britain.

Charles Rolls was so enthusiastic after his flight that he not only wanted his own *Flyer* but was also keen to become involved in exploiting the brothers' invention. At the time they were involved in ultimately fruitless negotiations with the British government and Rolls suggested the Short Brothers, who had built balloons for both him and Brewer, could construct the aircraft.

The enthusiastic reports sent from France by the British aviators who were treated to flights aboard the *Flyer* not only prompted Oswald's comment about the future direction of aviation but also persuaded Eustace to travel to France to meet Wilbur and make a flight. On Wilbur's second visit in December, Eustace took another flight, returning to persuade Horace to go and see the *Flyer* for himself. Horace did so and also made sketches of the craft. While at Pau he made what the Wright Brothers later admitted was the first complete drawing of their machine.

But instead of a major sale to the British government, the Wright Brothers had to settle for a deal with the Short Brothers which Rolls had pressed them to conclude and Brewer to negotiate. Brewer, who also persuaded the Wrights to appoint him as their British patent agent, was able to convince the Wrights of the Short Brothers' competence. It was therefore agreed that the Shorts would build *Flyers* under licence and that the Wrights would receive £1,000 per copy. It was a modest sum even by the standards of the day. The Shorts' profit was about £600 per aircraft.

It was clear that the railway arches at Battersea were too restrictive to accommodate these new activities and the Short brothers were again seeking new premises. However, the deal with the Wrights was negotiated while they were still at Battersea, as were orders for completed aircraft. Before returning home, the Wrights visited the Shorts' new works at Eastchurch and also the old premises at Battersea where the first of the *Flyers* was taking shape. The Short brothers were later to claim that they were the 'first manufacturers of aircraft in the world', and although this has been disputed, they were certainly the first in Britain. Despite their move to the Isle of Sheppey and subsequently to Rochester, the Battersea balloon factory remained in use.

The Short brothers move to Kent did not end Battersea's association with the manufacture of heavier-than-air craft. It is not clear why Mulliner, the well-known builder of bespoke bodies for luxury cars, chose to take a lease on a former skating rink at 2-16 Vardens Road, Battersea, in December 1910. According to its advertising material, 'Mulliner's Aerocraft Works' was 'the best organised and most extensive aeroplane works in Great Britain'. Certainly the accompanying photographs showed a large unobstructed building with numerous aircraft under construction. Although Mulliner exhibited a monoplane at the March 1910 Olympia Aero Show, it seems that this factory was used mainly for the construction of machines designed by other people and for the repair and rebuilding of damaged aircraft. The Mulliner monoplane was, however, praised by *Flight* for its high-standard of finish and light weight.

The prototype was built at Mulliner's Northampton factory and constructed mainly of ash with its wings and tail surfaces covered by Dunlop fabric. The machine was designed by Gordon Stewart and featured wings built up on two main spars, the rear pair of which were hinged together to facilitate roll control by warping, and operated by a car-type steering wheel. Wingspan was 33ft and overall length 27ft. The wings were braced to a tubular steel extension to the main frame.

The 35 hp 8-cylinder JAP engine was carried ahead of the wing leading edge with the exposed pilot's seat located 2ft behind the trailing edge. The machine was supported on a pair of spoked wheels mounted in a diamond-shaped frame across the centre of which was stretched an elastic spring which served as the suspension.

According to *Flight*, the Mulliner monoplane was 'mainly remarkable for the skeleton-like frame that has been adopted and the high finish of the workmanship'. But there was concern about the robustness of the machine's construction. The journal added: 'There are some parts, however, that we shall expect to see strengthened within a short while of this machine commencing its practical trials.'

This comment produced a tetchy response from the designer. Gordon Stewart said that the 'erroneous' impression that the machine lacked strength was probably due to the incomplete state in which it was exhibited at Olympia. He conceded that it was a light-weight machine – 'one of the lightest that has been constructed' – but he insisted 'its strength will be adequate for its purpose.' He expected that physical trials of the machine would begin at the end of May.

At the following year's Olympia show Mulliner displayed the Kny-Plane, designed by the firm's Danish manager. This was a two-seat monoplane with a boat-like body. 'Apart from this characteristic,' *Flight* reported, 'the most important structural detail is the method of swivelling the wings and depressing the leading edge so as to alter their attitude and camber simultaneously.' The wings were mounted on a central bearing to enable the angle of incidence to be altered during flight, while a system of pivoted rods, toothed sprockets and chains acted on the flexible leading edge. The undercarriage featured a pair of wheels on an axle with coil spring suspension. A central skid was hinged to the axle with a coil-sprung central support.

According to Mulliner's publicity, the Kny-Plane was 'the only machine that calls for serious attention and creates sensation in aeronautical circles here and aboard'. The reality, though, appears to have been rather different because later in 1911 Mulliner decided to quit aircraft manufacture and concentrate on its core business of building bodies for Daimler and Rolls-Royce cars. Accordingly the Vardens Road premises were vacated to make way for a rather more successful aeronautical business.

This was the firm of Hewlett and Blondeau formed by Hilda Hewlett and French engineer Gustave Blondeau. Hilda Hewlett was one of the few British women to have played a part in the early development of aviation. She and Blondeau became joint owners of a Farman biplane and attended the Farman school in France to learn how to fly it.

On returning to Brooklands they decided to start the first flying school there in September 1910. Many aviators would gain their first experience of flying at the Hewlett and Blondeau school, including Thomas Sopwith. In the 18 months it was operating 13 pupils graduated from the school which, remarkably, suffered no accidents during that period.

On 29 August 1911 Hewlett became the first woman in the UK to earn a pilot licence.

Hewlett also taught her son Francis to fly; he earned his pilot certificate, dated 14 November 1911, and went on to have a distinguished military aviation career in both the UK and New Zealand, making him the first military pilot to be taught to fly by his own mother. He was awarded the Distinguished Service Order in 1915 and rose to the rank of Group Captain in the RAF and Air Commodore in the RNZAF.

The flying school could not afford to employ a full-time mechanic so Blondeau himself had to check the aircraft before every flight, tuning the engine and tightening stay wires as well as carrying out any necessary repairs. He seems to have done this so well that he and Hewlett were asked to check aircraft for prospective purchasers. The pair therefore decided to close the flying school and go into aircraft manufacture, forming a limited company. They leased the former Mulliner factory in Battersea which they called the Omnia Works and there they built Farman, Caudron and Hanriot aircraft under licence. Having sunk most of their capital into equipping the Omnia Works, the principals could not afford to employ any office staff so most administrative tasks and book keeping fell to Hewlett. She was also running her home in North London, so she rented a flat at 34 Park Mansions, Prince of Wales Road, Battersea.

In addition to the production of complete machines, including Hanriots for the French and Russian governments, the company also offered fittings like turnbuckles, wire strainers and a type of stranded cable for which Hewlett and Blondeau represented the only source. By this time the company was employing twenty-five staff. In 1912 it was contracted to build aircraft for the Royal Navy and the army. Records quoted by south London aviation historian Patrick Loobey state that it built two BE2as for the navy, 18 BE2cs for the army and two AD Scouts for the army.

In 1913 Hewlett and Blondeau built a single-seat monoplane designed by George Dyott, a New York-born electrical engineer educated and resident in the UK who had gained pilot certificate no 114 in August 1911. His neat and well-thought-out machine showed how far aircraft design had progressed in just a few years, although it still featured roll control by wing warping.

Its rectangular-section fuselage was built up around four longerons connected by struts and cross-members braced by strong diagonal wiring. Aluminium sheeting partially enclosed the 50 hp Gnome rotary engine and extended beyond the cockpit. The 29 ft span wings comprised two rectangular-section main spars made up of three laminations of ash and spruce. The ribs were also of ash and spruce. The wings and rear fuselage were covered with doped linen.

The pilot sat well down in the fuselage in a wicker-work seat mounted in a welded tubular metal frame. Facing him was a dashboard containing an engine revolution counter, an altimeter and petrol and oil gauges. In the centre was a compass made by Kelvin and James White Ltd. The landing chassis comprised a pair of skids on which was mounted the axle. It was suspended from the body by four struts. Two of these machines were apparently completed, but not at Battersea.

In the expectation of further government orders Hewlett and Blondeau decided to seek larger premises offering scope for expansion which Vardens Road did not. In June 1914 the firm moved to a 10-acre (40,000 sq m) site at Leagrave, Bedfordshire, where it remained in business until after the Armistice. During the war the company employed over 700 people and turned out over 800 aircraft, mostly BE2cs, Armstrong Whitworth FK 3s and Avro 504s. After the war the business diversified into farming equipment, but the factory had closed by the end of October 1920. The site remained unsold until 1926.

Howard and Warwick Wright may be somewhat less well-known than their namesakes from Dayton, Ohio, but they were also notable pioneer aviators and aircraft manufacturers. For around five years, they rented railway arch number 80 at Battersea, next door to the Short Brothers. Later, as their business expanded, they took numbers 81 and 82.

As early as 1907 Howard was advertising that 'any kind of machine can be built to inventor's specification.' This may well have brought the Italian inventor Frederico Capone from Naples to the Wrights' door with a request to build a helicopter. The machine featured a welded tubular steel frame with two 20ft rotors to provide lift together with two smaller propellers for forward motion. All were driven by a 50 hp Antoinette engine. The machine was taken for trials to Norbury golf course but failed to lift itself more than 2 ft.

Capone then asked Howard Wright to build a more powerful version which was transported to Naples immediately it was finished. Further craft, equally unsuccessful, were built at Battersea before Capone lost heart. But in 1908 the brothers were asked by their neighbours, the Short brothers, to fit a 12 hp Buchet engine to a biplane originally built as a glider for John Moore-Brabazon.

This encouraged the Wrights to build a biplane of their own design, which was displayed at the 1909 Olympia Aero Show. It bristled with novel features including a framework entirely of tubular steel and the use of co-axial contra-rotating propellers. *Flight* explained that this was not to balance the torque from the 50 hp Metallurgique engine but to neutralise the propellers' gyroscopic effect.

The pilot sat in a linen-covered pod mounted between the biplane wings with the engine behind the cockpit. The box-kite tail was carried by a framework projecting from the wings. Another unusual feature was the undercarriage. There were single wheels mounted beneath the central chassis with another at the tail. Smaller bicycle-type wheels were mounted beneath the tips of the lower wings. The idea behind this arrangement, *Flight* explained, was that

> the embryo aviator will be able to learn something of the control of the machine without leaving *terra firma* by driving it about over the ground on two wheels only; in this way it is anticipated that he will learn to steer and balance the machine.

The craft carried a price tag of £1,200, which might explain why no orders were forthcoming. More successful, however, were the monoplanes which followed, which were designed by William Oke Manning. The first, known as the *Golden Plover*, was fitted with a 30 hp Anzani engine, later replaced by a 35 hp unit and completed in December 1909. Initial trials took place at Brooklands in the hands of the Hon Alan Boyle, founder of the Scottish Aeroplane Syndicate. By April the aircraft was achieving straight flights, before flying circles the following month. At the 1910 Wolverhampton meeting, Boyle was able to stay aloft for almost eight minutes.

Four further aircraft, now known as Avis, were built for the syndicate including one example which Boyle wrecked at the Bournemouth meeting in July, but not before using it to gain pilot certificate No 13. Another was sold to racing driver J.H. Spottiswood, while *Avis IV*, originally built to replace Boyle's wrecked machine, was sold at auction at Brooklands when the syndicate was dissolved. In what was claimed to be the first-ever auction of an aeroplane, the machine was knocked down for £50 to the circuit's press officer, Eustace Gray.

Meanwhile, Howard Wright and Manning were working on an improved version of the Avis for Warwick Wright's use. It was displayed at the Olympia Aero Show in March when, *Flight* noted, it combined timber and steel in the construction of its chassis and frame. The following month it made its first flight at Eastchurch. Further outings were made at Brooklands but were terminated by Warwick's immersion in the notorious sewage farm.

In what sounds like a scene from the movie *Those Magnificent Men in their Flying Machines*, Warwick swerved to miss a group of spectators and hit a boulder marking the edge of the sewage farm. The undercarriage was wiped off and the machine careered into the sludge.

Howard, meanwhile, was hedging his bets with another Voisin-type biplane. This was more conventional than his previous design, several examples of which were produced for customers. Among them was T.O.M. Sopwith whose machine differed from the others in featuring a tailwheel rather than a skid and single cabane strut in place of a pair of kingposts. Sopwith used this machine to set British duration and distance records. It had a wingspan of 36ft and, although it had the appearance of lightness, 'the construction is very strong,' *Flight* noted. Power came from a water-cooled 60 hp ENV engine driving a two-bladed pusher propeller. Twin radiators supplied by the Spiral Tube Company were mounted on either side of the engine on the lower plane.

In 1911 Howard Wright's share of the business was acquired by the Coventry Ordnance Works. Two biplanes designed jointly by him and

Manning to fulfil War Office requirements were assembled at Battersea from parts mostly produced at Coventry. *Flight* was impressed by its first sight of the aircraft, praising its 'marked originality, its excellence of design and construction and its business-like – more than that – its warlike appearance'. The journal added: 'It has a certain atmosphere about it that brands it as a machine intended for harder and more serious service than mere aerodrome work.'

The aircraft had side-by-side seating for two in its cockpit, but *Flight* noted in a description of the aircraft published in May 1912 that the aircraft had actually lifted four people under the power of its 100 hp Gnome engine. This unit was mounted in the nose and drove a two-bladed propeller via a chain, an arrangement which provided a 2:1 reduction. In some respects, the aircraft appeared to be ahead of its time, although it was a conventional biplane with the top wing having a greater span than the bottom. It was constructed mainly of ash, and wing warping provided lateral movement.

The aircraft underwent a series of military trials at Salisbury Plain in August 1912 but neither example particularly distinguished itself and no orders were forthcoming. This brought Howard Wright's connection with Battersea to an end (see box on page 102).

GRIFFITH BREWER

A recognised authority on patent practice relating to aircraft, Griffith Brewer was better known for his close friendship with Wilbur and Orville Wright. Brewer, who had made his first balloon flight in 1891, met Wilbur in France in 1908 and was the first Briton to fly as a passenger with the American inventor. He was to become a close friend and supporter of Wilbur and Orville, making thirty trips to the USA to visit them. Later he became the Wrights' patent agent in Britain and in 1914 arranged for the British government to secure the rights to use Wright's patents for £15,000. This freed British aircraft manufacturers from the threat of litigation from across the Atlantic.

Griffith Brewer was born in London in 1867 and later trained to enter his father's firm of patent agents in Chancery Lane. In 1891 he went to Leeds to take charge of the firm's office there, returning eight years later to run both the London and Leeds offices.

In the meantime, Brewer had become interested in aeronautics and made his first balloon ascent as a passenger in 1891. He became a pupil of Percival Spencer and in 1906 took part in the Gordon Bennett balloon race in Paris. He would later compete in three further Gordon Bennett contests and win a major international race from Hurlingham in 1908. Two years earlier he had married Beatrice Swanston who was the first woman to cross the English Channel by balloon.

A founder member of the Royal Aero Club, Brewer was also a leading light of the Royal Aeronautical Society, becoming its president from 1940-42. He was also president of the Chartered Institute of Patent Agents from 1930-31. Although he had learned to fly in the USA in 1914 it was not until 1930 that Brewer qualified as a pilot in Britain. He subsequently bought a de Havilland Gipsy Moth.

Griffith Brewer died in 1948 at the age of 80.

HILDA HEWLETT

As an Edwardian wife and mother, Hilda Hewlett was probably unique in starting her own aircraft manufacturing company.

Hilda Beatrice Hewlett (née Herbert) was born in London in February 1864, the daughter of a Church of England minister. She was an early bicycle and automobile enthusiast who participated in several car rallies. In 1888 she married barrister-turned-novelist Maurice Hewlett and they had two children, a boy and a girl. The Hewletts separated in 1914, partly due to Hilda's growing interest in aviation. Maurice went to live in Wiltshire and died there in 1923.

Hilda attended her first aviation meeting at Blackpool in 1909, and the same year met ex-patriot French aviator Gustave Blondeau at Brooklands, where in September 1910 they started a flying school. On 18 August 1911, Hewlett became the first woman in the UK to earn a pilot licence when she received certificate No 122 from the Royal Aero Club after completing the test in her biplane at Brooklands.

The First World War success of the Hewlett and Blondeau aircraft manufacturing company contrasted starkly with the lack of orders which followed the Armistice. The company folded and Hewlett emigrated to Tauranga, New Zealand. Her son, daughter and family were eventually to follow her. Having escaped what she called the 'three Cs of Europe – crowds, convention, and civilization,' she enjoyed the outdoor life in New Zealand, especially camping and fishing. Her family gave her the nickname 'Old Bird'.

In June 1932, Hewlett was present at the inaugural meeting of the Tauranga Aero and Gliding Club and the following month was elected as the club's first president. In January 1939, at the opening of the Tauranga airport, New Zealand's Minister of Defence, Frederick Jones, formally named a nearby road after Hilda Hewlett and her son Francis, in recognition of their services in pioneering aviation in Tauranga.

Hilda Hewlett died in Tauranga in August 1943. Following a service on the railway wharf, she was buried at sea. In 1979 the link between Hilda and Battersea was commemorated when the name Hewlett House was bestowed upon a new local authority development at Havelock Terrace.

THE OTHER WRIGHT BROTHERS

Britain's Wright brothers, Howard and Warwick, were born at Dudley in the West Midlands, the sons of foundry owner Joseph Wright and his wife Grace, née Tinsey. Howard was born in 1867 and Warwick nine years later. When Joseph retired in 1887 his sons carried on the Neptune Foundry business and also Wright's Patent Heater and Condenser Company which Joseph had originally founded.

The company failed in the late 1890s and Howard Wright found employment as works manager with Hiram Maxim's electrical engineering and export company, while Warwick joined the Vickers

Maxim company. Warwick became involved with the motor industry and, like Charles Rolls, was an agent for Minerva cars and later Darracq. When Maxim's business folded Howard worked as an engineer and inventor for a while before becoming associated with aviation through the activities of Italian pioneer Federico Capone with whom he joined forces to build a piloted helicopter.

Warwick's affairs meanwhile had prospered and in 1905 he joined Rolls and John Moore-Brabazon in ordering a balloon from the Short brothers. By 1908 both Wright and Short brothers realised that heavier-than-air machines represented the future of aviation and, while Warwick went to France to learn to fly, Howard decided to build a biplane of his own design. He assembled it and subsequent examples in premises he had acquired in Battersea where he devised a production system which enabled him to complete customer machines in two weeks. For a brief while he was one of Britain's foremost aeroplane constructors.

In late 1911 Howard and Warwick's business association came to an end and Howard Wright's part of it was acquired by the Coventry Ordnance Works. Howard and his designer, William Manning, worked for the company which also employed Sopwith as test pilot. This was to be a brief association, however, as Sopwith had his own fledgling business to attend to. He later taught Howard Wright to fly.

In 1912 Howard became general manager and chief designer for an aircraft manufacturing offshoot of Isle of Wight-based shipbuilders J. Samuel White, building a variety of machines including seaplanes and a quadruplane fighter which was tested by the RAF. White Aircraft closed in 1919 but by then Howard was no longer involved. He died in 1945.

After wartime service in the Royal Naval Air Service, Warwick resumed his connection with the motor trade through Warwick Wright Ltd which dealt in prestige cars, including the American Stutz brand. An association with Sunbeam-Talbot-Darracq led to involvement with racing and record-breaking in the 1920s but STD folded and was acquired by the Rootes Group. Warwick died in 1945, the same year as his older brother.

Chapter 8

The Aviators' Island

Push on through the village of Leysdown-on-Sea on the Isle of Sheppey, which is separated from the Kentish mainland by a channel known as The Swale, past the fish and chip restaurants and kebab houses that line the A2500 and you will eventually come to the Muswell Manor Holiday Park.

From here the road loops seawards towards Shellness Point, the most easterly feature of an island which the local tourist authorities are pleased to call Treasure Island. With frequent memorials to the pioneers of flight, commemorative plaques and models of the Wright *Flyer*, coupled with prominent references to the area's aviation history on Trip Advisor, Aviators' Island might be more appropriate.

Open the iron side gate at the entrance to Muswell Manor, walk past the rows of mobile homes and holiday makers' parked cars and you suddenly come upon the sixteenth century manor itself. The superficial changes made to it over the past 100 years or so cannot conceal the fact that this is one of the most significant buildings in British aviation history. Indeed, a plaque of the wall proclaims it to be the 'birthplace of British aviation'.

In 1909, then known as Mussel Manor, it was acquired by the Aero Club for use as a clubhouse for those of its members who had made the hour-long journey from London. By this time the facilities for the operation of primitive flying machines were rapidly being added to the flat countryside.

And Sheppey certainly is flat. On one side of Muswell Manor's electronic entrance gates the sandy beach shimmers across to the sea, which at low tide seems a very long way off. On the other side, an equally flat field is brightened in the summer by a riot of wild flowers waving gently in the breeze. This is the area the pioneer aviators referred to as

Shellness or Shellbeach. Today this section of the A2500 is known as Shellness Road

On 4 May 1909 Mussel Manor was expecting some rather special visitors, and the journal *Flight*, which was also the Aero Club's official organ, sent a man down to cover it.

So, as he concentrated on the dozen smartly-dressed men posing for him that day, what thoughts might have been passing through his mind as he prepared to take the picture? Was he, perhaps, thinking he was on the verge of a major scoop? Did he realise he was about to take one of the most famous photographs in aviation history which would still have the power to amaze more than a century later?

Who knows? What is clear, though, is that the names of the formally-dressed men lined up for his camera sound like a roll-call of aviation's most revered pioneers. Seated in the front row are Wilbur and Orville Wright, inventors of the aeroplane, who the day before had received the Aeronautical Society's Gold Medal. Flanking them are John Moore-Brabazon, the first Briton to fly an aeroplane in Britain, and Charles Rolls, another pioneer aviator and motorist whose partnership with Frederick Royce led to some of the world's most prestigious cars and aero engines.

Standing behind them are the three Short brothers, Oswald, Horace and Eustace, founders of one of Britain's most significant aircraft manufacturing companies who had just concluded an agreement to build the Wrights' *Flyer* under licence. Among the others in the picture are Griffith Brewer, who brokered the deal, Frank Hedges Butler, one of the founders of the Aero Club, and Warwick Wright, one half of Britain's Wright brothers who were also aircraft builders.

The picture first appeared in the issue of *Flight* for 8 May 1909, together with other images taken on the day of the Wright brothers' visit. In the morning the Wrights had inspected the Short Brothers' premises at Battersea where construction of the six machines covered by the agreement between them and the Shorts was just beginning. During their time in London the Wrights were guests of honour at banquets arranged by the Aeronautical Society and the Aero Club.

They were then driven to Sheppey for the first of three visits they would make in 1909, by Charles Rolls in – what else? – a Rolls-Royce

Silver Ghost. There they saw the Shorts' new premises at Shellbeach and posed for that photograph, a copy of which hangs on a wall in Muswell Manor.

Earlier that week the Wrights had been invited to meet Secretary of State for War Richard Haldane, leading to speculation that the government intended to acquire copies of the Wright *Flyer*. As it turned out Haldane had no intention of doing so; most generals were quite happy with balloons and horses. Instead of a major sale to the War Office of replicas of *The Flyer* they had to settle for a deal with the Short brothers.

Considering what the Wrights had been expecting, the proceeds of the deal were very modest. To place the operation on a sound financial footing, four Aero Club members, the Hon Maurice Egerton, Frank McClean, the Hon Alec Ogilvie and the Hon Charles Rolls, formed the British Wright Company Limited with capital of £6,000. Of this sum £3,000 was issued to Orville Wright as a shareholding and effectively financed the licences for the Short Brothers to build the *Flyer* replicas. Later the company managed the Wright's British patents culminating in the British government's payment of $75,000 to Orville for use of the Wrights' control system.

According to the *Guinness Book of Records*, the agreement with the Wrights led to the Short brothers establishing the world's first aeroplane factory, although Gordon Bruce, former Shorts company secretary, is more cautious. He will, however, allow that Short Brothers was the first firm in Britain to design, build and sell aircraft as proven commercial vehicles and that the contract with the Wrights represented the first agreement negotiated in Britain for the batch production of aircraft.

The Short Brothers' handwritten order book for 1909 shows that in March of that year the Wright Brothers ordered 'six aeroplanes, plans and details'. It does not say who acquired them but it is known that the first went to Charles Rolls and that subsequent machines were sold to Alec Ogilvie, Frank McClean, John Moore-Brabazon (but sold before delivery to Maurice Egerton) and Cecil Grace. The sixth was ordered by Ernest Pitman but later acquired by Rolls.

Because his engine was not delivered until August 1909, Rolls may have used his first machine initially as a glider, flying it from Standford Hill, Eastchurch. In February 1910 *Flight* reported that Rolls, Egerton and Cecil Grace were making regular flights at Eastchurch with their Short-Wright machines. Egerton was said to have flown over six miles. Rolls was reported to have added a horizontal tail to his machine.

Correspondence between the Shorts and the Wrights, now in the Library of Congress, shows that in December 1909 the Shorts were able to report that all six had been sold and that 'up to the present the machines have given every satisfaction to the owners.' The engines, though, had 'given the usual minor troubles'.

Although the first four Short-Wright machines had been completed by July 1909, they were kept waiting for their engines, which had been ordered from the French manufacturer Léon Bollée. As a substitute Frank McClean used the engine from his car but it was not a success. Alec Ogilvie took delivery of his No 2 machine at Camber Sands, Sussex, in November. He remained there until his lease ran out and then moved back to Eastchurch. The last two machines were delivered by mid-March 1910.

After Rolls' death the Shorts bought No 6 from his executors and sold it less engine to Ogilvie, who had fitted wheels to his first machine, and planned a series of modifications for No 6 to enable him to enter events for all-British machines.

Intriguingly, the letter to the Wrights refers to a seventh machine. 'As you told us to hold one of the six machines for you, we are putting in hand another for yourself, which will be number 7, as requested,' the letter said. It also noted that Shorts had booked two definite orders for the 1910 machine and received a lot of enquiries.

'If you can supply us with the necessary drawings for the alterations you intend making in the 1910 type we will at once push the work ahead,' the letter continued. 'We believe if we had a dozen more machines ready for delivery by the end of March we could sell them by then.' There is, however, no record of further Short-Wright copies being built.

In the order book, McClean is listed as Shorts' first customer for 'one aeroplane (Shorts No 1)' which was delivered in July 1909. In April

Moore-Brabazon ordered 'one aeroplane complete without engine but including fittings, everything complete'. The following month Rolls ordered a glider, which was delivered in July, while Ernest Pitman ordered 'a set of drawings as per quotation'.

In June the Blair Atholl Aeroplane Syndicate ordered 'one aeroplane to plans and specification complete without engine but including all fittings'. This machine, one of John Dunne's tailless designs, was delivered in November. Charles Rolls ordered a second glider in August but there is no record of its delivery.

The original order book is on display in the Ulster Folk and Transport Museum in Belfast.

Griffith Brewer had already leased a site in the south-east corner of the Isle of Sheppey which he planned to transform into a golf course. But in discussion with Eustace and Oswald Short, who had been appointed engineers to the Aero Club, it was decided that a better use of the site would be the development of flying machines. This land was duly acquired in February 1909 on behalf of the Aero Club, together with a small hotel near Leysdown to accommodate members. This was Mussel Manor, then owned by Mr Andrews.

Apart from the flat terrain, this island, roughly 9 miles long and 4.5 wide on the southern side of the Thames Estuary, had further attractions for the Aero Club and its members who had been looking for a suitable location for their experiments with heavier-than-air flight. Sheppey offered an area relatively free of trees and other obstructions and fairly sparsely populated with land for both flying and the construction of supporting infrastructure readily available.

It is very likely that many in the Aero Club were already aware of the island's suitability. Most of their balloon ascents had been made from the London area and, with the prevailing winds usually blowing from the west, the shores of the Thames estuary were familiar to the aeronauts. The Wrights also agreed with the selection. According to *Flight*, Wilbur thought it 'the best flying ground I have ever seen. It is much superior in every way to those we have used elsewhere.'

Another reason which may have had a stronger influence on the Shorts' choice of Sheppey than previously thought was the availability of suitable labour. Even though the dockyard at Sheerness was now involved with steel-built steam-driven warships, there were still plenty of men working there who were skilled carpenters and sailmakers, trades that could be useful in the manufacturer of aircraft. In addition, there were many small yards at nearby Sittingbourne and Faversham which were still building wooden sail-driven craft.

According to local legend, the Short brothers recruited many of their workers by going to the dockyard at Sheerness as the workers were knocking off to go home and offering suitable candidates an additional shilling (10p) more a week than their current wage. Whatever the truth of this, within three months Shorts had a workforce of eighty.

That March a firm of builders called W. Harbrow descended on the island to start erecting workshops for the Short brothers, together with two sheds for aeroplanes and bungalows for their eighty workmen. The main shed was 140ft long and 45ft wide. W. Harbrow, based at Bermondsey in south-east London, was a specialist in the construction of iron buildings. Those it erected at Shellbeach were of galvanised metal with timber covering and lined inside with felt. *Flight* noted in its issue of 15 May that they had been constructed 'solidly and with extraordinary dispatch'. Consequently, the journal reported,

> Messrs Short brothers have not only been able to take possession but have been able to get actively to work well in advance of all other proceedings. Already the building is completely full and Mr Short is lamenting that he did not have it made twice as big to start with; in fact, at the first opportunity it is to be extended in length by 100ft.

When *Flight*'s man looked inside he saw Moore-Brabazon's crippled *Bird of Passage* undergoing repairs following a recent crash, together with a Léon Delagrange owned by Ernest Pitman, and Frank McClean's unfinished Short No 1. The reporter also commented on some of the equipment in use including 'a handy little gas plant for welding'. This device, which might have raised health and safety concerns in the twenty-first century, comprised a can containing petrol through which air was blown by a bellows 'for purposes of carburetion'. *Flight* explained:

'In a place like this where there is no mains supply of coal gas available, the petrol serves a most useful purpose.'

Next to this building was another which Harbrow's had nearly finished by the time of *Flight*'s visit. This 'fine, lofty, dry "flyer-house" would be used by Aero Club members to house their machines. 'Nearby,' *Flight's* reporter observed, 'was a neat little pavilion fitted with a stove and a sink, where, presumably, comforts for the inner man will be available.' The site overlooked the sea and included a substantial flat area of tufted grass which would serve as a flying ground. It was understood that the farmer would move his sheep whenever the aviators wanted to fly.

The pioneer aviators had several means open to them of reaching their flying ground on the Isle of Sheppey. They could take the South Eastern and Chatham Railway service from London's Victoria station to Queenborough. There they could transfer to the Sheppey Light Railway, which ran between Queenborough and Leysdown calling at Eastchurch. This service opened in 1901 and closed in 1950.

Those aviators who opted to travel from London by road had the choice of going via Chatham or Maidstone. *Flight* advised its readers to go via the county town. Even though it took longer it was clearly the prettier route. 'There can be no question whatever,' the journal noted, 'of the advantage of proceeding via Maidstone to anyone who has the least eye for scenery.' The Chatham route was 'thoroughly unpleasant from start to finish'.

The first machine to use the members' shed was Moore-Brabazon's French-built Voisin *Bird of Passage*. The previous December he had become the first Briton resident in Britain to learn to fly. He had done so in France, because, as he explained in a letter to *Flight*, 'everybody in England is so ready to discourage one, to ridicule one and look upon one as an amiable lunatic.'

But now things had changed. Moore-Brabazon was back and about to put Sheppey on the aviation map. Over the weekend 29 April to 2 May, a few days before the Wright brothers' visit, he made three sustained flights, of 150, 200 and 500 yards in *The Bird of Passage* to become the first Briton to fly a powered aeroplane in Britain. Many years later, Moore-Brabazon would recall how slim was the margin between success and failure. With the Voisin, he said, 'I knew that if I could not persuade its engine to turn at 1130 instead of 1100 rpm it would never think of getting up. But if it was feeling good, then it was all right for a hop, though only with my coat off, no boots and half a gallon of petrol.'

But it was to take nearly thirty years for this feat to be officially recognised in the face of competing claims. In evidence to the Gorell Committee in 1926/9, Oswald Short said Moore-Brabazon's flight was the first he had ever witnessed. 'I was one of several persons who held on to the tail of the machine while the engine was being run for warming-up purposes,' he reported. Liz Walker, chairperson of the Short Brothers Commemoration Society, quotes him as saying:

> When the pilot wished to start I failed to see the signal 'Let go' and was dragged along the ground for some distance when the machine started to move. After running along for some distance, the machine rose into the air to a height which I estimate to have been from 50 to 80ft and a distance of from a quarter to half a mile from a position in front of the workshops on the marshes at Leysdown towards a house known as Mussel Manor. On making a left-hand turn the machine lost height and, touching the ground with one wing, crashed. With others I ran towards the spot and we were relieved to find the pilot unhurt.

On 2 May 1999, Moore-Brabazon's grandson, Ivan, 3rd Baron Brabazon of Tara, who had been a transport minister in the governments of Margaret Thatcher and John Major, unveiled a plaque to commemorate the 90th anniversary of his grandfather's achievement. It is now fixed to the wall of Muswell Manor.

Moore-Brabazon wrote many years later that his main anxiety had not been about his engine but the aerodrome surface because 'it was so full of dykes and ditches that landing could be very dangerous if not made in precisely the right place.'

In his autobiography, published in 1956, Moore-Brabazon explained that his aircraft had been struck by a sudden gust of wind. 'The whole aircraft, of course, tipped sideways and the impact was so sudden that I had no time to do anything but try to correct my position in the air by heaving on the rudder control.' He went on:

> This I did, but in my anxiety I proved a little over-zealous and suddenly discovered to my horror that the control to the rudder had broken. So there I was in mid-air and absolutely unable to control my machine. There was nothing to be done but glide down – canted at an angle of 35-degrees – and this I did.

The problem now was getting down more or less in one piece. The tip of his left-hand wing had struck the ground in an impact which shuddered through the flimsy machine snapping wires and struts. The engine was dislodged and hurtled past the pilot, missing him by inches to bury itself in the ground. 'It was a startling and disconcerting experience but through good fortune I wasn't personally damaged,' Moore-Brabazon recalled. He was bruised and dazed and recovered to find himself being licked by his two dogs which had chased the aircraft during its flight.

Next Moore-Brabazon turned his attention to another prize: the £1,000 offered by the *Daily Mail* for the first one-mile circular flight to be made in Britain. He asked Shorts to build him a new machine for the attempt. It was the second of the original design the brothers had produced. The Short No 2 was powered by a 40-60 hp Green engine and differed from the Wrights' *Flyer* in several respects. Wing warping was dispensed with and instead there were small planes – ailerons, in effect – pivoted between the ends of the wings. The rudder was mounted in front and the two propellers rotated in the same direction instead of opposing ones.

Like the *Flyer*, however, the machine was launched from an 80 ft long rail. At one end of the rail rose a pylon about 18 ft tall with a pulley at the top, over which ran a rope. The rope ran down inside the pylon with a half-ton weight attached to its end. A trolley, which was essentially a railway sleeper attached to a set of wheels, supported the aircraft itself. To launch it the rope was passed over the pulley at the top of the pylon, under a further pulley at the pylon end of the rail, and then along the rail and back to the aeroplane to which it was attached by a quick-release mechanism. The main drawback of this arrangement was that once the whole thing had been set in position, using a sturdy horse, the wind might well have changed and everything had to be moved.

Once the engine was warmed up and running flat-out, the pilot operated a trigger which released the weight, pulling the machine rapidly along the rail. Moore-Brabazon explained what happened next: 'You were doing about 40 mph and you had to do something about it by pulling your elevator. After that, if you got into the air, well, it was your job to get on with it.' Indeed, with no recognised techniques to fall back on, the pioneer airmen were very much on their own to discover for themselves the rudiments of control. Moore-Brabazon recalled that it was 'in essence an adventure into the unknown'.

It was not unusual for the machine, on reaching the end of the rail, to fail to soar into the air. In such cases it would fall back onto its trolley and probably break its undercarriage skids leading to more repair bills. And these bills were very much the bugbear of pioneer aviators. Moore-Brabazon called them 'frightful'. He wrote: 'Every time you went out something was smashed and had to be put right.' It was rumoured that Charles Rolls' weekly repair bill often reached £200.

When he was ready for the attempt on the *Daily Mail* prize, Moore-Brabazon notified the Aero Club and the newspaper. Official observers were to be the club's secretary, Commander Perrin, and Charles Hands representing the *Mail*. Choosing the most favourable conditions for flight meant the aviators getting up early to be ready at dawn when the air was at its most still. Hands stayed at Mussel Manor with Moore-Brabazon, and every morning for a fortnight they rose at 0300hr.

Finally came the day when conditions were right. It was 30 October when the aircraft rose from its launch rail and flew uneventfully for half a mile. It was at that point that Moore-Brabazon had to make a turn. As the advantages of banking into a turn had yet to be discovered, he did so 'perfectly flat with no bank at all'. He then noticed that the wind, instead of blowing straight into his face, now blew from the side but without adverse effects. He rounded the post which indicated his turning point without difficulty and landed 'just where I had started'. The aircraft had never been more than 20ft from the ground; it had been 'a feat of some dexterity'. The flight had taken 2min 36sec.

In hailing his achievement, *Flight* struck a slightly sour note by pointing out that Moore-Brabazon was already a wealthy man and was now £1,000 richer. But it did acknowledge that 'seldom was a prize more thoroughly deserved'. The journal noted that the 25-year-old

> has devoted the whole-hearted, youthful enthusiasm which served him so well in motor racing to the cause of flight, and although he may be counted among the youngest – if he is not quite the youngest – of the flying men, his experience with aeroplanes is more extensive than that of many of the aviators who have recently come before the public eye.

Moore-Brabazon used part of his prize money to buy a cup to commemorate the event. Later he used the same machine to fly from Shellbeach to Eastchurch, a distance of four miles, to compete in the British Empire Michelin Cup for the longest flight in a British-built aeroplane. With the engine running flat-out, which was standard practice for the time, the machine soared up to 500ft with the pilot completely exposed in a seat about the size and shape of a dinner plate with his legs stuck out on slides to operate the ailerons. His right hand held the elevator control and his left the rudder. There was nothing between the pilot and the ground. 'It was exceedingly draughty,' Moore-Brabazon recalled.

He managed eighteen miles before there was a violent clanking noise from the engine, which suddenly stopped. Later, he discovered that the crankshaft had burst through the crankcase. But at the time Moore-Brabazon was too preoccupied to worry about the engine. The machine pitched sharply upwards in a 'quick and vicious' stall, something he had never experienced before. At the time he was at an altitude of 100 ft. He put the aircraft into a dive and glided towards the ground. 'All might have been well,' Moore-Brabazon recalled, 'if I had not fouled a small dyke but even so the skids were so well made that no great harm was done.' It was his first forced landing.

On 5 November 1909, Moore-Brabazon took up his first passenger. Years later he revealed that he had been prompted by the *Daily Mirror* to borrow a piglet from a local farmer called Love to prove that 'pigs might fly'. He promptly christened the piglet *Icarus II* and the terrified animal was squeezed into a wicker basket strapped to one of the aircraft's struts a few feet away from the engine. Attached to the basket was a sign proclaiming 'I am the first pig to fly.'

In the 1950s, Sheerness blacksmith Herbert Jarvis, who assisted Moore-Brabazon, recalled: 'I put the first pig to fly in the 'plane.' The pilot himself thought that the piglet

> should have been pampered in life and preserved in death in the British Museum. But all that happened was that it was sold next day slightly above its market price. Why, I never understood; I could not have improved its taste by taking it on its historic flight.

The aviators present at Sheppey at the time were described by Moore-Brabazon as 'remarkable'. They included Ernest Pitman, The Hon Maurice Egerton, Percy Grace, Cecil Grace, Charles Rolls and James Dunne. The latter was a refugee from Farnborough following the failure of his advanced machine to fly in secret trials conducted at Blair Atholl in Scotland. Together with Samuel Cody, his services had been rejected by the War Office and he arrived at Leysdown in late 1909.

There erected a shed and arranged with the Short Brothers to construct to his drawings an inherently stable tailless biplane, with V-shaped wings, as a continuation of his efforts in Scotland. This was the first attempt in Britain to build a stable powered aeroplane. Dunne was assisted by Richard Fairey who later managed the Short Brothers factory after its move to Rochester. Fairey later founded his own aircraft manufacturing company and was knighted for his achievements.

The forced landing had not diminished Moore-Brabazon's enthusiasm for flying, although he was thoroughly disenchanted with the method of launching his aircraft. He asked Shorts to build him another machine, but this time based on the French Farman with a wheeled undercarriage. By this time, though, operations had moved from the bumpy Shellbeach to a smoother site at Eastchurch.

There had been frequent accidents at Shellbeach due to the bumpy ground until one of the Shorts' employees hit on the idea of burning the grass in the hollows, which would show the position of the dips clearly from the air. But this was to represent a short-term solution thanks to the generosity of Frank McClean.

In November 1909 he bought the 400-acre Stonepit (sometimes rendered as 'Stonepitts') Farm on the south side of Standford Hill, Eastchurch, from the Ingleton family. He also paid for it to be transformed into a flying ground. The buildings which Harbrow's had erected at Shellbeach were moved to the new site, while those occupied by the Short brothers were transferred to land bought from McClean for £25.

The move to Eastchurch was virtually complete by the end of April 1910. It meant that the Short brothers now had much improved accommodation and facilities for the manufacture and repair of aeroplanes. According to local historian Bill Croydon, this was the signal for Eastchurch to become, over the next four years, 'the focal point of aviation in Britain'. On 20 November 1910, a Short-built Wright piloted by Charles Rolls became the first aircraft to land at the new airfield. Later the same day McClean's Short No 1 arrived by road from Leysdown. By the end of the year he and Rolls were making full use of the new flying ground, while Dunne and Professor A.K. Huntington were beginning experiments with machines designed to be inherently stable.

On 8 March 1910 Moore-Brabazon received the Royal Aero Club's pilot certificate No 1. A week earlier, he had flown 18.75 miles, and during the same month Cecil Grace and Charles Rolls flew from Shellness to Eastchurch, via Queenborough, returning to Eastchurch without landing. They then circled over Shellness before finally landing at Eastchurch. On Good Friday Rolls also made a lengthy flight under bad conditions.

The summer of 1910 was notable for the increased interest in flying all over the country. By September, eighteen sheds to house aeroplanes had sprung up at Eastchurch. Their occupants included McClean, Percy and Cecil Grace, the Hon Maurice Egerton, Professor Huntington, John Moore-Brabazon, L.W. Travers, Howard Wright, Alec Ogilvie and Leon Jezzi. An aerial photograph taken in 1911 indicates that they had been joined by J. Dare, A. Batchelor, V.C. Colmore and Major Brocklehurst.

According to contemporary reports, Leon Jezzi, who was described as a 'City gent', arrived at Eastchurch with a bundle of calico under one arm, an old packing case on the other and an old motor cycle engine on his back. His friends had told him he was mad and would end up killing himself, but Jezzi persisted to such effect that he not only built an aircraft but flew it in August 1910.

The achievements of Paul Georges Leon Jezzi have been overshadowed by those of better-known aviators based at Eastchurch, yet he was awarded the Royal Aero Club's pilot certificate No 44 in January 1911 and was widely admired for his energy and enthusiasm for flying. He commuted regularly between his home in Bromley and his hangar at Eastchurch on his 2.75 hp Douglas motor cycle.

Jezzi's first flight, actually little more than a hop, covered about 250 yards at a height of 6ft above the ground. Remarkably for the time, the landing was trouble-free. In fact, in over 900 subsequent landings Jezzi was reported to have suffered just one broken wheel and a landing skid. Towards the end of 1911, Jezzi began the construction of a small tractor biplane powered by a 33 hp JAP engine. This was assembled at Eastchurch and in 1912 it was reported to have achieved a speed of 65 mph.

But if history has generally ignored him, Jezzi's activities were regularly chronicled in *Flight*. On 15 October 1910, for example, the journal reported that 'as usual' he had been hard at work throughout the preceding weekend when his performances in his self-designed biplane 'continue to show marked improvement'. The report added: 'He now flies three or four times around the course at about 30ft quite comfortably.' In late November Jezzi was said to be flying well, 'keeping a nice angle and showing a good turn of speed'.

Frank McClean and Cecil Grace were particularly active at Eastchurch during October and November 1910. Over two days in early October McClean was reported to have made half a dozen flights in his Short biplane, now with Gnome engine, averaging 20 minutes per trip and flying at around 100 ft. On one Sunday in October, McClean flew for a total of around six hours.

In late November McClean and Cecil Grace flew their Short biplanes from Eastchurch to Sheerness, the latter continuing towards Southend before turning for home. Before landing he passed the village at a height estimated at between 1,500 and 2,000ft. These demonstrations of flying prowess led to the belief that one of them would win the de Forest prize. However, T.O.M. Sopwith arrived on 18 December at the controls of a Howard Wright biplane powered by an ENV engine. He used this machine to fly to Thirlemont, Belgium, a distance of 177 miles in 3.5 hours, to claim the £4,000 prize for the longest flight from England to the continent of Europe.

Cecil Grace left Eastchurch soon after Sopwith but the weather worsened and he joined some of the other contestants sitting it out at Swingate Downs, Dover. After one failed attempt to cross the Channel, Grace arranged to try again, this time following a cross-channel ship. But it was delayed and Grace set off unescorted and without a compass. He was sighted by a fishing boat but failed to make it to the other side. A fortnight later his cap and goggles were washed up on a Belgian beach.

PART OF THE NATION'S DEFENCES

In the early twentieth century when the pioneer aviators were active, the Isle of Sheppey represented an important element in Britain's defences. It had done so for many centuries. In the sixteenth century Henry VIII ordered the construction of a fort there to guard the River Medway and protect the recently completed dockyard at Chatham.

In the 1660s work began on the construction of a stronger fort together with a dockyard in which Secretary to the Admiralty Samuel Pepys was largely instrumental. But war broke out with the Dutch and in 1672 the still incomplete fort was insufficient to prevent the enemy, commanded by Admiral de Ruyter, occupying the dockyard and laying waste to it as a preliminary to the humiliating destruction of the British fleet at Chatham.

The dockyard was rebuilt in the 1670s and again in the 1860s. Over the centuries many significant warships were built there, the last being the sloop HMS *Cadmus*, launched in 1903. By 1909 Sheerness Dockyard had become a centre for the repair and maintenance of

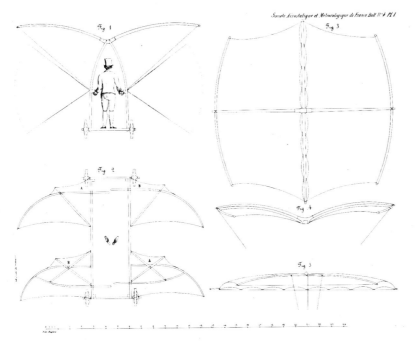

Original drawings for a man-powered flying machine designed by Sir George Cayley. (*Library of Congress*)

A replica of a glider designed by Sir George Cayley that can be seen at the Yorkshire Air Museum. (*Courtesy of Nigel Coates*)

A.V. Roe pictured in a Roe Triplane III at Brooklands circa 1910. (*A Flying History*)

Lieutenant John Cyril Porte flying a Deperdussin at Hendon circa 1911. (*A Flying History*)

Lieutenant Charles R. Samson at the controls of a Short S.27 at Eastchurch, 1911. (*A Flying History*)

A sculpture commemorating the three Short Brothers, Oswald (1883–1969), Eustace (1875–1932) and Horace (1872–1917), that can be seen on Shellness Road near Muswell Manor on the Isle of Sheppey. It was unveiled in May 2013. (*Author*)

A commemorative plaque in front of Muswell Manor. The inscription includes the following: 'Originally known as Mussel Manor, it was from here that a group of aviation pioneers planned the first powered flight by a Briton'. (*Author*)

Located by the entrance to Muswell Manor, this plaque informs the visitor that 'the first powered flight in this country by a Briton, J.T.C. Moore-Brabazon, took place near this spot on 2nd May 1909'. (*Author*)

This commemorative plaque, unveiled on the 90th anniversary of Moore-Brabazon's flight, can be seen on the wall of Muswell Manor. (*Author*)

Located in the grounds of Muswell Manor, this memorial, unveiled by the Airfields of Britain Conservation Trust, remembers the existence of Leysdown Airfield, which opened in February 1909 and closed in November 1937. (*Author*)

The flat beach at Leysdown near Muswell Manor. (*Author*)

Some of the original buildings used by pioneer airmen at Eastchurch still exist, albeit in dilapidated condition, at HMP Standford Hill. (*Author*)

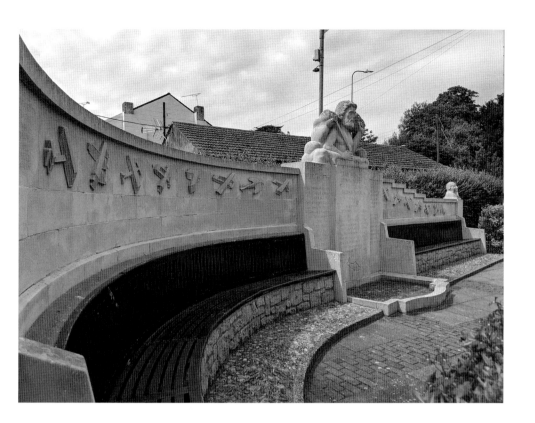

The memorial to the 'Home of Aviation' that can be seen at the junction of the High Street and Church Road in Eastchurch. It was unveiled in 1955 to commemorate the Royal Aero Club of Great Britain flying grounds at Leysdown and Eastchurch, and the first Royal Navy aviators based at Eastchurch from 1911. (*Author*)

Another memorial unveiled by the Airfields of Britain Conservation Trust, this one, located beside the Eastchurch Aviation Museum remembers the Eastchurch landplane airfield which was in use from 1909 to 1947. The Museum itself contains much interesting information about early aviation on the Isle of Sheppey. (*Author*)

A replica of A.V. Roe's triplane and shed that can be seen at Brooklands Museum. (*Author*)

torpedo boats and torpedo boat destroyers. The dockyard closed in 1960.

Following the training of the Navy's first aviators by members of the Royal Aero Club, the Royal Naval Air Service opened a training establishment at Eastchurch and, with the creation of the Royal Air Force in 1918, it became an RAF station. During the Second World War it was operated by Coastal Command. The airfield closed in 1946.

In the twenty-first century most of the old airfield site is occupied by Standford Hill open prison which has been there since 1950. HMP Standford Hill forms part of a complex of three prisons which also includes the category B HMP Swaleside and the training prison HMP Elmley. Still visible at Standford Hill are some of the (now dilapidated) hangars occupied by Frank McClean and others, together with Second World War concrete pill boxes as well as the hill from which Charles Rolls launched himself in the glider built for him by the Short Brothers.

Opposite the prison coffee shop and next door to an establishment selling honey and run by the prisoners is the single-storey Eastchurch Aviation Museum which contains much interesting information about the area's connection with pioneer aviation. Outside is a memorial dedicated to the memory of the units based at the airfield during nearly four decades of operation. The names of the roads in the prison complex also reflect the area's aviation history: Rolls Avenue, Airfield View, Shorts' Prospect and Wrights' Way.

EUSTACE AND OSWALD SHORT

It was Albert Eustace, the middle of the three Short brothers, born in 1875 in Chilton, County Durham, who really launched the family name in aeronautics and led to the creation of one of Britain's leading aerospace companies.

At first, Hugh Oswald, born in 1883 at Stanton-by-Dale in Derbyshire and therefore eight years younger than Eustace, was initially swept along by his brother's enthusiasm. However, it was Eustace who effectively ran the company from 1917 until 1943 when it was nationalised. The oldest brother, Horace, came late to the partnership but provided its driving force during its formative years (see Chapter Ten).

If Eustace was said to look more like a poet, his appearance concealed an astute business brain. He transformed his initial enthusiasm for ballooning into the dedication and expertise that led to him and Oswald becoming the foremost balloon designers in Europe, if not the world, with a flourishing export business for civil and military customers based at the railway arches at Battersea.

In 1906 they won a prize for excellence of balloon construction and this was followed by their appointment as official balloon makers to the Aero Club of Great Britain. It also led to their association with the Wright brothers and their subsequent move to the Isle of Sheppey. But it was Oswald, also an astute businessman, who provided the driving force for the brothers' move into powered heavier-than-air flight. He sensed that interest in ballooning was being replaced by a public craving for the excitement provided by powered aeroplanes.

In this enterprise they were joined by Horace and it was as a result of his visit to Pau in February 1909 that the brothers secured manufacturing rights to the Wright *Flyer*. The arrangement covered the construction of six aircraft. Orders for these machines were detailed in a handwritten order book, to which King George VI added his signature during a visit to the Shorts' Rochester factory in March 1939.

The move to Eastchurch coincided with the Short brothers' interest in water-borne aircraft and was followed by a steady stream of designs so that by 1913 virtually all of the Shorts' work was on seaplanes for the Admiralty. This necessitated a further move to larger premises and a new factory beside the River Medway which was constructed at Rochester in 1913/14. It was in full production by the time the First World War broke out.

Between the wars Shorts built a wide variety of aircraft including a succession of airliners for Imperial Airways culminating in the C-Class Empire flying boats which set new standards in luxurious long-distance air travel. These aircraft led to the Sunderland patrol flying boat for the RAF of which nearly 750 were built. At the same time the company produced the RAF's first four-engined heavy bomber, the Stirling.

During the 1930s the company established a new factory at Queen's Island, Belfast. Production was progressively transferred to Northern Ireland and in 1943 the company was nationalised with Oswald effectively sidelined.

After the Second World War the company continued to turn out a flow of original designs which included research aircraft, guided weapons and the highly successful Skyvan/SD330/SD360 family of light transports. Shorts remained in public ownership until it was sold to the Canadian company Bombardier in 1989. In the twenty-first century Bombardier is Northern Ireland's largest manufacturing company producing around ten per cent of the province's total manufacturing exports.

Eustace died in April 1932 after suffering a heart attack at the controls of the Mussel II seaplane. He was taxiying the aircraft after landing on the Medway. He was 57. Oswald became sole manging director following Eustace's death and chairman when it became a public company in 1935. He died in 1969 having lived long enough to see the realisation of his 1918 prediction that long-distance air travel would become commonplace.

The Short Brothers' great, great niece Liz Walker believes they have not received the recognition due to them as true pioneers of British aviation. 'They were working class boys who were never driven by thoughts of money,' she told me.

JOHN MOORE-BRABAZON

As the first Briton to fly a powered aeroplane in Britain and the holder of the Royal Aero Club's pilot certificate No 1, John Theodore Cuthbert Moore-Brabazon occupies a unique place in British aviation.

He was also a Member of Parliament, a minister in Winston Churchill's wartime government and chairman of the government-appointed committees charged with recommending the type of airliners Britain would need when peace returned.

Moore-Brabazon was born in London to Lieutenant Colonel John Arthur Henry Moore-Brabazon and his wife, Emma Sophia. He was educated at Harrow and read engineering at Trinity College, Cambridge, although he did not graduate. His vacations were spent working for Charles Rolls as an unpaid mechanic and he became an apprentice at Darracq in Paris after leaving Cambridge. He became a successful racing driver and in 1907 won the Circuit des Ardennes in a Minerva.

Following Rolls' death in 1910, Moore-Brabazon promised his wife he would give up flying but on the outbreak of the First World War he joined the Royal Flying Corps. He served on the Western Front where he played a key role in the development of aerial photography and reconnaissance. With the creation of the Royal Air Force he became a staff officer and by the end of the war had attained the rank of lieutenant colonel and been awarded the Military Cross.

Between the wars he was Conservative MP for Chatham and then Wallasey. In October 1940 he became Minister of Transport and appointed to the Privy Council. The following May he succeeded Lord Beaverbrook as Minister of Aircraft Production but was forced to resign following ill-judged remarks about the Soviet Union made in public.

Ennobled as Lord Brabazon of Tara, he was appointed to chair the committees tasked with planning the shape of post-war British commercial aviation from which emerged such airliner types as the

Vickers Viscount, the world's first turbine-powered airliner, and the de Havilland Comet, the first jet transport.

Moore-Brabazon was president of the Royal Aero Club and chairman of the Air Registration Board, predecessor of the Civil Aviation Authority. He died in 1964 and is buried in Stoke Poges Memorial Gardens, Buckinghamshire.

Chapter 9

London's Aerodrome

In the early years of the twentieth century Hendon aerodrome was a major aviation centre. People flocked there in their thousands to watch the spectacular air displays that had become synonymous with the airfield. There was even talk of it becoming 'the Charing Cross of the air'.

In the twenty-first century, though, Hendon aerodrome is the site of a housing estate, the Metropolitan Police College and the RAF Museum. Virtually none of the aerodrome remains, although some of the original buildings survive and elements of the factory established by the charismatic pioneer aviator Claude Grahame-White have been incorporated into the RAF Museum.

In the middle of the eighteenth century Hendon was situated in the countryside between the villages of Colindale and Mill Hill in the county of Middlesex, just eight miles north-west of Charing Cross. Aviation first came to the area in 1862 when two balloonists, Henry Coxwell and James Glaiser, made an unscheduled landing on 25 August. They had earlier set off from Crystal Palace in their 93,000 cu ft craft called *The Mammoth* with five passengers.

At the time Coxwell and Glaisher were Britain's premier balloonists. Later that year they would ascend to 30,000ft, or nearly six miles, to set a record that was to stand for nearly forty years. In 1870 Coxwell would be involved in balloon operations from Paris during the Prussian siege. But in August 1862 they were making a series of ascents on behalf of the British Association for the Advancement of Science. At dusk on 25 August they resumed an interrupted flight by taking off from a site near the Welsh Harp Reservoir, named after the nearby public house, the Old Welsh Harp. In Victorian times the area was a popular place for walks and cycle rides.

It was not until 1909 that the first powered flight was made at Hendon. Stanley Spencer's 88-foot non-rigid airship had been built by the well-known and long-established family firm of C.G. Spencer and Sons of Highbury. Spencer carried a passenger, an Australian suffragette called Muriel Matters. The same year, H.P. Martin and G.H. Handasyde attempted to fly from the site in an aeroplane they had built in the unused ballroom of the Old Welsh Harp. Their efforts were unsuccessful but the two men later formed a partnership called Martinsyde which, based at Brooklands, became Britain's third biggest aircraft manufacturer during the First World War.

Inspired by Louis Blériot's cross-channel flight, E.J. Everett, a director of Everett, Edgecumbe and Co, a local firm of instrument makers, began building an aeroplane of his own design in a shed he had erected on a field off Colindale Avenue. The machine was powered by a 35 hp JAP engine and was nicknamed *The Grasshopper* – appropriately as it turned out, for it made a series of hops but failed to get airborne.

Yet a trend had been started. In 1910-11 the site was adopted by a number of pioneer aviators, including Louis Blériot and also Grahame-White who subsequently manufactured aircraft there and whose ambition was for Hendon to be the aerodrome for London.

This field was to have a significant influence on British aviation as the site of experiments conducted by various pilots. It would also be the location of Louis Paulhan's departure on his dramatic prize-winning London to Manchester flight when he beat Grahame-White to the £10,000 *Daily Mail* prize.

Fresh from his successful first cross-channel flight, Blériot established a flying training school for pilots at Étampes near Rouen in late 1909, and early the following year, a second was opened at Pau. Between 1910 and 1914 these establishments trained around 1,000 pilots. In fact, nearly half the aviators holding the Aero Club de France pilot brevet on the outbreak of the First World War had been trained by the Blériot schools.

When he decided to expand across the English Channel, Blériot chose Hendon as the site for his first British flying school. This was in September 1910 and he erected eight hangars there. Three of them were leased to a company called the Aeronautical Syndicate Ltd, which had produced a strange-looking tailless monoplane known as the *Valkyrie*. This machine achieved modest success and was the only successful pusher monoplane built in Britain. The favourite party piece of its creator and pilot Horatio Barber was to demonstrate its short-field performance by charging at the spectators from 50 yards before lifting off and zooming over their heads.

Blériot filled the rest of his hangars with replicas of his Channel-crossing monoplanes, all powered by Gnome rotary engines. Pierre Prier was appointed chief instructor and the first pupil was wine merchant Frank Hedges Butler, the well-known balloonist and founding member of the Aero Club of Great Britain.

Among Blériot's pupils at Pau was a car dealer from London's West End who had become interested in ballooning. Claude Grahame-White made several ascents from Battersea but his frustration at flight destinations being largely determined by the wind direction led him to take an interest in heavier-than-air craft. This led him to France where he bought a Blériot XII, which he helped to assemble. After his course of lessons at Pau, Grahame-White became the first internationally-recognised British pilot, being awarded Aero Club de France certificate No 30 in January 1910.

He immediately ordered six Blériot Type XIs to establish his British Flying School at Pau. Like Blériot, he decided to expand into England and he too chose Hendon as the most suitable site mainly because of its proximity to London. It was within easy reach of Watling Street and Hendon stations on the Midland Railway network. By mid-January Grahame-White was reassembling the machine at the Everett & Edgecumbe shed at Colindale. He made three short flights in the reassembled aircraft before taking an option to buy 207 acres of the pasture land between Colindale and Hendon which he planned to establish as an airfield.

Although Louis Paulhan won the race to be the first to fly between London and Manchester it was the gallant and plucky loser, Grahame-White, who was to become a household name and Britain's first aviation hero. His reputation was enhanced by a hectic schedule of exhibition flights which made headlines nationwide.

While Grahame-White was barnstorming his way around Britain, aviation enthusiasts were gathering at Hendon on 16 May, Whit Monday, for an impromptu air display. It was to be the first of many to be held on the site. The same weekend, Everett made further unsuccessful attempts to persuade the *Grasshopper* into the air. More successful was an aviator, identified as A. Rawlinson, who became the third pilot to take off from Hendon.

Following his successful round-Britain tour, Grahame-White received a lucrative offer to appear at flying meetings in the USA. On 1 September he arrived in Boston accompanied by two mechanics, B.C. Hucks and R.H. Carr, to look after his Farman and 100 hp Blériot. During the course of this trip, Grahame-White won the Gordon Bennett International air race held at Belmont Park, New York, which resulted in Britain hosting the following year's event at Eastchurch.

On his return to the UK in January 1911 Grahame-White was able to move his operation from Brooklands to Hendon where he joined existing occupants Horatio Barber's Aeronautical Syndicate, McArdle and Drexel and the Blériot Flying School. Two months earlier, in November 1910, one of Blériot's pupils, J.G. Weir, who was to become Controller of Aircraft Production in the Ministry of Munitions during the First World War, became the first Hendon trainee to qualify as a pilot.

In partnership with Blériot and Sir Hiram Maxim, Grahame-White attempted to float a company to develop Hendon into an international aviation centre. The partnership was established on the basis of an ambitious prospectus which envisaged share capital of £200,000 to be raised by the sale of 5-shilling shares. These plans were ridiculed by most sections of press, with the exception of Lord Northcliffe's newspapers, and consequently the issue failed with only £75,000 subscribed.

Grahame-White responded by returning all the subscriptions and trying again using his own not inconsiderable resources. He formed the Grahame-White Aviation Company, in which he invested all the cash he had earned during his US trip with additional share capital subscribed by friends and relatives.

The new company took a 10-year lease on Hendon's 207 acres along with the right to buy the freehold together with additional land. He immediately started to clear and level the pasture to form an aerodrome two miles in circumference. It was Britain's third aerodrome after Brooklands and Eastchurch. Richard Gates was appointed general manager with Clement Gresswell put in charge of the flying school.

At first it cost 100 guineas (£105) for a course of lessons although this was later reduced to 75 guineas. Additional sheds were erected for the aviation companies wishing to establish themselves at Hendon. Early in 1911 another significant personality turned up at Hendon to excite the spectators. Gustav Hamel, who had learned to fly on the continent, arrived at Grahame-White's school and, in a borrowed 50 hp Blériot, proceeded to demonstrate his prowess as a pilot. Despite his Teutonic-sounding name, Hamel was British, the Eton-educated son of the Royal Physician. He had a penchant for large and powerful Mercedes cars as well as aviation. Hamel had learned to fly at the age of 26 at the Blériot school at Pau in 1910 and in March 1911 he flew from Hendon to Brooklands in a record-breaking 58 minutes. As with Grahame-White, his name was seldom out of the headlines.

But it was a Frenchman, Pierre Prier, chief instructor at the Blériot School at Hendon, who was making the news – and filling the aviation record books – in April 1911 when he became the first to fly non-stop from London (i.e. Hendon) to Paris (Issy-les-Moulineaux) in a 50 hp Gnome-powered Blériot. It took him 3hr 56min. Prier's route took him over Chatham, Canterbury, Dover, Calais, Boulogne, Abbeville and Beauvais. He encountered bad visibility, except over the Channel, but in spite of the mist he was able to maintain his course. Prier also set a world record for distance flown in a straight line.

There were, however, far-reaching consequences when Hendon-based aviators flew over the Thames while the annual Oxford v Cambridge boat race was in progress. Hamel, Gresswell and Prier flew Blériots, while Grahame-White and Hubert were in Farmans. They were joined by Graham Gilmour from Bristol on a Bristol biplane, who proceeded to entertain the crowds by repeatedly zooming up, cutting his engine and gliding down over the boat race competitors. This was abruptly terminated by a forced landing on Chiswick Polytechnic cricket ground when he ran out of fuel. The officials were not amused and there were to be consequences.

Gilmour was hauled up before the Royal Aero Club to be questioned over this and other incidents. The club also investigated further reports of low flying over populated areas. But even though officials did not censure the aviators, the damage had been done. The Air Navigation Bill was before Parliament at the time and provided for stiff penalties for low flying over towns or crowds of people. Following the Boat Race incident, the Bill passed all of its Parliamentary stages and received Royal Assent within just seven days.

This did not deter Gilmour. His response was a low-level flight over the Thames from Weybridge to Wapping and back, which attracted considerable press attention. Not content with this exploit, Gilmour returned to the Thames to 'beat up' the crowded river during the Henley Regatta. At one point he flew so low that his wheels were touching the water. This was too much for the Royal Aero Club, which called him before the committee and suspended him for a month.

Gilmour's employer, the Bristol Aeroplane Company, appealed against this penalty. It had entered its star pilot for the Circuit of Britain Race for which the *Daily Mail* had offered another £10,000 prize. Bristol took the RAC to court and eventually the Court of Appeal ruled that the club's action had been *ultra vires*. By that time it was too late: the race had been run. On a happier note, Grahame-White organised a special 'benefit' meeting at Hendon for Jules Védrines, runner up in the Circuit of Britain. A crowd, said to have been 50,000 strong, attended the meeting to watch three pilots, including Védrines and Grahame-White, give a stirring display of flying despite a 30 mph wind.

The next noteworthy event on the Hendon calendar for the year was a demonstration staged for the Parliamentary Aerial Defence Committee. Attendance included members of the Royal Family and senior ministers such as prime minister Herbert Asquith, Secretary of State for War Lord Haldane, First Lord of the Admiralty Reginald McKenna and Home Secretary Winston Churchill, together with senior army and naval officers. *Flight* put the number of MPs attending at 300.

They watched several aeroplane types – including Farmans, Blériots, Howard Wrights, Avros, Barber's *Valkyrie* and Samuel Cody's *Flying Cathedral* – performing military-style tasks, including bomb dropping using sacks of flour. Some of the guests were treated to flights, including the leader of the opposition Arthur Balfour who went up with Grahame-White. As *Flight* reported somewhat lyrically:

> Starting away at quarter past three, hatless with his silver hair gleaming in the brilliant sun, this very distinguished passenger was sped around the aerodrome for a couple of circuits. Then came a run along the ground with the wheels just grazing the grass, to rise again before alighting. Naturally there was somewhat of a rush to ascertain Mr Balfour's views upon his experience but those who were near required no words from the leader of the opposition to leave any doubt as to the enjoyment which he had experienced. His smile and his face were too expressive.

When Gustave Hamel turned up from Aldershot he was greeted with 'great applause' from spectators but his arrival was eclipsed by Cody and his *Flying Cathedral* which approached at a height of 1,000ft. *Flight* reported:

> …before his machine had reached the limits of the aerodrome, he had shut off his engine and from that point made a beautifully slow and impressive *vol plane* completely round the aerodrome getting down close to earth in parallel with the enclosures.

A demonstration of erecting and dismantling a Blériot monoplane showed that it could be assembled in just nine minutes, with the reverse operation taking little more than two minutes longer. The monoplane was then returned to its transport wagon drawn by two horses. There were demonstrations of bomb and missile dropping, machine gun and ammunition carrying, and reconnaissance flights with officers as observers. 'Never for a moment was the air free of one or two machines circling around at various heights,' *Flight* noted.

A sequence of photographs published alongside the journal's six-page report showed Balfour animatedly telling a group of fellow parliamentarians about his flight with Grahame-White, while in another Churchill and his wife Clementine are seen watching the display in company with the Chancellor of the Exchequer and future prime minister David Lloyd George. The journal's verdict on the day was that it had been

> one of the most impressive demonstrations that could possibly have been devised for the bringing home, not only to the government but to the entire British public, of the marvellous strides which, in the short period of about three years, have been made in aviation.

The only sour notes were struck by the authorities' refusal to allow Horatio Barber to fly his *Valkyrie* and by the crash suffered by Alexander Drexel. This mishap destroyed his Blériot but left the pilot unhurt. It seems that a mechanic had crossed the elevator controls with the result that when Drexel pulled the stick back to take-off, the machine nosed over.

By June, however, Barber had a new machine built especially for racing. He flew it from Hendon to Brooklands in 20 minutes at a speed of 60 mph despite misty weather. The return journey took 30 minutes due to a head wind. Historian Dallas Brett called it 'a very splendid performance on the part of both machine and pilot'. Barber went on to produce further machines, two single-seaters and a pair of two-seaters, which he presented to the government.

One of the two-seaters was specifically designed for training pilots and fitted with a primitive form of dual control; until then pupil pilots had been instructed by leaning over their instructor's shoulders and feeling the stick in his hands. After one or two flights the pupil was sent off alone with instructions to make a straight flight before progressing to turns, half-circuits and circuits of the airfield.

In September, an army pilot, Lieutenant R.A. Cammell, was detailed to collect the first of the gift *Valkyries* from Hendon. Before flying it back to Farnborough it was arranged that he should familiarise himself with the aircraft by flying it around the airfield for thirty minutes. But it seems he was over-confident and soon began to make a series of steep turns. He cut his engine to attempt a gliding turn but lost control and the machine side-slipped into the ground. Cammell was thrown out and killed. Barber went on to establish the Valkyrie flying school at Hendon.

The same month, Britain's first air mail service was launched between Hendon and Windsor as an experiment supported by the Post Office. Special envelopes and postcards went on sale in London stores and were soon in demand, the idea having caught the public imagination. The care of the mail was entrusted to the staff pilots of the Blériot and Grahame-White schools.

Undeterred by high winds, Gustav Hamel took off at 04:58 on 9 September with the first bag of mail. Ten minutes later he was in Windsor having averaged just over 105 mph. There was no service the following day, Sunday, but over the next few days nineteen bags of mail were delivered. The service was interrupted by bad weather and mechanical failure and the experiment was concluded on the 29th. By that time Hamel and three other pilots had made 21 flights and carried more than 130,000 letters and postcards in 39 bags. On the debit side, one of Grahame-White's instructors, Charles Hubert, had crashed his Farman on take-off while carrying eight mail bags and broken both his legs. He received £500 compensation from the Post Office.

Most of the flights had taken about 30 minutes to cover the 21-mile route, but the experiment actually proved very little except that the aeroplane was not quite reliable enough for a regular mail service and also that it was vulnerable to bad weather. The Post Office damned the experiment with faint praise, considering that it had been 'of great public interest that would not be repeated for the time being'.

Two months later, Mrs Cheridah de Beauvoir Stocks became only the second woman to gain a Royal Aero Club pilot certificate (No 153) when she passed her test at Hendon using a 50 hp Farman biplane. She had been a pupil at Grahame-White's school for some months and celebrated the event by giving a joy ride to her friend, the wife of the school's general manager, Richard T. Gates.

By the end of 1911 several new companies had been established at Hendon. In fact, the aerodrome had become a thriving business enterprise, so much so that its first full year's income of over £11,000 was £1,000 more than Grahame-White's original projection even though it was a figure which, at the time, had seemed wildly optimistic. But Grahame-White now had other ambitions.

CLAUDE GRAHAME-WHITE

With his good looks, resourcefulness and talent for public relations it was inevitable that Claude Grahame-White should become widely recognised as one of Britain's most successful pioneer aviators.

He was born in 1879 at Bursledon, Hampshire, near the site of what is today the London Air Traffic Control Centre, to John White, a successful cement merchant and keen yachtsman, and his wife Ada. White later adopted the name of Grahame-White.

Claude was educated at Crondall House School, Farnham, and Bedford Grammar School and was later apprenticed to an engineering firm. After that he worked for an uncle who was a Yorkshire wool magnate before forming his own company to service motor vehicles in Bradford. His interest in aviation was sparked by Louis Blériot's cross-channel flight in 1909, which prompted him to attend the Rheims aviation meeting. There he met Blériot himself and enrolled at his flying school. He became one of the first to qualify as pilot in England, becoming the holder of Royal Aero Club certificate No 6, which he received in April 1910.

His elevation to celebrity status came the same month when he competed with Louis Paulhan for the *Daily Mail* £10,000 prize for the first flight between London and Manchester in under twenty-four hours. Although Paulhan was victorious, Grahame-White's achievement in making the first night flight won him wide acclamation.

In July in his Farman biplane Grahame-White took the £1,000 first prize for a flight of 1hr 23min 20sec at the Midlands Aviation

Meeting at Wolverhampton. Even more spectacular was his victory in the Gordon Bennett race at Belmont Park, New York. For this he was awarded the Royal Aero Club's Gold Medal. That October Grahame-White flew over Washington DC and landed on West Executive Avenue near the White House. Rather than being arrested for this intrusion he was widely fêted.

In 1911, in addition to establishing Hendon aerodrome and his flying school, Grahame-White also began his attempts to commercialise aviation with regular flying displays and to promote the military application of air power with his 'Wake Up Britain' campaign. He was also involved in the experimental carriage of various weapons on aircraft.

Grahame-White also established an aircraft manufacturing enterprise at Hendon but on the outbreak of the First World War the airfield was requisitioned by the Admiralty. He was commissioned in the Royal Naval Air Service and flew the first night patrol mission against an expected German Zeppelin raid on 5 September 1914.

He resigned from the RNAS in 1915 to concentrate on building aircraft for the government. His company produced 600 of the 8,430 Avro 504 trainers built during the war. But a contract for 700 de Havilland DH 6 trainers for the Royal Flying Corps led to major differences of opinion between Grahame-White and the Air Board. Having borrowed heavily to finance the expansion of his business, Grahame-White faced mounting debts as the factory stood idle due to a shortage of raw materials.

With bankruptcy looming, he diversified into furniture and car manufacture, and there was some success with post-war aircraft designs, notably the Bantam single-seater biplane. But Grahame-White's efforts to take a leading role in the development of civil aviation were frustrated by the legacy of the wartime DH-6 fiasco and the Air Ministry's refusal to return Hendon aerodrome to his ownership.

This led to a protracted legal wrangle which caused Grahame-White to lose his enthusiasm for aviation. Instead he turned his entrepreneurial talents to property development in Britain and the USA.

Claude Grahame-White died in Nice in 1959. Memories of his exploits live on at Hendon aerodrome however. After RAF flying operations there stopped in the 1960s, the site was largely redeveloped as a housing estate which was named Grahame Park. An original aircraft factory hangar has been relocated to the Royal Air Force Museum, where it houses the museum's First World War collection. It is named the Grahame-White Factory.

Chapter 10

Birth Of An Industry

While Alliott Verdon Roe had been busy at Lea Marshes following his eviction from Brooklands in 1908, there had been a crucial change of personnel at the Surrey speed bowl. Clerk of the course Ernst Rodakowski, who had so disapproved of Roe and his activities, had departed. It was considered that Rodakowski's enthusiasm and energy had been essential to launch the Brooklands motor circuit, but now the track had become established there was seen to be a need for a quieter, more methodical approach. Major (later Colonel) Frederick Lindsay Lloyd, who succeeded him, also took a different attitude towards aviation compared to his predecessor.

Lloyd had been secretary of the War Office Committee on mechanical transport and had become interested in the potential of all forms for military use. He had been elected to membership of the Aero Club the previous February and his appointment to Brooklands brought to the track a man who appreciated that aviation went hand-in-hand with motoring.

Under the new regime the BARC had offered a prize for the best flight of more than fifty yards at the 1910 Easter Monday meeting. It sounded a modest enough target, and the winner, Lionel Mander, actually flew ten times the distance, although he hit a parked roller on landing. Among the contestants was A.V. Roe, whose return to Brooklands was no doubt encouraged by Rodakowski's departure. He flew a new triplane which he had christened *Mercury*. True to form he crashed.

Roe's return to Brooklands had coincided with an upturn in his fortunes. Not only had he managed to coax one of his machines into the air to official recognition but he had announced in January the formation of his company, A.V. Roe and Co. It would not become a limited company for a further three years but, according to *Flight*, its intention was to build and sell monoplanes, biplanes and triplanes.

Financial backing had come from Roe's father and brother. Workshop space had been provided at Humphrey Roe's elastic webbing company at Brownfield Mills, Manchester, which made Bullseye Braces. 'This gave rise to the joke that Avro aeroplanes were kept up by Bullseye Braces, which was financially true at least,' wrote historian Philip Jarrett.

Roe started advertising his products soon afterwards. Complete aircraft started at £450 and were guaranteed to fly five miles, a somewhat ambitious promise from a man who had only managed to fly 500 yards the previous July. He also offered to build machines to clients' order or act as a consulting engineer.

Mercury was in fact A.V. Roe and Co's first product. It was displayed in Manchester and at the Aero Show at Olympia in March 1910. In June Roe used this machine to fly a series of complete circles at Brooklands, the first he had been able to manage. This was despite the fact that he had yet to devise a satisfactory control system and, indeed, to realise that control in yaw and roll was necessary for coordinated turns. On 11 March, Roe made four short flights in his second triplane, the best covering half a mile. After modifications Roe used this aircraft to compete for the BARC's prize but it did not fly any appreciable distance. It was dismantled by the end of April.

Mercury was retained for further experiments and for use by Roe's newly-established flying school at Brooklands but was damaged in further mishaps. In its rebuild Roe added ailerons and settled for what was to become the standard three-axis control system already adopted by the Wright brothers. This made *Mercury* Roe's first genuinely practical aeroplane.

Handicap races for aeroplanes soon became a feature of Brooklands' aviation meetings. The first was the twelve-mile race around the circuit at the Whit Monday meeting in 1910. The handicapping, as with the car races, was organised by the redoubtable A.V. 'Ebby' Ebblewhite, the circuit's legendary timekeeper. The race was run in two heats and the overall winner was Fred Raynham flying an Avro biplane. Raynham was to be one of the contestants for the £10,000 prize awarded by the *Daily Mail* for the first non-stop trans-Atlantic crossing by aeroplane. At Brooklands he was followed home by Collyns Pizey in a Bristol biplane and L.F. McDonald (R.E.P. Vickers monoplane).

The event was watched by a large crowd who had paid a shilling a head for admission to the site. As the BARC was offering more and more ambitious programmes over the next few years, the extent of the flying and the growing public interest attracted the attention of the famous ticket agency Keith Prowse. In February 1911 representatives visited Brooklands to arrange for admission tickets and tickets for flights to be sold at their offices. The charge for a short flight was 2 guineas, one involving three circuits cost 4 guineas, while a cross-country flight could be had for 10 guineas.

By the end of May 1910 Roe was working on his first customer aircraft in his hangar number 14. It was one of the biggest at Brooklands and now housed three machines. Roe soon had two customer orders for Farman-type biplanes and was generating additional income by supplying fixtures and fittings to other manufacturers. A third triplane design was also completed during mid-1910 and it soon proved capable of executing figures of eight.

Howard Pixton, who had been employed by Roe as a mechanic, made several hops in this machine. Pixton worked without pay in return for receiving flying instruction; soon he would be flying with Roe as his passenger. Pixton would become an accomplished pilot and, later, winner of the prestigious Schneider Trophy race. Roe, meanwhile, gained pilot certificate No 18 flying the new triplane.

By October a fourth variation on Roe's triplane theme – and the last – had been completed and joined the flying school at Brooklands. Despite being dumped into the sewage works by a pupil making his first flight, this machine was to become the workhorse of the Avro Flying School. Pixton used it to demonstrate his rapidly developing flying skills by describing figures of eight at a height of 200ft. But after he lost control, he too ended up in the sewage farm. In January 1911 he received pilot certificate No 50.

Later that year a biplane based on the last of Roe's triplanes made its appearance at Brooklands. Powered by a 35 hp water-cooled four-cylinder Green engine, it represented a significant milestone in the evolution of Avro aircraft. It made its first flight in April in Pixton's hands. Despite a strong wind, the new machine created a favourable impression. *The*

Aero reported that it 'promises uncommonly well'. Compared with the triplanes, the journal observed, 'it strikes one as being an improvement in every way.'

Pixton later made several long flights in this machine, on one occasion reaching 1,000ft. He found it an outstanding machine with no vices and would report that, despite its low power, it could carry a passenger with ease. This machine, retrospectively designated the Avro Type D, would become the mainstay of the flying school.

It was said that a pilot was not fully qualified until he had crashed into the sewage farm. If that was so, then the A.V. Roe school must have been one of the most successful as one of his later triplanes used for tuition was said to have spent more time in the sewage farm than in the air.

The Avro school would remain active at Brooklands until the early autumn of 1912 when the bulk of it moved to Shoreham in West Sussex where permanent hangars and an impressive new clubhouse had been built following the airfield's opening in 1911. By this time Roe had virtually given up flying to concentrate on the business of building aircraft.

Meanwhile other schools had arrived to take its place, including Hewlett and Blondeau, Hanriot, Spencer and Deperduissin, Sir George White's British and Colonial Aeroplane Company (later Bristol), and Vickers. These establishments trained a combined total of 44 pilots in 1911 and 90 the following year.

Vickers, which had started aircraft manufacture in 1911, took its first machine, a licence-built R.E.P., to Brooklands for its first test flight, but it crashed on take-off, necessitating repairs which were undertaken on-site. At the same time, Vickers began to recruit staff from British and Colonial for its newly-established flying school.

There were some notable names among both students – Trenchard and Joubert de la Ferte were examples – and instructors. Among the latter was Major Frank B. Halford, who would become technical director of the de Havilland engine company and designer of, among a range of notable power plants, the Gipsy series of engines.

Some pilots decided to teach themselves. One of them was 'Tommy' Sopwith whose desire to learn to fly was sparked by a £5 introductory joy-ride with Gustave Blondeau in a Farman. Following that first flight, Sopwith taught himself to fly using a Blériot-type monoplane built by Howard T. Wright at Battersea. It was delivered to Sopwith at Brooklands on 21 October and the following day he took to the air for the first time but crashed on landing after travelling about 300 yards.

The machine, an improved version of Howard Wright's Avis, built for the Scottish Aeroplane Syndicate, was repaired, but Sopwith crashed it again. He abandoned it in favour of a Howard Wright-built biplane based on the Farman design. He flew it immediately and without instruction, receiving Royal Aero Club pilot certificate No 31 on 22 November.

A confident Sopwith entered for the British Empire Michelin Cup for which a prize of £500 was offered to the British pilot who covered the greatest distance in a closed circuit by the end of the year. Sopwith covered just over 150 miles in 4hr 7min at Brooklands on 31 December, but he lost out to Samuel Cody who pipped him to the prize at Farnborough later in the day.

Sopwith went on to establish a flying school at Brooklands and later became a notable manufacturer. But as there was limited space at Brooklands for him to pursue his ambitions he acquired a disused skating rink at nearby Kingston-upon-Thames. All Sopwith aircraft were taken to Brooklands for assembly and test flying.

In 1910 French-born artist-turned-aviation-pioneer José Weiss, who had earlier flown a series of gliders near Littlehampton in West Sussex, began testing his new *Sylvia* monoplane – named after one of his five daughters – at Brooklands. The pilot was racing driver and engineer Eric Gordon England who, according to *Flight*, 'attained a height of 40ft flying the length of the ground'. But the machine appeared to lack agility and while attempting a turn heeled over so far that it crashed, Mr England claiming acquaintance with the sewage farm.'

England later wrote that, with Weiss watching, he and *Sylvia* had passed over the Brooklands paddock at 100ft but that while over the sewage farm 'something gave way in the structure of the machine'. He reported: 'With more luck than judgement I kept the machine the right way up in a form of stall and the machine hit the softest and slimiest part of the sewage farm, turned right over and forced me head downwards into the glutinous mess.'

Sylvia was one of two monoplanes built by Weiss, the other being called *Elsie* after another of his daughters. It was powered by a three-cylinder Anzani engine. By the time it arrived at Brooklands, *Sylvia* had a V8 ENV engine, bought with the proceeds of the sale of a painting. The machines were flown at Littlehampton Sands, which Weiss and his helpers regarded as their aerodrome. The base for these operations was Littlehampton Fort, owned by the Duke of Norfolk, on the south-east corner of Littlehampton golf course and overlooking the harbour.

The following March, *Flight* ran a three-page article on the Weiss monoplane, reporting that 'there is no more interesting machine at Brooklands today.' The journal reported that it was

> the outcome of many years' painstaking experimental work by Mr José Weiss, who was one of the most persistent investigators of that branch of aerodynamics concerned with the principle of automatic stability. It is to this side of the problem of flight that Mr Weiss has devoted most of his energy and model after model was made and flown on the hillsides near Arundel long before the habitués of Brooklands received him and Mr Gordon England, who piloted a man-lifting model of that period, as newcomers amongst them.

Weiss returned to Sussex where he continued his experiments with gliders until his death in 1919.

Meanwhile, there was more aeronautical competition at Brooklands. In January 1911 the BARC and the owners of Hendon aerodrome jointly put up a £50 purse for the fastest return flight between the two locations on the same day. The winner was Gustave Hamel flying a Blériot XI. In May there was another race, from Brooklands to Brighton, organised as a handicap by Ebby Ebblewhite. Four starters competed for the £80 prize, including Howard Pixton in the Avro biplane. Despite three postponements due to bad weather, Hamel was again the winner. He duly circled the balloon at Brighton Palace Pier, which marked the finish point, and landed at Shoreham.

But these two events were dwarfed in scope and significance by something much grander: the *Daily Mail*-sponsored Round Britain Air Race, which offered a £10,000 prize to the winner. From Brooklands the twenty-one competitors were to fly more than 1,000 miles over five days on a route which would take them via Hendon to Edinburgh with intermediate stops at Harrogate and Newcastle-upon-Tyne. They were to return via Shoreham with stops at Stirling, Glasgow, Carlisle, Manchester and Bristol. It was to be a contest even more gruelling than the European event staged the previous month. No changes of machines were allowed and parts of the engines and airframes were sealed to avoid substitutions.

To *Flight*, the race marked the point at which interest in aviation events at the Surrey venue surpassed enthusiasm for motor racing, with a crowd estimated at 50,000 present to watch the start. Among them was the brother of the German Kaiser. Two entries crashed on take-off and one – that of A. V. Roe – had come to grief on a test flight on the morning of the race.

So it was that seventeen aircraft took off for Hendon, but any hopes of a home win were soon to be dashed when the race quickly resolved itself into a contest between two French pilots, Jules Védrines and André Beaumont, the pseudonym of a French naval officer. There was to be no flying on the Sunday.

The race had attracted huge public interest. Spectators' cars, parked side by side, stretched around the banking for two miles. At Hendon 500,000 people turned up to watch the first competitor flagged away at 0400 hrs on Monday. Some had camped in neighbouring fields. Three hours later there were 150,000 spectators at Harrogate.

Only three competitors completed the second stage in a single day and by Wednesday it had come down to a straight fight between Védrines and Beaumont who both opted to forgo the scheduled night stop at Shoreham. Beaumont returned to Brooklands over an hour ahead of his compatriot.

The race demonstrated that British aircraft were well behind their foreign counterparts in terms of performance and reliability. In fact

Samuel Cody was the only pilot of a British-built machine to complete the course – three days behind the winner. Two other British competitors, James Valentine and Gustav Hamel, who had been forced out with engine trouble at Dumfries, were considered to have done well even though Valentine had finished two days in arrears. Jules Védrines was awarded a consolation prize of £200.

During 1911 Brooklands hosted seven aviation meetings at which prize money totalled £800. Awards were made for flights of over fifteen minutes and for the three best flights of the season. It was during that year that Brooklands witnessed its first fatal flying accident. Gerald Napier's Bristol Boxkite stalled while he was making a sharp turn at about 50ft. His passenger, who was occupying a second seat, escaped with minor injuries.

Regular handicap races, overseen by Ebblewhite, continued to be a Brooklands speciality. Collyns Pizey won the first of 1912 flying a Bristol Boxkite. The race was run in April over a six-mile course to Chertsey Bridge and back. The following day's event, over a nine-mile course, was won by Sopwith. Another of the year's winners who was later to win fame was John Alcock. The first man to fly an aeroplane non-stop across the Atlantic won a two-lap speed handicap flying a Henry Farman. It was his first race.

In May 1912 there was another fatal accident at Brooklands and it shook the flying community to its core. E.V.B. Fisher had been one of the first occupants of a shed at the airfield in January 1910 and, together with Howard Flanders, had built a small monoplane of original design. He received his pilot certificate (No 77) in May 1911 and was widely considered to be a fine pilot. He was also secretary of the original shed holders' committee and later organiser of the Brooklands Aero Club.

On the evening of 13 May he was flying a Flanders monoplane powered by a 60 hp Green engine with a passenger, American industrialist Victor Mason. The aircraft made several circuits of Brooklands but crashed after attempting a left-hand turn. The wreckage immediately burst into fire.

As well as being a tragedy involving a well-liked and highly respected aviator and his passenger, this crash was significant for another reason.

It was the first in Britain to be the subject of a formal professional investigation. The Royal Aero Club's Public Safety and Accidents Investigation Committee blamed Fisher for causing it. The investigators found that he had lost control during the turn and thought it possible that he might have moved the elevator control involuntarily, causing the aircraft to pitch downwards. At a time when aircraft were not required to be equipped with seat belts, Fisher had been catapulted from the aircraft. The investigators considered that had he been strapped into his seat he might have retained control of the aircraft.

In October, Harry Hawker, who had received his pilot certificate the preceding month, won the British Empire Michelin trophy. Flying a Sopwith-modified Wright biplane powered by a 50 hp ABC engine, Hawker won the trophy and a £500 cash prize with a flight of 8hr 23min. He also set a new British duration record.

The following year Hawker flew the Sopwith Three-Seater to a new British altitude record of 11,450 ft. Hawker also used it to win the twelve-mile cross-country handicap in bad weather. Even more eye-catching was a neat and compact side-by-side two-seater which made its first flight at Brooklands in November 1913. Fitted with floats, this machine won the 1914 Schneider Trophy race at Monte Carlo with Pixton at the controls.

In 1913 one aviator showed it was possible to learn to fly in a single day. Noel Pemberton Billing (sometimes rendered with a hyphen) was the brother of the proprietor of Brooklands' popular Blue Bird café. Earlier he had attempted to create an aerodrome from 3,000 acres of marshland at Fambridge, Essex. The venture failed but one of his collaborators had been Frederick Handley Page who would found the first British public company to build aircraft.

Among the venture's first products was a machine claimed to possess outstanding stability. During a conversation with Handley Page, Pemberton Billing (see box on page 147) claimed that stability was immaterial and that it was possible to learn to fly in a single day. A £500 wager was agreed and the next morning Pemberton Billing set out to win the bet. He approached several of the flying schools at Brooklands but all were reluctant to take on the challenge. Pemberton Billing therefore bought a Farman biplane and persuaded one of the Vickers instructors to accompany him on his first flight. He went solo after twenty-five minutes but rain prevented further flying. A Royal Aero Club observer was sent for and Pemberton Billing completed the requisite tests. On 17 September he was awarded his pilot certificate (No 632). Handley Page duly paid up and handed over a sum that would be worth somewhere between £50,000 and £500,000 in twenty-first century values.

Later that month Brooklands was the location for the manoeuvre known as looping the loop to be performed for the first time in Britain. Earlier that year Adolph Pégoud had become the first to loop-the-loop and it was subsequently announced that he would come to Brooklands. Pégoud and his aircraft arrived during the summer and began several weeks of testing before he was ready for a public display. On Saturday, 25 September, witnessed by a crowd said to be the biggest yet seen at the track, the Frenchman created a sensation when he looped the loop.

In 1914 Brooklands would begin its association with attempts to win the £10,000 prize offered by *Daily Mail* proprietor Lord Northcliffe for the first non-stop crossing of the Atlantic by aeroplane. Among the first to rise to the challenge was Canadian-born banker Edward Mackay Edgar, who approached Gustav Hamel with the suggestion that he should compete for the prize.

Edgar subsequently approached Brooklands-based Martin and Handasyde (later Martinsyde) with an order for a monoplane with a 65 ft wingspan and powered by a 215 hp Sunbeam engine. It would have been the largest aeroplane yet designed in Britain but, although construction had already begun, the project was abandoned when Hamel disappeared in May during a flight from France to England.

War broke out on 4 August 1914 and Hugh Locke King offered Brooklands to the War Office. It duly took possession the following day. All further competitive fixtures at the venue were cancelled. The Blue Bird café became the officers' mess and the flying schools which had turned out more qualified pilots than any other UK location were taken over by the military.

But Brooklands was about to take on another role. In the period up to 1914, sixteen different aircraft builders were in operation there. Most would be short-lived and are barely remembered today, but from the sheds previously emblazoned with names like Avro, British and Colonial (later renamed Bristol), Martin & Handasyde, Sopwith and Vickers would spring a mighty industry that would make Brooklands one of Britain's leading aircraft manufacturing sites.

A.V. EBBLEWHITE

Albert Victor Ebblewhite's name is more usually linked with Brooklands where he was from its inception the official starter, timekeeper and handicapper. But before the First World War 'Ebby', as he was universally known, also officiated at many of the early aviation meetings in Britain.

Born in London in 1871 the son of John and Amy Ebblewhite, Ebby followed his father into the craft of musical instrument making. Away from his shop in Aldgate High Street in London's East End, he acted as starter at the fourth Bexhill motor race meeting held in 1905. He moved on to Brooklands when the track opened two years later.

Other events at which Ebblewhite acted as timekeeper included the Blackpool, Lanark and Bournemouth meetings as well as the London to Manchester flights by Louis Paulhan and Claude Grahame-White for the *Daily Mail*'s £10,000 prize. He performed a similar function at the 1910 Gordon Bennett race held in Britain in 1910.

Ebblewhite was, however, at his busiest and most influential at Brooklands. From 1907, races there followed horse racing practice with drivers wearing different coloured smocks like jockeys. Later in the year cars were numbered, a change the British Automobile Club had initially been reluctant to adopt.

A guiding force in the decision was Ebblewhite, who over the years became a constant and reassuring figure with his pipe, three-piece suit and trilby hat. Another horse racing practice adopted by the BARC was handicapping. It was Ebblewhite who persuaded officials that handicapping by distance was unworkable and that it should be done on the basis of time.

He had been recording times at Brooklands since the first meeting using a sophisticated method involving pneumatic rubber strips separating a system of duplicated copper contacts stretched across the track surface. When a wheel passed over the strips, a circuit was completed and the recording mechanism actuated. A feeder-led tape, running at a rate of one foot per minute, went past three ink-line traces. The middle trace recorded a blip when passed over the pneumatic strip and the lower trace was a back-up in the event of the first trace failing.

Ebblewhite remained at Brooklands until 1939. He died the following year.

NOEL PEMBERTON BILLING

Soldier, businessman, aviator, publisher: Noel Pemberton Billing was all of these and more. As a member of Parliament he became a controversial figure who seldom missed an opportunity to promote aviation and air power.

Born in Hampstead, north London, in 1881 into a middle-class family, he ran away from home aged 13 and travelled to South Africa where he became a policeman and later fought in the second Boer War. On his return to England he opened a garage in Surrey but soon became interested in aviation.

In 1909 he acquired 3,000 acres of marshland at South Fambridge, Essex which he planned to develop into an aerodrome with extensive facilities. Among the aviators to sample these facilities was French-born pioneer José Weiss. He was joined by Eric Gordon England, who acted as his assistant. Frederick Handley Page was another tenant and both he and Pemberton Billing worked with Weiss to develop his first monoplane.

Flight was so impressed by Pemberton Billing's plans that it ran a three-page article describing them in detail in February 1909. The journal reported that in addition to the land, Pemberton Billing had acquired buildings which had previously been used by an engineering works manufacturing hydraulic cranes. These buildings, the journal reported, would be transformed into 'aero docks', together with sheds that could be rented out for £50 a year. There was also a row of four-roomed bungalows which could be used by aviators.

'The only stipulation which Mr Billing desires to make with those who share the use of his property,' *Flight* reported,

> is that they shall give evidence of a patriotic side to their work. And this they shall do by associating themselves with his general scheme…that of founding the nucleus for an aerial fleet, which it is proposed to call the 'Imperial Flying Squadron'. It will be observed that Mr Billing's proposals are of a very ambitious and praiseworthy nature and that they are essentially intended to imbue the sporting side with a militant national aspect of a definite kind. As such we hope that this 'Colony of British Aerocraft' (as Mr Billing proposes to call it) may meet with immediate success.

It did not, as most British aviators continued to favour places like Brooklands, Eastchurch and Hendon. Undaunted, Pemberton Billing used the £500 he won from Frederick Handley Page to establish an aircraft manufacturing business. The intention was to build 'boats that fly rather than aeroplanes that float.'

Based on the River Itchen near Southampton, the company set out to build marine aircraft, and the single-engine PB1 was displayed at the 1914 Olympia Aero Show. It failed to fly, but the PB7 was advertised as a flying lifeboat in which the wings and rear fuselage could be detached leaving the forward part as a boat.

Two were under construction for the German government when war broke out in August 1914 and the order was cancelled. The Admiralty placed orders with the company for aircraft designed by other firms but Pemberton Billing's next original design was the PB9 scout biplane also known as the 'Seven Day Bus' because it was reputedly built in that number of days. Other designs included the PB23/25 for the RNAS and the eccentric quadruplane, known as the Nighthawk, for intercepting Zeppelin.

When Pemberton Billing joined the Royal Naval Air Service, he sold his share of the business to his works manager, Hubert Scott-Paine, who renamed it Supermarine after the company's telegraphic address. In 1916 Pemberton Billing became an MP. His used his seat in the House of Commons to call for the creation of an independent air force and for a bombing campaign against Germany.

He also founded a journal which he used to attack, among other groups, Jews and financiers. But it was his extreme homophobic views which landed him in court in a sensational libel case. He represented himself and won the case. Failing health forced Pemberton Billing to quit politics in 1921. Subsequent attempts to win another Parliamentary seat were unsuccessful but he turned his talents to writing plays and inventing new types of sound recording systems and cameras.

Noel Pemberton Billing died in 1948. He was buried at Burnham-on-Crouch just across the river from South Fambridge.

THE FIRST ACCIDENT INVESTIGATORS

Concern over the growing number of accidents involving British flyers led the Royal Aero Club, then the nearest thing to an aviation regulator which issued pilots with their certificates of competency, to take action.

What particularly concerned the club, as well as the whole aviation community, was the loss at Bournemouth in 1910 of Charles Rolls, whose aircraft had broken apart in mid-air. Although the aircraft was not one of the six Short-built Wright *Flyers*, having been built in France to the Wright design, Horace Short was involved in investigating the cause of the crash.

In February 1912 therefore, the club decided to establish a Public Safety and Accidents Investigation Committee under the chairmanship of Colonel Henry Holden who had earlier supervised the construction of the banked race track at Brooklands. Its membership included George Cockburn, who would later become Britain's first chief inspector of accidents, Frank (later Sir Francis) McClean, Alec Ogilvie and Mervyn O'Gorman, superintendent of the Royal Aircraft Factory at Farnborough.

The Fisher accident at Brooklands represented the committee's first investigation but its method of work was said to have been inspired by Horace Short's probe of Rolls's crash. Its last investigation was completed in 1914. In June 1912 *Flight* commented that 'the chief value of these exhaustive enquiries and the evidence they produce is that they place at the disposal of those interested the means of avoiding similar happenings in the future, and that is the main justification of the expenditure of time and trouble to which the members of the committee have pledged themselves.'

By that time the committee had appointed two or three committee representatives at each of the major flying grounds, such as Eastchurch, Brooklands and Hendon.

Chapter 11

Married Officers Need Not Apply

In 1907 Lord Tweedmouth, First Lord of the Admiralty, wrote to the Wright Brothers to tell them that the Admiralty was not interested in acquiring the machine they had invented. Aeroplanes, he wrote, 'would not be of any practical use to the naval service'.

At about the same time, Field Marshal Sir Henry Wilson, Chief of the Imperial General Staff, was expressing similar sentiments. Aviation, he declared, was a 'useless and expensive fad, advocated by a few individuals whose ideas are unworthy of attention'.

A change of heart was not long in coming.

By 1908 the British government was beginning to recognise the military potential of aircraft. The following year, prime minister Herbert Asquith approved the formation of a body called the Advisory Committee for Aeronautics together with an Aerial Sub-Committee of the Committee of Imperial Defence. Both bodies comprised politicians, army and Royal Navy officers.

That July Captain Reginald Bacon, a member of the sub-committee, submitted to the First Sea Lord, the redoubtable Sir John Fisher, that a rigid airship based on the German Zeppelin be designed and constructed by Vickers. After much discussion by the Committee of Imperial Defence, the suggestion was approved, but not until May 1909. The resulting airship, despite its name *Mayfly*, never flew and broke in half in September 1911, leading Fisher's successor, Sir Arthur Wilson, to recommend that rigid airship construction be abandoned.

Meanwhile, in June 1910, Lieutenant George Colmore had become the Royal Navy's first qualified aeroplane pilot, having paid for his tuition out of his own pocket. He made his first flight in Frank McLean's Short S.27 covering 11 miles in 20 minutes. On the 20th, Colmore passed the Royal Aero Club's test and was awarded pilot certificate No 15, which he received at a club meeting the following day.

It was inevitable that the naval officers stationed at Sheerness would be curious about what was going on at the club's airfield at nearby Eastchurch. Encouraged by this interest and by Colmore's success, the club offered both the army and the navy the opportunity to train their personnel as pilots. The offer, made in November 1910, included the use of the airfield at Eastchurch together with aircraft and the services of its members to act as instructors.

The army declined and the Admiralty, still pinning its faith on the *Mayfly*, demurred. It was, however, persuaded to accept when it was pointed out that the club's offer was free of charge. The commander-in-chief, the Nore, Admiral Sir C.C. Drury, who was responsible for the protection of the entrance to the port of London, promulgated the scheme to the officers under his jurisdiction. It was stipulated that applicants had to be unmarried and be able to pay the club's membership fees. It was also made clear that they would receive six months' leave of absence from duty, forgo any prospect of commanding a ship, and pay for any damage to their aircraft while training.

Despite these restrictive conditions, the response showed the degree of interest in aviation within the service: 200 applications were received. Lieutenant Charles Rumney Samson, Lieutenant Arthur Longmore, Lieutenant Reginald Gregory and Lieutenant Wildman-Lushington were accepted. The latter, however, was found medically unfit and was replaced by Lieutenant Eugene Gerrard of the Royal Marines.

Cecil Grace was originally scheduled to be the flying instructor but following his death George Cockburn took on this responsibility. Horace Short was in charge of ground instruction. Basic flying tuition comprised three lessons. In the first the student taxied the aircraft around the airfield before progressing to make a few straight flights. Lesson three involved making a turn within a 440-yard radius. The student would normally take 2½ hours before making a solo flight but there was no flying if the wind velocity was over 4 mph.

All four officers completed their training successfully. The course lasted six weeks, during which there were only two crashes, neither serious. In addition to flying training, the officers received technical instruction at the Short brothers' aircraft factory, visited French aeronautical centres and attended the military aeroplane trials at Rheims to study foreign developments.

The original agreement between McClean and the Admiralty was that two machines should be lent for instructing RN pilots. One of these two machines was, however, being flown by Cecil Grace when he disappeared over the Channel, so another was built in its place. An older one, known as 'the Dud', was added. The first three machines were Short No 26 with Farman-type 50 hp Gnome engine (the Dud), Short No 28, first with 60 hp Green engine and then 50 hp Farman-type Gnome, and Short No 34.

These machines were later supplemented by four more aircraft, a Blériot monoplane, Short No 36 (70 hp Gnome engine) and two twin-engined aircraft, Short No 239 and Short No 27, both powered by 50 hp Gnomes. On 25 April 1911 Samson, Longmore and Lieutenant Wilfred Parke, who had learned to fly at Brooklands, were awarded pilot certificates 71, 72 and 73 respectively. A few days later Gregory and Gerrard received certificates numbers 75 and 76.

In May 1911 the Aero Club secretary noted

The four Naval officers who have been undergoing a course of instruction in flying at the Club's flying grounds at Eastchurch, under the guidance of Mr G.B. Cockburn, have all succeeded in obtaining their aviators' certificates in accordance with the new rules. The committee at its meeting on Tuesday last unanimously passed a resolution warmly thanking Mr. Cockburn for the generous way in which he had devoted himself to the instruction of the Naval officers.

Parke, like Colmore before him, had paid for his own tuition. He had his first flying lesson at the Avro school at Brooklands in April 1911 at a time when dual-control instruction was almost unknown. He was therefore in sole charge of the aircraft in which he had been told to try taxying. But, to the surprise of onlookers, he opened the throttle and made a series of short hops from which he managed to land without damaging the aircraft. At his third attempt a few days later, Parke managed to fly a half-circle in a stiff breeze, landing with only minor damage to the undercarriage. A week after his first hops he passed the pilot licence test in a Bristol Boxkite.

Parke was, however, killed in December 1912 when the bird-like Handley Page Type F monoplane he was flying from Hendon to Oxford crashed at Wembley. His passenger, Alfred Hardwick, manager of the Handley Page factory, also died in the accident. It was found to have been due to loss of engine power, combined with the decline of airspeed caused by turning. This was exacerbated by wind disturbances due to the local topography, especially the presence of a belt of trees on the windward side of a ridge. There is a stained glass window dedicated to Parke's memory in Uplyme parish church in Devon where his father was rector.

Some of the newly-trained pilots remained at Eastchurch where they tested Short-built aircraft. In June 1911 Samson flew to Brooklands and back, while Gerrard set a world record by flying a ten-mile course. Accompanied by another officer, he remained airborne for 4hr 13min. Three days later Samson, flying solo, set a British endurance record of just under 5hr.

Samson also tried to convince his superiors that more pilots should be trained to fly. His task was made easier by the loss of the *Mayfly*. By December 1911, McClean had bought additional land so that the navy could establish a flying school at Eastchurch, with Samson as its first commanding officer. The initial flying course opened on 2 March 1912, which, it should be noted, was before the Royal Flying Corps, with its Naval and Military Wings, had been formed. The establishment of the RFC was announced later that month, by which time seventeen naval officers had qualified as pilots.

For administrative purposes the Eastchurch unit became part of Nore Command based at Sheerness, but operationally, at least on paper, it would be part of the RFC's Naval Wing. Although it had been assumed that all flying training, military or naval, would take place at the Central Flying School at Upavon, the navy continued to use Eastchurch for this purpose. Trainees followed a programme similar to that of the RFC but were encouraged to see themselves as part of a distinct naval service.

This was promoted through a series of courses which introduced students to notions of discipline and service while creating an understanding of the mechanical and scientific basis of the machines they flew. This process was also designed to replicate the rigours of the long training process required to inculcate the values of hierarchy and control through days of classes and physical activity. In other words, pilots were sailors first and pilots second.

By June 1913, 44 naval officers and 105 other ranks had been trained at the Central Flying School and at Eastchurch, while 35 officers and men had been trained in airship work. In 1913 a seaplane base on the Isle of Grain, the spit of land between the Thames and Medway estuaries, and an airship base at nearby Kingsnorth, were approved for construction.

The service also conducted experiments there, particularly in the use of wireless for air-to-ground communications, dropping bombs and mounting Lewis guns on aircraft. Three non-rigid airships built for the army had been taken over by the navy. Close liaison was maintained with Shorts. It was not until June 1913 that Eastchurch became an RNAS station, an event which pre-dated the formation of the Royal Naval Air Service on 1 July 1914.

The Short brothers' designs continued to evolve over this period. The S.27 represented an advance in aeronautical design because it featured two engines, a 50 hp Gnome mounted 2ft behind the pilot's head and driving a pusher propeller, and another similar unit mounted in front driving a tractor propeller. This aircraft was known as the Tandem Twin. Horace Short also devised a wing folding mechanism which enabled aircraft to be stored aboard ship.

The association with the navy inevitably led Shorts to consider aircraft able to operate from water. Oswald designed pneumatic flotation bags to enable them to make emergency landings on water. In December 1911 Longmore took off from Shellbeach in an S.34 equipped with flotation gear and made a successful landing on the Medway. Things were taken a stage further with a take-off from the pre-Dreadnought battleship HMS *Africa*.

Staging was erected on the ship's foredeck, running over the forward gun turret to the bows with rails to guide the aircraft. Samson took off from Eastchurch on 10 January 1912 and flew across the Medway to Cockleshell Hard. The aircraft was then taken by lighter to the *Africa*, which was anchored in the Medway, and hoisted aboard by the ship's derrick.

The ship's crew tested the strength and stability of the rails by jumping up and down on them. Then, while the ship was under way, they held the Gnome-powered modified Short S.27 fitted with air bags as Samson prepared for the first British shipboard take-off. The aircraft moved quickly down the runway, dipped slightly after leaving it, but then pulled up and climbed easily. It was 2hr 20min since he had left Eastchurch.

Samson circled *Africa* several times to the cheers of the crew, although on one pass he came uncomfortably close to the ship. After a few minutes, he climbed to 800 ft and landed safely ashore. *Africa*'s flight equipment was transferred to the cruiser *Hibernia* in May 1912.

The 15,000-ton warship was cruising at 10.5 knots in the Channel off Weymouth during the Portland Naval Review when Samson gave a repeat performance of his *Africa* take-off and landed ashore at Lodmore near Weymouth. The following day he flew round the fleet and in the evening was among the officers who dined with the King aboard the royal yacht. Another aircraft, designated the S.41 and fitted with floats, was also aboard the cruiser but was lowered into the water by crane, enabling it to fly away as a seaplane.

The S.41 'Hydro-Aeroplane', as it was known to Shorts, was a two-seat tractor biplane powered by a 100 hp Gnome engine. This appeared in 1912 equipped initially with wheels, although they were quickly exchanged for floats. Following the Weymouth review, the Admiralty ordered twenty-five new seaplanes, most of which were to be built by Shorts. The S.41 was the ancestor of all Shorts' seaplanes and flying boats although the basic design underwent many subsequent changes.

The navy conducted further experiments with seaplanes later in the year. Lieutenant L'Estrange Malone flew a 70 hp Gnome-powered Short from Eastchurch to Sheerness. There it alighted on the water alongside the battleship HMS *London* which then hoisted the machine aboard and set course for Portsmouth. When the ship was 19 miles from its destination and steaming at 15 knots, Malone took off from the warship's deck and landed ashore.

In July, Samson, accompanied by Lieutenant Trewin and Lieutenant Spencer Grey, accompanied by Lieutenant Sheppard, used similar aircraft to make the 196-mile flight from Eastchurch to Portsmouth. Grey, however, had to land at Newhaven to remedy engine trouble but reached his destination the same day. Samson was able to fly non-stop, arriving at Portsmouth a little over three hours later to complete the longest cross-country point-to-point flight yet made by a British pilot.

Although seemingly overshadowed by these naval activities, the civilian aviators at Eastchurch remained active. Indeed, the 1911 Gordon-Bennett air race was held there. The series had been established two years earlier by the rich and somewhat eccentric American publisher who took a keen interest in aviation.

Because Claude Grahame-White had won the 1910 race held in Long Island, it fell to the Royal Aero Club to organise the following year's event. After some consideration, officials decided to stage the event at Eastchurch. A 3.76-mile course was laid out over which competitors were required to complete twenty-five laps. Disappointingly however, this prestigious international competition attracted few entries. German and Austrian competitors withdrew at the last moment, leaving entries from Britain, France and the USA to fight it out.

Grahame-White dropped out early because he was unable to find a suitable machine, while the locally-based RN pilots were banned by the Admiralty from entering. This left only Alec Ogilvie and the German-born but naturalised British Gustave Hamel to face three entries from France and one from the USA. Apart from Ogilvie all the competitors were flying Blériot or Nieuport monoplanes which had been built for speed. Ogilvie's Wright Baby, similar to that flown by Sopwith to win the Forrest cup and powered by a 50 hp NEC machine, was the only biplane. Its chances of success seemed to depend on a high rate of attrition among the other competitors.

On race day morning, 1 July, a special train packed with spectators left London's Victoria Station for Eastchurch. Other spectators travelled on the Queenborough to Sheerness light railway, went by car or simply walked. The eventual number was put at 10,000. A favoured vantage point was Standford Hill. Although just 165ft high, many of the spectators watching from there were actually looking down at the competitors as they zoomed past. Catering, apparently, was not up to much, lacking the copious champagne of previous races. 'I've seen worse,' grumbled the editor of *Flight*, 'but I cannot recall when.'

Before the race Hamel decided to lop a yard off his machine's wingspan in an attempt to boost its speed. But this probably did little more than upset the aerodynamics. Soon after taking off at 1445 hrs Hamel's left wing hit the ground as he was rounding a pylon. The machine was almost totally destroyed in the resulting crash but Hamel crawled from the wreckage suffering from concussion and bruises.

Ogilvie, meanwhile, continued to lumber round the course, being lapped by the other competitors. Things got worse when he ran out of fuel on his twentieth lap and, embarrassingly, was forced to land to refuel in front of the main spectator enclosures. He eventually completed the course at 1900 hrs. When times were compared it was seen that the winner was the USA's Charles T. Weyman who had taken around 71 min and averaged over 75 mph in his 100 hp Gnome-powered Nieuport.

In February 1912 C.G. Grey, the highly opinionated editor of *The Aeroplane*, noted:

Busy Eastchurch is one of the busiest, most workmanlike and cheerful places in this country. It now has 28 sheds all with authentic aeroplanes in them, various cosy bungalows, a manufacturing establishment where the Short brothers can really turn out machines in quantities and, on a moderately fine day, half a dozen or more machines in the air at a time.

Typical of the 'cosy' dwellings that had sprung up at Eastchurch was Leinster Lodge which was shared by Maurice Egerton and George Cockburn. Live-in servants, a married couple, the Russells, looked after the pair of aviators.

In August 1912 Frank McClean, benefactor of the Navy, the Royal Aero Club and, indeed, pioneer aviation as a whole, created a sensation with a spectacular demonstration of his own flying prowess. On that Sunday morning, McClean took off from Harty Ferry in the Swale in his float-equipped S.27. He followed the coast around Sheppey to Sheerness and continued up the Thames to Westminster. On the way he passed under eight bridges, including Tower Bridge, and landed opposite the Houses of Parliament.

McClean's motive was to demonstrate to the government in the most graphic terms how aviation had advanced without official help. It was said that the idea came to him from a French aviator, Lieutenant Conneau, who boasted that he would be the first to show Londoners what an aeroplane looked like. Conneau, however, failed in this objective because he crashed on take-off from France.

The day after McClean's feat the newspapers were full of images of his aircraft negotiating Tower Bridge with its folding spans in the closed position and lined with spectators. *The Times* reported: 'The engine ran smoothly and the machine was always under complete control.' *The Graphic* of 17 August published a picture of McClean's aircraft on the water with Big Ben in the background. It reported that his flight

> ranks among one of the most remarkable feats of airmanship. He left the anchorage on the Swale at 06:30 hr and just an hour later flew between the bascules and the overhead footway of the Tower Bridge, plunged down, and shot under Cannon Street bridge, Southwark and the two Blackfriars bridges, Waterloo and Hungerford bridges and stopped in the water before 08:30. Attempting a return flight, the aviator collided with a barge, and the waterplane, which, by the way, is British built, was damaged.

Predictably, the authorities were not amused. The police made McClean taxi back to Shadwell Basin, while the Royal Aero Club later banned all flights over the Thames pending consultations with the armed forces and the police. When McClean was permitted to take off, he collided with a barge and damaged a float. The machine had therefore to return to Eastchurch, somewhat ignominiously, by road. A point, though, had been made.

Soon afterwards, Winston Churchill, who had become First Lord of the Admiralty in 1911 and was an influential supporter of naval aviation, arrived at Eastchurch in November 1912 with the intention of learning to fly. He may well have been the first cabinet minister to do so but the fact was that it was still considered too dangerous to let Churchill fly solo.

'He was a keen learner and was reported to go up in the air over ten times a day,' according to Rachel Boon of the London Science Museum. 'Fears about Churchill's safety grew after one of his instructors, Captain Lushington, was killed in a plane crash in Kent. Churchill reluctantly gave up his hobby in 1913 following pleas from his friends and wife Clementine.' He did so reluctantly. 'This is a wrench,' he reflected. 'Anyhow, I can feel I know a good deal about this fascinating new art... well enough to understand all the questions of policy which will arise in the near future.'

The man who was said to be his favourite instructor, Royal Marines officer Gilbert Wildman-Lushington, was killed in a flying accident at Eastchurch in December 1913. Holding the temporary rank of captain, Wildman-Lushington was the first officer of the RFC's Naval Wing to be killed while flying on duty. He was over Sheerness in a Henry Farman biplane with a fellow Royal Marines officer, Captain Henry Fawcett, when he lost control. When the machine hit the ground, Wildman-Lushington was crushed by the fuel tank. Fawcett suffered only slight injuries. Wildman-Lushington was interred at Portsmouth. Churchill sent a wreath with the message: 'In deepest regret for a gallant officer of achievement and promise.' The First Lord also sent a message of sympathy to Wildman-Lushington's fiancée.

In 1914 McClean pulled off another spectacular feat of airmanship when he flew up the River Nile in a Gnome-powered Short pusher biplane fitted with floats. The aircraft, adapted to carry a crew of four, weighed about 1.6 tonnes with 37 gallons of fuel which restricted its speed to 72 mph. The wings spanned 67 feet and were constructed on the Shorts patented folding principle.

McClean was accompanied by Alec Ogilvie, Horace Short and flight mechanic Gus Smith. The aircraft arrived from Liverpool at the naval dockyard at Alexandria disassembled in crates. It was most likely assembled by Smith. On 3 January, with passengers and crew aboard, McClean steered the flimsy craft into the air, watched by, among others, a reporter from *The Times*. The machine's limited range meant that the journey south had to be undertaken in a series of short hops. Petrol supplies had been stored at points along the route.

The aircraft was plagued by engine trouble and there were thirteen breakdowns. Extended delays caused by awaiting the delivery of spare parts meant that the flight to Khartoum – perhaps 1,500 miles, at an altitude of around 200 feet above the Nile – took almost three months. The Short biplane was overtaken by French airman Marc Pourpe, who was flying a monoplane fitted with wheels and reached Khartoum in around ten days. The British party did not reach Khartoum until 22 March – not that there appears to have been any question of a race between the two aircraft. It seems, though, that the prospect of a three-month return journey prompted the decision to dismantle the machine and ship it back to Eastchurch from there.

Both McClean and Gus Smith flew with the Royal Naval Air Service in the First World War. McClean was knighted in 1926 and Smith worked as a flight instructor between the wars. He died in 1942 at the age of 58. A few days later, his sister received a letter on Royal Aero Club stationery. It read: 'Though it is a long time since my days at Eastchurch and on the Nile, Gus was so much a part of those days and of the struggle to make machines fly that no recollection is complete without him, and it was in great part due to him that failure was avoided.' It was signed 'F K McClean'.

Meanwhile, Leo Jezzi remained active at Eastchurch. By December 1912 he had been hard at it for two years and in March had started building a new tractor biplane at his home in Bromley. According to *Flight*, Jezzi did not have much time to devote to his hobby due to 'strenuous days in the City' but thanks to 'equally strenuous evenings, and more often, nights, had put together an interesting little machine'.

It was built mostly of spruce with ash used for the landing skids that projected ahead of the wheels. There were two tail skids. The pilot controlled the aeroplane via a universally-jointed vertical lever – the sort that would later be called a 'joystick' – which operated the elevators and wing warping gear. A pivoted foot bar operated the rudder. A 35 hp JAP engine drove a two-bladed propeller, but despite the lack of power the machine was said to be capable of reaching 65 mph.

Jezzi often flew with a 12-stone (153 kg) passenger for trips around the Eastchurch flying ground and on one occasion carried one who tipped the scales at 16-stone. Jezzi had worked hard to cut wind resistance with carefully streamlined struts and a comparative lack of bracing wires. But his machine's performance when carrying a passenger suffered accordingly.

While some of the Eastchurch aviators took residence there, Jezzi had a living to earn and continued to commute to Sheppey from his home in Bromley by motor cycle. According to *Flight*, he had partitioned off part of his hangar so that he could spend weekends there. He was often joined by a friend called Arthur Cooper, who cycled to join him at Eastchurch. *Flight*'s reporter joined Jezzi and his friends for a day's flying in mid-December, enjoying their hospitality at the end of it. 'Let us draw the curtain over the picture of a party,' *Flight*'s man wrote, 'exhibiting enormous appetites, rapidly becoming cheery under the comforting influence of honest bread, butter and jam and steaming tea, for it is all in a day's march when you are learning the gentle art of aviation.'

The arrival of the first four naval officers for flying training signalled the decline of Eastchurch as a centre for civilian aviation, for, unlike Brooklands or Hendon, there were no civilian flying schools there. Naval activities became more and more dominant alongside the rapidly growing aircraft manufacturing business created by the Short brothers. But by 1917 the company had moved again to bigger premises.

In a somewhat controversial contribution, an anonymous author writing in 1913 called Eastchurch a more important centre of aviation than either Brooklands or Hendon. 'From the first,' he noted, 'it enjoyed the favour of wealthy experimenters and it soon became the home of an aeroplane industry. Brooklands was rather the resort of the amateur designer. Hendon was chiefly the home of flying sport. It was largely at Eastchurch that aeronautical technology was built up.'

In September 1914, Eastchurch-based No 3 Squadron RNAS went to war under its CO, Commander Charles Samson, when it was transferred to France to support Allied ground forces along the French and Belgian frontiers.

HORACE SHORT

He may not have taken very much interest in the balloon manufacturing activities of his two younger brothers but he was the driving force in the manufacture of aeroplanes after he had joined Eustace and Oswald.

Horace Leonard Short was born in 1872 into a family of engineers living in Newcastle-upon-Tyne. He turned out to be a genius. C.G. Grey, editor of *The Aeroplane*, said of him: 'It was almost impossible to produce a subject about which Horace Short did not know as much as the leading authority on the subject.' His intellect was attributed to a head injury suffered during childhood which led to meningitis and abnormal brain development. It may also have led to the fatal brain haemorrhage which cut short his life at the age of 44.

Horace had grown up with a desire to see more of the world. He therefore left home to embark on a series of adventures which included trekking from the River Plate to the Amazon and being captured by cannibals in the South Seas who worshipped him as a god and taught him to fish for pearls. He became manager of a silver mine in Mexico, returning to Britain in 1896 after the death of his father. Two years later he patented the sound amplification device he had invented and called the Auxetophone.

In November 1908 he entered into a partnership with his two brothers, each of the three taking equal shares in what would become Britain's first aircraft manufacturer. Horace's energy and drive led to major success. Following completion of the six aircraft which were the subject of a licensing agreement between the Short brothers and the Wright brothers, a steady stream of designs flowed from the factory on the Isle of Sheppey, first at Leysdown and then Eastchurch.

Among the aircraft the Shorts constructed were the machine in which John Moore-Brabazon made the first flight in England of one mile by an all-British combination of pilot, aircraft and engine. In 1912 a Short Pusher became the first aeroplane to take off from a moving ship, while the Short Tractor biplane was the first naval aircraft to have a practical folding-wing mechanism and to launch a standard naval torpedo. The Triple Twin and Tandem Twin were the first aircraft to be powered by two engines.

In 1913 the company started the search for bigger premises which was to take it to a site on the banks of the Medway in Rochester. It was in full production by the time war broke out in August 1914. Three years later, Horace was dead, leaving the company, now well-established as a builder of naval aircraft, in the hands of Eustace and Oswald.

At Eastchurch Horace Short lived at Parsonage Farm with his wife Marie-Claire, usually known as Catherine, and three children, Leonard, Kathleen and Francis. Today a sculpture of the three Short brothers by Barbara Street stands opposite the entrance to Muswell Manor a few miles away.

THE FAMOUS FOUR

Of the original four Royal Navy pilots who received flying training from Royal Aero Club members at Eastchurch in 1911, three of them went on to achieve air rank in the Royal Air Force and one became a senior commander during the Second World War.

Arthur Murray Longmore was born in Australia but educated in Britain. He entered Dartmouth Naval College and was commissioned in the Royal Navy in 1904. Having gained his pilot certificate, he worked with Oswald Short in the development of streamlined flotation bags to enable aircraft to land on water.

In December 1911 Longmore took off from Eastchurch in the improved Short C.27 biplane, also known as the S.38, and landed on the River Medway off Sheerness. Later he became a flying instructor before commanding Royal Naval Air Service squadrons. In 1916 he served on the battlecruiser HMS *Tiger* during the Battle of Jutland.

He obtained a permanent commission in the Royal Air Force and after a succession of senior appointments rose to command

Coastal Command. As an air chief marshal, Sir Arthur Longmore commanded RAF Training Command on the outbreak of the Second World War. In 1940 he was appointed Air Officer Commanding in the Middle East but did not enjoy the full confidence of the prime minister. In 1941 he was relieved of his command when Churchill complained that he had failed to make proper use of the manpower and aircraft under his command. As a civilian, he stood unsuccessfully as a Conservative in a Parliamentary by-election in 1942. He died in 1970 at the age of 85.

Eugene Louis Gerrard was born in 1881 and commissioned into the Royal Marine Light Infantry in September 1900. After several sea-going appointments, he volunteered for pilot training. As a member of the Royal Flying Corp's Naval Wing, he became a squadron commander at the Central Flying School. He attempted to set a new altitude record of 10,000 ft in the prototype Royal Aircraft Factory RE7 carrying Major Hugh Trenchard as his passenger. On a subsequent flight, Gerrard set a record of 8,400 ft while carrying two passengers.

Soon after the outbreak of the First World War Gerrard was appointed to command No 1 Squadron, RNAS. Flying a BE2a, he participated in an attack on German airship sheds at Dusseldorf. He joined the RAF on its formation with the rank of colonel, later group captain. In the early years of peace, Gerrard was appointed to a succession of senior commands, culminating in that of Air Officer Commanding RAF Transjordan and Palestine with the rank of air commodore. He retired from the service in 1929 and died in 1963.

In thirty years of service Charles Rumney Samson rose from Royal Navy midshipman to RAF air commodore. He was the first pilot to fly an aircraft from a moving ship and he later commanded the first British armoured vehicles used in combat. Transferred to the Dardanelles, Samson pioneered the use of radio in directing the fire of battleships.

In 1916 Samson was given command of the seaplane carrier *Ben-my-Chree* whose aircraft patrolled the coasts of Palestine and Syria and he often flew combat missions himself. On one occasion he attacked a Turkish staff car carrying Mustafa Kemal Ataturk who later founded the Turkish republic.

When asked by the Admiralty why his ship was using so much ammunition, Samson replied that there was 'unfortunately a war on'. After the vessel was lost to Turkish gunfire, a court martial not only acquitted Samson of responsibility for the loss but commended his conduct. Posted back to the UK, his Great Yarmouth-based group shot down five Zeppelins.

Samson became a group captain in the newly-formed RAF and was appointed air officer commanding units in the Mediterranean. Promoted to air commodore in 1922, he was given command of 6 Fighter Group based at Kenley in Surrey. Ill health, however, forced his retirement from the service in 1929 and he died two years later to be interred at Putney Vale Cemetery. He was just 47.

In 1905 Reginald Gregory was promoted to the rank of lieutenant and, after receiving his pilot certificate in 1911, was appointed to command a Central Flying School squadron. In 1913 Gregory was given command of a group of naval air stations on the North Sea coast and by the outbreak of war had attained the rank of squadron commander. Like Samson, Gregory was to develop an expertise with armoured cars, which he deployed first in Belgium and later in Russia. After the war he was posted to HMS *Tamar*, the RN base at Hong Kong which took its name from a warship later replaced by an establishment ashore. He died aged 39 while still a serving naval officer.

FRANK McCLEAN

In its obituary published in August 1955 *The Times* called Frank McClean the founder of UK naval aviation as well as the founder of amateur flying in heavier-than-air machines.

Francis Kennedy McClean was born in 1876 the son of Dr Frank McClean FRS and he became a civil engineer working for the Indian Public Works Department. On his return home, he took up ballooning, getting his first taste of the sport in the 1907 Gordon-Bennett race with Griffith Brewer. After another attempt in the race he met Wilbur Wright in France and had a flight with him at Le Mans.

This led to McClean's association with the Short brothers. He was awarded Royal Aero Club pilot certificate No 21 in September 1910. Between 1909 and 1914 he owned sixteen different aircraft, all but one built by the Short brothers: Short No 1, Short-Wright No 3, Short biplane S.26 ('the Dud'), Short S.29 (lost with Charles Grace), Short S.28 (ex-Moore-Brabazon No 6), Short S.34 (later RNAS No 1), Short S.27 (ex-Grace No 2), Short S.32 (later rebuilt as No 14), a Birdling Monoplane, Short S.29 Triple-Twin (later RNAS 3), Short S.27 Tandem-Twin (rebuilt No 7), Short S.36 Tractor Biplane, Short S.33, Short S.32 (later RNAS 904), Short S.68 Tractor seaplane, Short S.80 ('Nile' seaplane; later RNAS 905).

McClean's generosity helped bring the pioneer aviators to the Isle of Sheppey and later provided the aircraft on which the Royal Navy's first four pilots were trained to fly. He was also a noted astronomer and as a pioneer of submarine photography his most notable achievement was taking pictures of the wreck of the SS *Oceana* which had sunk off the coast at Eastbourne after a collision with another vessel. Two months later, McClean created an even bigger stir with his flight up the River Thames to Westminster. In August 1914 he joined the Royal Naval Air Service and became chief flying instructor at Eastchurch.

On the formation of the RAF in 1918 McClean was offered a commission but resigned in 1919. He maintained his interest in aviation, however, and in the post-war years he was a familiar figure at major aeronautical sporting events, usually visiting them either by air or in his big white Rolls-Royce. In 1923 he was the entrant of the winning aircraft, a Sopwith Gnu flown by Squadron Leader W.H. Longton, in the first Grosvenor Challenge Cup Race.

In 1926 McClean was knighted in recognition of his services to British aviation. The same year, the Royal Aero Club awarded him its highest honour, the Gold Medal. A founder member of the club, he served as its chairman in 1923-24 and again from 1941-44. McClean was High Sherriff of Oxfordshire in 1932/33.

Chapter 12

Waking Up England

C laude Grahame-White was determined to make the nation aware of the exciting prospects offered by aviation, not only for recreation but as a means of transport and as a weapon of war.

His plan was to exploit his ownership of Hendon and its proximity to the capital by making it the centrepiece of a public relations campaign to promote aviation, particularly to the government. Using his flair for publicity, Grahame-White inaugurated weekly Saturday flying meetings at Hendon. Prominent aviators were invited to take part in exhibition flights, speed handicaps and races. Prizes and trophies were donated by newspapers as varied as the *Daily Mail* and *Tit-Bits* and also by leading companies like Mappin and Webb as well as wealthy supporters of aviation.

Members of the public were offered the chance to fly two circuits of the field in a Farman biplane emblazoned with the slogan 'Wake up England' for two guineas; for five guineas they could fly to Edgware and the Old Welsh Harp. Additional attractions included motoring events to the accompaniment of military bands playing a selection of popular tunes. Season tickets were available at two guineas for gentlemen and £1 11s 6d (£1 57p) for ladies. A full-time PR man was appointed and there was a press club with bar available on-site.

Around 15,000 people attended the first of these meetings on 5 April 1911. But even this was not enough for Grahame-White and his associates. They were now planning to stage an even grander event that would rival established social attractions like those offered by sailing at Cowes and horse racing at Ascot. Accordingly, the first Aerial Derby was staged at Hendon on 8 June. Sponsored by the *Daily Mail*, it took the form of an eighty-mile race around London with turning points at Kempton Park, Esher, Purley, Purfleet, Epping and High Barnet. The event attracted a crowd of over 45,000 which gathered at Hendon to watch the seven competitors being flagged away in a start delayed by bad weather.

To keep them entertained pending the return of the competitors a series of exhibition flights had been organised involving Samuel Cody in his 120 hp biplane, B.C. Hucks in a Nieuport monoplane and Fred Raynham in an ABC-powered Wright biplane. They did not have too long to wait: after just 1hr 23min T.O.M. Sopwith roared into sight in his 70 hp Blériot. *Flight* reported:

> Soon after 1800hr a speck was discerned low down over the trees in the Mill Hill direction. He [Sopwith] it turned out to be, and, reaching the aerodrome, he was welcomed with a burst of cheering, for he was naturally put down as the winner and an easy one at that. But the observers at Purley ruled otherwise. They said he had not rounded the mark properly; so, on that score, he was disqualified. Sopwith himself confessed to not having recognised it but reckoned on having gone well outside it for there he took an exceptionally wide turn.

Sopwith's appeal to the Royal Aero Club was upheld because visibility had been poor and he had, in fact, passed well outside the marker, unseen by the judges. He therefore took the £250 first prize and a gold cup. Behind Sopwith came the French pilot Guillaux in a Caudron but second place was snatched from his grasp when he ran out of fuel as he approached the airfield.

His loss was Gustav Hamel's gain. He was accompanied in his Blériot by a lady passenger, Miss Trehawke Davies – 'with whom he has flown so far and so often,' according to *Flight*. Behind Hamel came W.B. Rhodes-Moorhouse in his 50 hp Radley-Moorhouse. By now dusk was falling and Grahame-White took off in a Farman equipped with searchlights to guide latecomers home.

Photographer Ivor Castle accompanied Pierre Verrier in his Farman. In his account, published in *Flight*, Castle said the compass they had been expecting failed to arrive and so a map of the route was strapped to Verrier's back where Castle could see it to help navigate. Without the compass though, the pair got lost and eventually landed at Hounslow before struggling back to Hendon. Undaunted, Castle commented: 'I have been up in a good many aeroplanes but I can truly say that I have never been up in such a comfortable one.'

Back at Hendon the organisers were finding it difficult to persuade some spectators to depart at the end of the event. *Flight* reported: 'In the sixpenny enclosure trouble was experienced in getting the people to leave. Even at that hour they were still keen and wanted more flying.' The first Aerial Derby was considered a great success with an estimated 500,000 spectators watching the race around London. *Flight* commented,

> The race took a big hold on public imagination. As a sporting event, as an encouragement to the individual flyers or firms and as an advertisement to aviation generally, the flying Derby succeeded admirably and we can only hope that steps will be taken to ensure it as an annual event.

They were. The Aerial Derby was run in 1913 and 1914, suspended for the war years and held again from 1919 to 1923. The 1924 event was cancelled due to lack of entries and not resumed. However, the RAF Air Pageant, held at Hendon from 1920 to 1939, became a highly popular event and can even be considered a forerunner of today's Farnborough Air Display.

The Aerial Derby was unquestionably the most spectacular event at Hendon in 1911 but 1912 was significant in the development of the airfield for other reasons. By mid-year more than thirty sheds had been erected along the aerodrome's western edge. Of these eleven were occupied by Grahame-White, while the rest were divided among the flying schools and other enterprises. Among the new arrivals was a company which came to be known as AIRCO, an abbreviation of Aircraft Manufacturing Company, established by George Holt Thomas.

The newspaper magnate bought the assets of Horatio Barber's Aeronautical Syndicate. He had previously acquired a licence to build Henry and Maurice Farman designs which he intended to build at Hendon in sheds leased from Grahame-White, but a former Aeronautical

Syndicate employee, 20-year-old J.D. North, was hired as chief designer to produce new aircraft.

Another arrival was the Deperdussin Flying School. An offshoot of the British Deperdussin Company founded by John Cyril Porte, it had originally been established to act as an agent for the French manufacturer. Later it constructed its own designs from premises in London. The school had been established at Brooklands but by mid-1912 had moved to Hendon. The British Deperdussin Company was not a success and although several machines were ordered by the Admiralty, poor performance caused the order to be cancelled. The company was wound up in 1913.

The Blériot school continued to flourish and there was a new chief instructor, Henri Salmet, who made a tour of Britain to publicise the establishment. On 18 May he made what was only the second crossing of the Bristol Channel in his Blériot XI. A week later, Grahame-White's mechanic, Bentfield Charles Hucks, who would become one of Britain's foremost aviators, flew the first airmail from Hendon to Bath in another Blériot. He was carrying letters from the Lord Mayor of London to the Mayor of Bath and completed the 100-mile journey in 1hr 45min.

When 18-year-old Dorothy Prentice learned to fly at Hendon during the summer of 1912 she became Britain's youngest female aviator. Whether or not this gave Grahame-White the idea for his next wheeze is not known, but a Ladies' Day was staged at Hendon in July. It should have been what *Flight* called 'a red-letter day for British aviation' with a series of special competitions organised for lady pilots but bad weather put paid to that. The high winds were thought to be particularly risky for the ladies.

Only one actually flew that day, the redoubtable Mrs de Beauvior Stocks, who made three circuits of the field in an Anzani-powered Blériot to win the *Daily Mirror* prize. She also became the first female pilot to fly with a lady passenger when she took up Mrs Richard Gates, wife of the airfield's manager. *Flight* reported: 'She flew exceedingly well, the monoplane being very steady indeed. She made a good landing, too, though just a trifle bouncy. This flight certainly deserved the round of applause accorded it at the finish.' The magazine's report included two pictures of Mrs Stocks, one with demure expression and fetchingly attired with a parasol, and the other in flight.

Despite the weather, and the counter-attraction of the Henley Royal Regatta, the meeting attracted a large attendance. This was no doubt due to the series of races organised for the day which included such well-known competitors as Hamel, Hucks, and Grahame-White himself. Even more successful was the first illuminated night flying display in September. In fact, it proved to be one of the most popular events yet organised at Hendon. More than 10,000 lamps of different colours were used to illuminate the enclosures while five aeroplanes went up, also outlined in electric lights. This inspired *Flight* to publish a dramatic drawing depicting Captain Tyrer flying as a passenger in a Henry Farman biplane, dropping 'bombs' on a dummy battleship.

A second night flying exhibition was planned for 5 November to celebrate Guy Fawkes' day but bad weather meant it was postponed until the 9th. Again, a large crowd, estimated at up to 20,000, was attracted to Hendon. One of the stars was the Australian Sydney Pickles whose Caudron biplane, powered by a 60 hp Anzani engine and illuminated by numerous electric lights, flew over the airfield silhouetted against the rose-tinted sky. 'It was undoubtedly a pretty sight,' *Flight* commented.

The meeting was also distinguished by the first ever nocturnal aviation accident. Richard Gates flying the Farman displaying the 'Wake up England' slogan became disorientated and collided with a clump of trees. His Farman biplane was wrecked but Gates escaped with concussion and a few cuts. He had been intending to 'destroy' a dummy fort but his mission had to be fulfilled by Louis Noel and Sydney Pickles. A few days later Pickles provided an account of what it was like to fly at night and to answer the question: was there any danger? He wrote:

> I would say no, providing that you do not attempt to fly in anything but practically a dead calm, that you do not attempt any fancy tricks, that you keep well within the confines of the aerodrome, and that you remain constantly on the alert, confident that, should your engine stop, you could land on clear ground.

The year had undoubtedly been successful for Hendon aerodrome. During 1912 it had staged around thirty flying events attended by over 500,000 paying spectators, making it another profitable year for the Grahame-White Aviation Company. For 1913 Grahame-White decided to build on this success with even more meetings. The full flying calendar for the year now stretched from February to November.

Hendon was flourishing in other ways too. At the start of 1913 no less than eight flying schools had become established there: Beatty, Blackburn, Blériot, Deperdussin, Ewen, Grahame-White, Hall and Temple. There was now a steady stream of aspiring young aviators making their way to Hendon, including baronets, gentlemen sportsmen as well as military officers like Lanoe Hawker, who was to become the third airman to win the Victoria Cross and fall victim to von Richthofen, 'the Red Baron'. A student of the Deperdussin School, Hawker was awarded pilot certificate No 435 by the Royal Aero Club in March.

Other successful students included J.B. Hart–Davis who went on to set a record of 34hr 39min to cover the 886 miles from Land's End to John o'Groats and E. Bentley Beauman who was giving exhibition flights within days of gaining his certificate. In some cases, flying school instructors were pilots who had held their certificates for little more than three months; the Grahame-White School's William Birchenough was another. All the Hendon schools now charged 75 guineas for a course of tuition. To gain their pilot certificate candidates had to complete two flights of at least two miles involving five figures of eight, reach an altitude of at least 350ft, and land with the engine cut within sixty yards of a special mark.

The year's first night flying display was held in June and, as in 1912, attracted a large crowd. It did not please local residents. This, the local newspaper reported, was due to 'the ribald singing and chatter in the streets and the roar of omnibuses as thousands of strangers passed up and down the thoroughfares until nearly midnight'. The noise, the paper observed, was 'deafening'.

Even more people attended the August Bank Holiday meeting but the highlight of the season was the second Aerial Derby on 20 September when 65,000 spectators flocked to Hendon to watch the start and finish of the 95-mile race around London. The winner was Gustav Hamel in an 80 hp Morane-Saulnier monoplane, who took 1hr 15min 49sec to complete the course at 76 mph and take home the 200-guinea prize put up by the *Daily Mail*. Second was H. Barnwell in a 120 hp Austro-Daimler-powered Martinsyde, with Harry Hawker in a Sopwith and Fred Raynham fourth in the prototype Avro 504 biplane.

The spectators certainly received their money's worth for there were some spectacular flying displays. In one, Pierre Verrier flew a Maurice Farman biplane with a passenger. At one point both pilot and passenger were seen to stand up in the aircraft's nacelle and wave to the crowd below. Louis Noel, Grahame-White's chief pilot, topped this feat by taking up four passengers. Two climbed out and clambered to the wing tips, where, according to *Flight*,

> they sat down with their feet dangling underneath. The two other passengers in the meanwhile stood up and moved about in the nacelle, and yet the bus was flying steadily as ever.

Commenting on the event itself, the journal noted that 'such an animated scene had not been seen since the Circuit of Britain…the field was literally swarming with aeroplanes, pilots, officials, mechanics, reporters, photographers and others. There were no fewer than 18 aeroplanes scattered around No 1 pylon…'

But the day ended on a less happy note. Sydney Pickles was flying with Mrs Stocks as passenger when after a series of sharp turns their Champel biplane dived to the ground from 60 ft. Both pilot and passenger were rushed to hospital. Stocks was unconscious and remained so for three days. Pickles sustained a broken leg while Stocks was found to be suffering from concussion and back injuries. She recovered from her injuries but never flew again. There was worse news the following day. M Debussy, one of the runners in the Aerial Derby, was killed when his Breguet biplane crashed during his return flight to France.

A third naval and military day was held at Hendon in late September and on 2 October Louis Noel made history. He was piloting a Grahame-White Type X biplane, *Charabanc*, which carried a record nine passengers, with a combined weight of over 1,370lb (623 kg), on a twenty-minute flight over Hendon. The *Charabanc*, one of the first passenger-carrying aircraft, was designed by Grahame-White's chief designer, John Dudley North, who from 1913 produced a series of original designs. They included the *Popular*, the *Type VI*, which was designed for military use, and the *Type XIII* of 1914, originally conceived as a seaplane but converted to a landplane. In 1917 North moved to Boulton and Paul Aircraft as chief designer.

November proved to be a particularly active month for London's aerodrome. The first night speed handicap, which involved four laps of the airfield, was won by Noel in a 70 hp Renault-powered Maurice Farman with R.H. Carr in a Grahame-White biplane (50 hp Gnome engine) second and Marcus Manton third in a similar aircraft. The Hendon–Brighton–Hendon handicap race was won by Verrier in a Maurice Farman with Hamel (Morane-Saulnier) second and Walter Brock (Blériot) third.

On 29 November Bentfield 'Benny' Hucks became the first English pilot to loop the loop. This manoeuvre had been pioneered by French pilot Adolphe Pégoud at a time when aviators were wary of adopting any unusual attitude because it was generally considered that if an aeroplane flew vertically on its side, much less inverted, it would become uncontrollable and crash. Pégoud had proved this wrong.

Hucks had been inspired by Pégoud's feat and travelled to France to watch the man who was Louis Blériot's star pupil. While there he ordered a specially-strengthened Blériot with reinforced wing bracing. On return to Hendon, Hucks practised by strapping himself into a purpose-built inverted seat, progressively increasing his time upside down until he could read a newspaper for fifteen minutes without suffering any ill-effects.

Hucks' feat was watched by a crowd estimated at 15,000. He repeated it several times over the next few days. *Flight*, which published a dramatic drawing, reported,

He climbed steadily for some time and we noticed that while he was doing so his engine was not running at its best. In fact, he told us on landing that it stopped on several occasions owing to a derangement in the pressure-feed system for the petrol. Eventually, however, he reached an altitude of about 3,000 ft, from which height he made two S's, in one of which he remained up-side down for about ten seconds. His altitude was then 2,000 ft, and after flying a little towards the centre of the aerodrome he made two complete loops, one after the other. He was not more than 1,000 ft up when he had completed the second loop, after which he made a dive to about 700 ft, and then, much to everyone's surprise, he made another loop before descending. When he did descend there was a pandemonium of cheering, clapping of hands and hooting of motor horns, which was emphatically repeated when he was carried along the enclosures on the Grahame-White land bus.

Further entertainment was provided by Harry Hawker in Sopwith's trim little Tabloid biplane. He was reported to have arrived at 'a great rate' and to have made two circuits of the field at an 'astounding speed', reported to have been at least 90 mph.

A week later Hucks was looping the loop again at Hendon despite high winds. Among the spectators was a recovering Sydney Pickles. Watching from a car, his leg still in plaster, the Australian was said to have been 'much impressed' by Hucks' flying. Looping displays would soon become a regular feature of Hendon meetings. Grahame-White organised a special 'Upside Down' dinner for his former mechanic at the Royal Aero Club. The tables were suspended from the ceiling and the menu was served back-to-front with diners served coffee to start the meal and soup at the end.

By the end of 1913 no less than fifty-one meetings had been held at Hendon which dominated *Flight*'s coverage of British aerial activity. More than a million people attended the meetings which had become the social events that Grahame-White had hoped they would. They were attended by the rich and famous together with show business stars, the sort of people who would today be called 'celebrities'.

But Grahame-White was still not satisfied. He believed that despite the formation of the Royal Flying Corps the government was still apathetic in its attitude towards aviation. The considerable publicity generated by the aerial activities at Hendon was harnessed in a lobbying campaign to the series of books written by Grahame-White in collaboration with Harry Harper, the *Daily Mail's* tireless air correspondent.

Gustav Hamel lost no time in emulating Pégoud and Hucks. Two days into the new year he was flying his friend Miss Trehawke Davis in her Blériot to experience the thrill of inverted flight. In doing so she became the first woman to experience looping the loop. Eleanor Trehawke Davies had earlier become the first woman to fly the English Channel when she flew with Hamel as a passenger. Two weeks later Lady Victoria Perry, daughter of Lord Limerick, became the second. Hamel was again the pilot and Hendon again the venue. In March, R.H. Carr looped a Grahame-White machine specially designed for aerobatic and exhibition flying, to become the first British airman to perform the manoeuvre in a British machine. In September Pégoud himself visited Brooklands where he performed a series of aerobatics including looping the loop.

During the first six months of 1914, Hendon and the aviation community were mourning the loss of several airmen. Gordon Lee Temple died in a crash during a meeting in January, while Phillipe Marty, a French aviator who had become an instructor with the W.H. Ewen Aviation Company's school at Hendon, became the sixth aviator to be killed there when he crashed his 80 hp Morane-Saulnier. Worse was to come. Gustave Hamel, idol of air show spectators, disappeared on 23 May while *en route* from Paris to Hendon. He had just collected a new 80 hp Morane monoplane which he intended to enter for the third Aerial Derby.

At a time of high international tension there was speculation that Hamel, son of a naturalised German, had been the victim of sabotage. No trace of the pilot or his aeroplane was ever recovered and it remained speculation, but the tension continued and restrictions were imposed on civil flying. As a result, French long-distance record-breaker Marcel Brindejonc de Moulinais, who had been invited to participate in the Whit Sunday Hendon meeting and had flown in from Bremen, Germany, found his victory in the thirty-mile cross-country race disallowed. The Royal Aero Club alleged that he had contravened government restrictions on overseas flights, leading to a bitter dispute between the club and

Hendon's management. Both Grahame-White and Gates resigned from the club and declared the Frenchman to be the winner whatever club officials ruled.

Even the absence of the popular Gustav Hamel failed to depress attendance at the Aerial Derby held on 6 June. Among the 75,000 spectators was Queen Alexandra, the Queen Mother. Despite the quality of the entry, which included Howard Pixton in the 100 hp Sopwith Tabloid, and John Alcock, in a 100 hp Maurice Farman, the flying proceeded without incident. Perhaps aviation was maturing. *Flight* observed: 'If the third Aerial Derby was not a success from a spectacular point of view, it was a magnificent triumph for the modern pilot, who got the better of about the only thing left for a pilot to fear – fog and mist.'

The Derby was won by the American pilot Walter Brock in his Morane-Saulnier monoplane with 80 hp Gnome engine. Second was R.H. Carr and third Pierre Verrier, both in 80 hp Henry Farman biplanes. Walter Brock was on something of a roll that summer for he went on to win the London–Paris–Hendon race in his Morane which was said to have covered over 1,000 miles without major repair. Roland Garros was the only other contestant to complete the course the same day, but the French pilot had returned to Hendon to be told that he had missed the turning point at Harrow church. *Flight* reported: 'He at once took wing again and flew back and rounded the point.' Garros returned to clinch his second place.

Brock also won the final handicap race at Hendon. It was held on 3 August, the day Britain before declared war on Germany. The government immediately clamped down on civil flying. Home Secretary Reginald McKenna, who had attended the military flying day at Hendon in 1911, issued an order which banned flying over the UK by any other than military or naval aircraft.

Of the 863 aviators who had learned to fly in Britain between March 1910 and August 1914, 185 had done so at Hendon, where, during this period, there had been eleven different flying schools in operation. Grahame-White's establishment had trained seventy-one of the total.

Many of these airmen would soon be fighting in the war that was about to engulf Britain and the rest of Europe.

Hendon was immediately requisitioned by the Admiralty as a Royal Naval Air Station to help defend London from air attack, and Grahame-White joined the service as a flight commander. By 1917 the airfield had become an RFC aircraft acceptance park, with ownership passing to the RAF in 1925. During the Second World War Hendon was used mainly for transport operations, although it did play an operational role in the Battle of Britain. A post-war reduction of military activity was followed by part of the site being sold for housing in 1968. The RAF station finally closed in 1988.

GUSTAV HAMEL

Good looking and highly accomplished as a pilot, it was hardly surprising that Gustav Hamel should have been an idol to the thousands of spectators who thronged to see him in action.

He was the only son of Dr Gustav Hugo Hamel, Royal Physician to King Edward VII, and his wife Caroline Magdalena Elise. He was actually born in Hamburg, Germany, as his parents' first child, but his family moved to England at the end of the century to live at Kingston-upon-Thames. They became naturalised British citizens in 1910.

Hamel was educated at Westminster School and, like many others of his generation, became fascinated by aviation. In 1910 at the age of 21 he learned to fly at the Blériot school at Pau, France. He gained his Aero Club pilot certificate in February 1911. His first flight of note was made the following month when he flew from Hendon to Brooklands in a record 58 minutes.

In September Hamel flew a Blériot from Hendon to Windsor, covering the 21 miles in 10 minutes to deliver the first official airmail to the Postmaster General. Included was a postcard Hamel had written en-route.

His attempt to carry newspapers from Hendon to Southend a few weeks earlier had not been so successful, as bad weather forced his machine down at Hammersmith in West London. In April 1913 he made the first non-stop flight from England to Germany and, in November, the fastest time in the London–Brighton–London race in which only four of the nine starters finished.

On 22 May 1914 Hamel flew to Paris to collect a new Morane-Saulnier monoplane which he had entered for the following afternoon's Aerial Derby. He was warned that the engine had been playing up but took off from Villacoublay at 0440 hrs and landed at Crotoy for breakfast at 0522 hrs. He left for the Blériot landing ground at Hardelot to refuel, arriving there thirty minutes later. He took off for Hendon at 1215 hrs but was never seen or heard of again.

The Admiralty sent out a flotilla of destroyers to search the Straits of Dover but nothing was found and the search was called off after two days and nights. In a rare tribute to a civilian from the armed forces, the Admiralty issued a statement praising Hamel's 'daring, skill, resource and modesty'.

A message of condolence to the Hamel family from Buckingham Palace also noted that the King and Queen, who had seen him fly at Windsor, 'were struck by the skill courage and mastery with which he controlled the aeroplane'.

B.C. HUCKS

'Benny' Hucks earned undying fame in a life cut short by illness as the first Briton to loop the loop, but he was also a noted test pilot and the inventor of a mechanical device for starting aircraft engines.

Bentfield Charles Hucks was born in 1884 in the small Essex village of Bentfield, after which he was named, to consulting engineer William Hucks and his wife Kate. He was expected to follow in his father's footsteps, but at the age of 20, fascinated by the internal combustion engine and its potential, he entered into an apprenticeship in the infant motor car industry.

His father helped him to buy a second-hand car but he soon fell foul of the speed restrictions and, after several prosecutions, Benny

Hucks was banned from driving for three years from 1907. This prompted him to look to aviation for his thrills. As he could not afford to fly, he became a mechanic for Claude Grahame-White. He accompanied the pioneer aviator on his highly successful visit to the USA in 1910 and by the time of his return to the UK had persuaded his employer to let him make a number of short flights.

Early in 1911 Robert Blackburn, the Yorkshire aircraft designer, tempted Hucks to move north to be test pilot and mechanic at a salary of £3 a week. But while flying Blackburn's second prototype monoplane at Marske near Filey, Hucks' lack of experience caught him out and he crashed onto the beach. He was unhurt, although the machine was substantially damaged. It was soon repaired however, and Hucks made many successful flights in it.

In May Hucks was awarded Royal Aero Club pilot certificate No 91 by which time he had been appointed chief instructor at Blackburn's flying school at Saltburn. Hucks was also entered to fly a Blackburn machine in the *Daily Mail* Circuit of Great Britain but he failed to finish after an accident that deprived the machine of its undercarriage.

By the end of the year Hucks had established a reputation as an accomplished pilot. He had made more than fifty flights, covered more than 1,000 miles and flown the Bristol Channel three times. As a result, Grahame-White offered him a six-month contract to fly a 50 hp Blériot in races and exhibition flights at Hendon as part of his 'Wake up, Britain' campaign.

Hucks later formed his own company and bought a 70 hp two-seat Blériot to make exhibition flights at various locations around the country. In September 1912 he won the Shell Trophy for the Aerial Derby sealed handicap. It was about this time that he heard of Adolphe Pégoud's aerobatic flying and decided to emulate the Frenchman by becoming the first Briton to loop the loop. In the early summer of 1914 Hucks teamed up with Marcus Manton to perform the first synchronised air display which involved the pair looping the loop in unison. Hucks also flew between the towers of Lincoln Cathedral.

By the outbreak of war Hucks was considered Britain's premier pilot renowned for his aerobatic ability. According to Dallas Brett, 'Hucks' handling of a Blériot was a joy to behold and his stunt flying fluid and effortless.' One of his specialities was the 'falling leaf' manoeuvre which gave the impression of his machine being out of control until it was a few hundred feet from the ground. 'I have seen others do this trick,' reported the *Daily Mail*'s Harry Harper, 'but none of them with quite the artistry which Benny managed to impart to it.'

Hucks joined the RFC in August 1914 and was posted to the Western Front, but he was invalided out of the service after an attack of pleurisy. He continued flying however, and became chief test pilot for AIRCO. He is also credited with inventing the Hucks mechanical aircraft engine starter. He succumbed to pneumonia in November 1918 just a few days before the end of the war and was buried in Highgate Cemetery.

Chapter 13

Britain's First Military Airfield

Salisbury Plain might have been created as a playground for soldiers and aviators alike. Covering 300 square miles of southern England, it is a flat, sparsely-populated area occupying much of Wiltshire and part of Hampshire.

Not only is the area rich in archaeological and historical sites like Stonehenge but, due to the number with restricted access, provides a habitat which allows rare species of wildlife and plants to flourish undisturbed.

Salisbury Plain was first used by the army for exercises in 1898 and the War Office continued to purchase land there until the Second World War. Today it is Britain's largest military training area with some areas permanently closed to the public. Military camps include Tidworth, Larkhill, Bulford and Warminster with nearby facilities like Middle Wallop and Boscombe Down continuing to operate on the plain. The Royal School of Artillery is reputed to use it for live firing for as many as 340 days a year.

By 1910 the major military powers had begun experimenting with powered flight, and with Salisbury Plain offering the perfect arena for pioneer airmen, Larkhill, two miles north-west of Amesbury, became Britain's first military airfield. Along with nearby Upavon and Netheravon, Larkhill played a key role in the formative phase of military flying.

Because of the dithering of the War Office, it was private enterprise which made the first move. Frank Hedges Butler, one of the founders of the Aero (later Royal Aero) Club had been lobbying the War Office to allow the club's members to use military land for their aeronautical experiments. In February 1909, *Flight*, which was the club's official organ, reported, 'The War Office is prepared to grant the club facilities for the use of the War Department land for flight trials providing that there is no interference with military training.'

At this time, Britain's Wright brothers, Howard and Warwick, together with their designer, William O. Manning, were building aircraft under the railway arches at Battersea alongside the premises occupied by Eustace and Oswald Short. They too were feeling the pinch of insufficient space. While the Shorts had opted to move to the Isle of Sheppey, the Wrights decided on Salisbury Plain.

By this time they had teamed up with a 34-year-old entrepreneur called Horatio Barber to form the Aeronautical Syndicate Ltd (ASL). Barber had recently returned from Canada where he had made a fortune mining silver. On his way home he had added to his wealth with a big win at a New York casino. Although he had no engineering background or aeronautical knowledge, he did have a desire to fly together with some interesting ideas on how to go about it.

The syndicate received permission to rent a piece of land 100 yards square at Durrington Down on Salisbury Plain, an area that came to be known as Larkhill, Lark Hill, or even the Hill of Larks. It turned out to be a place of uneven, sloping down-land and seemed an unsuitable site for flying. But with the incentive of copious quantities of free beer from the Stonehenge Inn, local military personnel were recruited to help prepare the site.

In June a shed was erected there in which ASL could assemble and store its machine. It was an odd-looking device: the large single wing was mounted ahead of the pusher propeller which was powered by a 50 hp Antoinette V8 engine from a speedboat. The pilot sat behind the engine, facing the elevator mounted at the front of the lattice-work fuselage.

Barber, meanwhile, had installed himself at Amesbury to supervise operations. At the same time he rented lodgings for his chauffeur near the Stonehenge Inn. In an echo of Sir George Caley and his coachman a century earlier, Bertie Woodrow was given the job of test pilot, on the entirely logical grounds that as he drove Barber's car he should handle his aeroplane too.

Woodrow dutifully replied: 'Very good, sir,' but despite his best efforts, the ungainly machine refused to fly, probably because it was too heavy. It was sold and the syndicate tried again with another monoplane design, which was ready for tests by spring 1910. Woodrow, who had not received any form of flying training, gained experience of its handling by taxying the machine around the field.

When it hit a tuft of grass the machine was jerked 30ft into the air. Woodrow's response was to cut the engine and head for the ground as soon as possible. The machine landed heavily, damaging its port wing and undercarriage. Woodrow explained later: 'I just wanted to get the bloody thing back on the ground.' When testing was resumed, the aircraft managed to take off but flipped over and crashed into a field near Stonehenge. Woodrow escaped unhurt.

ASL's third machine was similar in concept to its predecessors but was given a name: *Valkyrie*. But after its initial trials ASL moved its operations to Hendon. Over the next two or three years ASL sold around thirty *Valkyries* before Barber decided to quit aircraft manufacture in the face of competition from bigger operators. The Larkhill shed was taken over by the British and Colonial Aeroplane Company (BCAC).

In June 1910 the BCAC established a flying school at Larkhill on 2,248 acres of land leased from the War Office. This and other schools operated by BCAC won a high reputation so that by 1914, 308 of the 664 Royal Aero Club pilot certificates awarded up to that time had been issued to its students.

Realising at last that some of its personnel should be trained to fly, the army accepted an offer from the Hon Charles Rolls to provide instruction. But Rolls was killed in July 1910 before the offer could be taken up. Cecil Grace would have taken his place but he too was lost in a flying accident so it was George Cockburn who stepped in.

Meanwhile, the Larkhill shed that Rolls was to have used was acquired by an ambitious young artillery officer called Captain John Fulton. Blériot's cross-Channel flight had inspired him to build an aeroplane similar to the French pioneer's but it proved too difficult and he eventually bought a machine from Claude Grahame-White. Cockburn, who acted as his mentor, had already taught his first official military student, Lieutenant Philip Broke-Smith. But in April 1911 Cockburn moved back to Eastchurch to instruct the first four naval student-pilots selected by the Admiralty.

Both BCAC and the War Office approached the Bermondsey company of W. Harbrow to erect several of its metal-framed sheds at Larkhill. The same company had undertaken similar commissions at Sheppey and also at Dover for Charles Rolls. It had adapted its own design of buildings used for church halls, chapels and schools. The sheds were metal framed with corrugated iron sheeting, sloping gabled roofs and doors that opened directly on to the landing ground.

It was clear, however, that military interest was crucial to the development of aviation and the proponents saw their chance of demonstrating the aeroplane's potential at the forthcoming military manoeuvres of September 1910. Nobody was more concerned to do this than Sir George White of BCAC. Its first Boxkite machine, based on an improved Farman biplane, had made its maiden flight on 30 July 1910 and the company was busy turning out further examples.

Following vigorous lobbying on his behalf by Lord Northcliffe, the War Office agreed that the company could participate in the manoeuvres. Accordingly, BCAC prepared three newly-built machines for this important test. No 9 was modified to carry a passenger and had a larger fuel tank and upper wing extensions, while No 8 also had an additional seat together with a wireless transmitter paid for by Northcliffe. The third machine was kept in reserve.

No 9 would be piloted by Bertram Dickson, a colourful character who had resigned his commission as a captain in the Royal Horse Artillery to concentrate on his flying. He had gained his pilot certificate in France in May 1910 and had since become a genuine *Boy's Own Paper* hero. In an article published in that journal in January 1913, he described his first flight. 'I was very nervous,' he admitted. He went on,

> however, I got much cooler and more at ease after a minute or so; then I went along right enough. I did two laps of the ground, which was, I understand, extremely good for an initial flight. My sensations on reaching *terra firma* once more were very mixed, but I remember that I felt quite pleased with myself and proud of my achievement; for one's first actual flight is a memorable thing.

By the time Dickson met White at the Bournemouth meeting he was a highly-regarded display pilot. His technique was much admired by other pilots and he was capable of commanding fees of up to £500 from event organisers. Dickson agreed to fly one of White's Boxkites at the manoeuvres, accompanied by his friend Lancelot Gibbs.

Northcliffe ordered the *Mail*'s newly-appointed air correspondent Harry Harper to Amesbury to shadow Dickson throughout the event. Over a drink in his hotel that evening Dickson confided to Harper that he thought he was being cold-shouldered by his former army colleagues and had not been properly briefed on what was expected of him during the manoeuvres.

The basic scenario was that the 75,000-strong Blue Force was advancing from the south-west towards London while the opposing Red Force was arranged in a defensive line from Salisbury to Bath. In the absence of detailed instructions, Dickson and Gibbs rose at 0430 hrs on 19 September and were driven to the BCAC sheds where the Boxkites were being warmed up for them. On the way they had noticed that there had been an autumn frost overnight.

Historian and author Timothy C. Brown described Dickson's preparations:

Dickson wasted no time and started preparing for his flight, dressing in two woollen cardigans, topped with a rough tweed jacket and breeches and overalls on top. He gratefully accepted Harper's offer of a pair of motorcycle leggings and the suggestion that he should further insulate them with sheets of newspaper. Finally, he placed a leather helmet…on to his head and Dickson was ready to go.

At 0525 hrs Dickson's engine was started, the machine rolled down a slight slope and lifted off into the early morning mist. Harper later reported that 'we lost sight of him quickly in the low-lying mist but could hear his engine for some time as he steered around the plain.' Dickson climbed to around 2,000ft and headed south-west for Stonehenge before turning north. During his thirty-mile flight he spotted Blue Force cavalry units and, according to contemporary reports, the noise of his engine caused several horses to take fright and bolt.

Over the next few days the Army's airship *Beta* flew over the area, covering over 700 miles in all. The ship was equipped with wireless and was able to pass messages to the ground, something which Dickson's Boxkite, lacking the necessary equipment, could not do. That meant he had to land to report his findings to Red Force officers who were breakfasting at the George Inn in the village of Codford. 'The mist had been a real drawback for him,' Harper reported later, 'but he was able to tell them enough of real significance from a military point of view.'

Harper added that the officers' initial indifference quickly turned to enthusiasm when Dickson was able to give them far more information on the opposing force's movements than their own cavalry scouts had been able to glean. Another reporter, covering the manoeuvres for the *Birmingham Gazette,* had also been present. He noted: 'Today should be a notable date in military calendars for it is the first on which this potent instrument of war has been used in British military manoeuvres.'

Also present at the manoeuvres were General Sir John French, who in 1914 would command the British Expeditionary Force in France, and Winston Churchill. The Home Secretary had cut short a visit to Turkey to be there and he later talked to Dickson about the part aviation could play in future military and naval operations. Dickson flew two more sorties that day before returning to Larkhill and handing his machine over to Lancelot Gibbs.

Harper later quoted Dickson's verdict on the success of his day's work: 'It has been shown that if one army possesses aeroplanes and another does not, the one which has the new arm can place the other at a hopeless disadvantage. Therefore, all doubt has been set at rest upon one hitherto controversial point – our army must have the assistance of a properly-equipped air corps.' Gibbs added: 'Seeing that the tests were carried out without any preliminary experiments, I think they were extraordinarily successful.'

Another pilot to make an impression during the manoeuvres was the actor and aviator Robert Loraine, who was recruited by BCAC to fly one of its Boxkites equipped with wireless. Over the preceding weekend Lorraine had brushed up on his Morse code in his London dressing room to prepare himself for his flight over Salisbury Plain on 26 September. *Flight* reported:

Some interesting experiments were made on Monday, on Salisbury Plain, by Robert Loraine, who, piloting a Bristol aeroplane, was able to send some messages by wireless telegraphy to a temporary station rigged up at Larkhill. The transmitting apparatus was fixed in the passenger seat of the aeroplane, and Mr Loraine operated the Morse key with his left hand while he controlled the machine with his right. Communication was maintained over a distance of about a quarter of a mile, and by way of a start may be considered a valuable achievement.

Lorraine continued the experiments for several days and then on the 30th the temporary receiving station at Larkhill was able to pick up transmissions from an aircraft flying over a mile away. It seemed possible that reception over much greater distances would be possible. *Flight* reported on the overall results of the manoeuvres from the aviators' point of view:

Considerable gratification has been felt at Bristol with the splendid results obtained in the Army manoeuvres with the two biplanes of the Farman type, built by the British and Colonial Aeroplane Co at Bristol, and piloted by Captain Dickson and Mr Robert Loraine respectively. Both these aviators made several flights of varying duration…Lt Gibbs also made some flights on a Bristol biplane, but most of his work was done on his racing Henry Farman machine.

Despite his success, Bertram Dickson would, however, play little active part in the future of military aviation. After the manoeuvres, he was flying at a meeting in Milan, Italy, on 3 October when he was involved in the first-ever recorded mid-air collision between aeroplanes. He was badly injured and seldom flew again. Indeed, there were many who thought the injuries he received eventually caused his death following a stroke in September 1913.

One result of the manoeuvres was to provoke second thoughts about the future of military aviation. Lord Esher had chaired an influential sub-committee of the Committee for Imperial Defence in 1904 and continued to maintain that flying machines could have no possible military value.

But by October 1910 he had received reports of the Salisbury Plain manoeuvres together with information about similar events in France and Germany. Britain, he now believed, should have 'a whole fleet of aeroplanes'. Otherwise, he thought, the nation would be 'in mortal peril and for this the Imperial Defence Committee would be rightly blamed'.

His change of views was typical of the way the military attitude towards aviation was now shifting. In May 1910 Richard Haldane, Secretary of State for War, had announced to the House of Commons that he had appointed a special committee to provide advice 'on scientific problems arising in connection with the work of the Admiralty and War Office in aerial constitution [sic] and navigation'.

This led to the formation of the Advisory Committee for Aeronautics which represented a major change in the government's attitude towards aircraft. Captain Fulton had already become the first serving officer in the armed forces to obtain a Royal Aero Club pilot certificate, and more recently Bertram Dickson had shown the value of aircraft in undertaking battlefield reconnaissance during army manoeuvres. A further demonstration of the War Office's new attitude followed when it was announced in October 1910 that the Balloon Factory's scope of activity would be broadened out to include opportunities for what it called 'aeroplaning' as well as ballooning.

A similar change of heart was expressed by the Chief of the General Staff, Field Marshal Sir William Nicholson, who had sat on the committee which had earlier stopped funding for further aircraft development. He wrote:

> It is of importance that we should push on with the practical study of the military use of air-craft [SIC] in the field.... Even with the present types of dirigibles and aeroplanes, other nations have already made considerable progress in this training and in view of the fact that air-craft will undoubtedly be used in the next war, whenever it may come, we cannot afford to delay the matter.

For *Flight*, action could not come too soon. 'All we have to say,' the journal observed in February 1912, 'is the sooner the better for we have got to a stage when literally every day counts.'

In February 1911 it was announced that the Balloon Section, School and Factory were to be replaced. The Balloon Section and School would become the Air Battalion of the Corps of Royal Engineers while the Factory became the Army Aircraft Factory. The Air Battalion was established on 1 April 1911 to create a body of expert airmen and to consider how the army should adopt air power. Service with the Air Battalion was not seen as a career in itself but rather as an extension of the training of a Royal Engineer.

Officers wishing to join the battalion had first to obtain their Royal Aero Club pilot certificate at their own expense. But as an incentive for those eager to join and learn to fly, the War Office would refund them the £75 private tuition fee upon gaining their certificate. Recruits were required to have 'experience of aeronautics, good map-reading, and field sketching, not less than two years' service, a good aptitude for mechanics and [to be] a good sailor'.

At the time of its formation, the Battalion's 14 officers and 176 other ranks were commanded by Major Alexander Bannerman with headquarters at Farnborough. No 1 Company, commanded by Captain E.M. Maitland, was also based at Farnborough, and was to be responsible for airships, balloons and kites. No 2 Company, commanded by Captain Fulton, was based at Larkhill and focused on aeroplanes. It was the first formation in the British Army devoted to heavier-than-air flying even though it was a small-scale operation: by August 1911 it had nine aircraft.

Even more significant developments were on the way. On 28 February 1912 another subcommittee of the Committee for Imperial Defence recommended that a flying corps be established. Details of the government's plans for implementing the recommendation soon followed: during the debate on the army estimates in the Commons in March, it was revealed that £320,000 had been allocated to the War Office for this purpose, with £90,000 to be spent on laying out a new aerodrome on Salisbury Plain. It was also stated that 36 new aircraft, of which 18 were of British manufacture, had been ordered to supplement the 16 the army already owned.

Similar details for the navy were not forthcoming and the White Paper published the following month contained scant information on the service's plans. The document did, however, lay out the government's intentions for the organisation of the new service. On 13 April 1912 the Royal Flying Corps was formed by Royal Warrant and formally came into being a month later when the Air Battalion was absorbed into the Military Wing of the new Corps. The RFC was to consist of three elements: a Military Wing administered by the War Office, a Naval Wing administered by the Admiralty and a jointly-run Central Flying School to teach pilots the skills required for operational flying.

The Military Wing was commanded by Major Frederick Sykes. Initially it comprised three squadrons. No 1, formed from the Air Battalion's No 1 (Airship) Company, remained an airship company; No 3 Squadron was formed from No 2 (Aeroplane) Company of the Air Battalion, while No 2 was formed from a nucleus of aeroplane pilots at Farnborough. Further squadrons were formed over the course of the following year with No 4 being created in August 1912 and No 5 in July 1913.

The Naval Wing was smaller, being formed from the cadre of naval aviators based at Eastchurch. It was commanded by Commander Charles Samson but did not establish squadrons of its own until it separated from the RFC in 1914 when the Royal Naval Air Service (RNAS) was formed.

The organisation of the Central Flying School provided for three courses a year, each of which was to last for four months with students receiving instruction in the maintenance of aircraft and engines, meteorology, navigation, photography and signalling in addition to flying training. Provision would be made for 91 military and 40 naval pilots, half of whom would be non-commission ranks, together with 15 civilians, to pass through the school every year. The major flaw was that all the Corps' naval personnel would continue to be administered and funded by the Admiralty.

Years later, historian Dallas Brett was scathing about this provision. 'It seems almost incredible,' he wrote during the 1930s,

> that anyone, even a politician, could have been so obtuse as to fail to realise that a scheme which involved joint command and administration of a force by the War Office and the Admiralty was doomed to failure. No intelligent person could anticipate for one

moment that the arrogant bureaucrats at the Admiralty would be content to take the inferior position demanded of them by this project and to submit to accepting orders from their fellow civil servants at the War Office. Nor was it probable that the Admiralty would consent to contribute towards the maintenance of the CFS so long as its administration remained in the hands of the 'junior' ministry.

Had it not been for this defect, Brett considered that the scheme would have been 'well-nigh perfect'. The CFS was established at Upavon. It covered 2,400 acres and was formally opened on 17 August. Construction had started in June on an elevated site about 1.5 miles east of Upavon village, near the edge of Salisbury Plain. It was also 6 miles from the nearest railway station. As the site expanded during its time under RAF control it was bisected by a public highway, the A342, with the airfield and hangars on the south side of the road, and all the administrative and some technical buildings and accommodation on the north side.

The school opened with eight of its planned complement of twenty-five aircraft. Captain Godfrey Paine RN who had previously commanded the naval flying school at Eastchurch was appointed the first commandant. But before taking up his post, Paine was ordered by the First Lord of the Admiralty, Winston Churchill, to learn to fly. This Paine duly achieved in ten days under the instruction of Lieutenant Longmore.

The Upavon site was not popular. Living conditions were certainly spartan in the school's early months. Those pupils billeted in the wooden huts found them cold and some staff members sought accommodation in Upavon village. Lieutenant Joubert de le Ferte, who attended the school early in 1913 and would rise to become an air chief marshal, called it 'a collection of weather board huts on a windswept hill'. He added: 'It must be awful in cold weather. Much wind and rain.' A correspondent of *The Aeroplane* observed that

> Taking its bad points first, the school has been located on the top of a mountain where it is open to every wind that blows.... One may expect that those aviators who survive the gorges and ridges,

the upward and downward turbulence…will develop into aviators of unsurpassed hardiness.

The weather was very poor that August and September and future Marshal of the Royal Air Force Sir John Salmond recalled his first impression: 'It was a very wet day with wind and rain scurrying over the downs and making the windows of the wooden mess rattle.' Salmond was also struck by another figure attending the first course. He recalled:

There were several people there, and it is interesting to realise how a strong personality will leap across and hit one immediately. For in the corner, sitting rather apart, was a dark glowering man with a parchment coloured face and a light behind his eyes, whom I was soon to know as Trenchard, and it was not long before I knew what that fire meant.

He was describing the man who would become the RAF's first chief of staff and be acclaimed as the 'Father of the RAF'. Trenchard had joined the army in 1893 and been severely wounded during the Boer War and was now being offered a place on the school's permanent staff. But first he had to learn to fly. In fact, he was given an ultimatum: he could take up his appointment if he learned to fly before his 40th birthday. This he did, enrolling at Sopwith's school at Brooklands, although Sopwith himself is reputed to have commented that Trenchard 'would never make a good pilot but what he lacked in natural ability he made up for with drive and determination'. Trenchard gained his pilot certificate on 17 August, the school's first day.

The ten army pilots on the first course at Upavon had all qualified for their Royal Aero Club pilot certificates, but none of the five naval officers attending had done so. One of these was Captain Charles Erskine Risk, who made his first flight under the guidance of one of the four instructors, James Fulton, on 22 August. It lasted fifteen minutes. Risk flew again on the 27th. In his diary he recalls that he

firstly [took] one joyride in Avro with Fulton, ten minutes in air; then went for first lesson with Fulton in the Short Sociable….I first of all just held the control lever lightly but after we had done half a circuit of the aerodrome, Fulton let go of the control column lever, I was so surprised that I pulled the lever slightly back and we shot upwards. Fulton put her straight again and then told me to try and take charge.

Risk passed the flying tests on 12 September after what would appear from his log book to be approximately 2hr 50min flying time. In those days flying instruction was only given on calm days when it took place at an area known as The Gallops. This was a long smooth stretch of ground over which students could fly and make practice landings in comparative safety.

But there was also a sense of urgency during the early days due to the belief that war with Germany was imminent. Salmond recalled:

> Our job at the Central Flying School was to turn out pilots to fill the squadrons that were now forming. We started at sunrise and finished at sunset with intervals for lectures and practical work in the shops.

Less than two months after gaining his certificate, Risk was appointed an assistant flying instructor, as was John Salmond. The speedy promotion to instructor of newly-qualified pilots highlights the lack of qualified personnel at the time. It also reflected the air of urgency in building up the RFC as quickly as possible. NCOs with technical knowledge were also sent for flying training. Risk records instructing Leading Seaman Brady. He appeared to be doing well enough for Risk to conclude that Brady was ready to practice solo straight flights. The first one, however, ended in a crash which damaged the machine but despite this Brady gained his certificate in January 1913.

Meantime, the War Office was giving thought to the future equipment of the RFC. Under-Secretary of State for War Colonel John Seely told the Commons in October 1911: 'We are arriving at a point where we think we see our way to choose what is the best type [of aircraft] first for teaching people to fly and secondly to buy for the purpose of war should war unfortunately break out.'

By the end of the year it was announced that trials to select the most suitable machines for the RFC would be held at Larkhill the following summer. The Military Aeroplane Competition was to be held in June 1912 but it was postponed for a month and then again until August.

It was a contest that had been eagerly awaited by both British and foreign aircraft constructors and it would represent the most searching test to which flying machines had so far been subjected, either in Britain or indeed anywhere else. There was a general consensus that British manufacturers should be encouraged to bid for orders.

A total of 31 machines from 20 different manufacturers were entered, although some dropped out subsequently. The great majority had foreign-made engines of which the Gnome rotary was the most popular. Among the British entrants were names like Avro, Bristol, Handley-Page and Vickers. With four machines entered, Bristol was the biggest entrant in terms of numbers (see box on page 199). Dallas Brett commented:

Altogether it was a formidable collection of aircraft and was fairly representative of the best efforts of both the British and foreign manufacturers. The majority of the machines were to a great extent experimental and formed a most interesting study both from the point of view of design and construction.

All entrants were required to complete a series of flying tests. They were expected to stay aloft for at least three hours with a passenger and climb to 1,000 ft at the rate of 200ft per minute. The competitors also had to demonstrate their ability to climb at a minimum angle of one in six and there were tests of fuel consumption, range, maximum speed and speed range. They were also expected to show they could take off in a short distance and remain airborne in a wind averaging 25 mph.

There were four judges, all of whom were qualified pilots: Brigadier General David Henderson, director of military training, Captain Godfrey Paine RN, commandant of the Central Flying School, Major Frederick Sykes, CO of the RFC's Military Wing, and Mervyn O'Gorman Superintendent of the Royal Aircraft Factory. Dallas Brett felt that the choice of judges had been a good one. He wrote:

Probably there has never been an important international competition
which occasioned less friction than did these trials. The competitors
grumbled at their engines, which were dreadfully unreliable, and at
the weather, which was appalling throughout, but no complaint was
raised during the meeting against these four officials who displayed
the utmost tact and amiability.

He was less complementary, however, about their judgement. Generally,
monoplanes performed better than biplanes and most observers thought
the Hanriots had been outstanding, being fastest in terms of outright
speed and rate of climb. But the judges placed Samuel Cody's complex and
clumsy-looking *Cathedral* ahead of all the others, with the Deperdussin
flown by Prévost second. The best of the Hanriots was jointly placed
third, together with Verrier's Maurice Farman biplane. *Flight* considered
that the Hanriots, together with the Deperdussin, had set the standard
for 'modern monoplane efficiency'.

Dallas Brett criticised the judges for their 'astonishing lack of
intelligent criticism' and for attaching 'exaggerated importance' to
relatively unimportant factors. It should have been obvious, he argued,
that the *Cathedral*'s complicated structure rendered it unsuitable for
quantity production and that it offered no protection against the elements
for pilot or passenger. It was, however, equipped with the most powerful
engine of any contestant – the 120 hp Austro-Daimler – and this gave it
a reasonable turn of speed together with the widest speed range of all.

Many observers felt that the winner should have been the one aircraft
that was not entered. Because it was built by the Royal Aircraft Factory,
the BE2 was ineligible, but it was used to perform in some of the tests to
provide comparative data. Flown by its designer, Geoffrey de Havilland,
it was also used to transport officials around the area.

According to Dallas Brett, it was easily the best all-round aircraft
present at the trials and 'must have been one of the best aeroplanes in the
world at the time'. *Flight*, however, was inclined to be more charitable
towards the winner. 'Whatever Cody has gained,' the journal observed,
'he has deserved for none can deny that he has worked hard and none can

deny that his machine went through with the flag flying.' It was, in short 'a triumph'. And it was British.

Cody won a total of £5,000 in prize money plus the Royal Aero Club's gold medal, its highest award, but no government orders for replicas of his Cathedral were forthcoming. Instead, it was the BE2 which reaped the reward with mass-production contracts divided between established British manufacturers.

The tests did not proceed without incident. R.C. Fenwick in the curious-looking Mersey Monoplane was killed when it dived into the ground during a trial flight, while the Avro cabin biplane was badly damaged in a crash. Flown by Lieutenant Parke RN, it had to be returned to Manchester to be rebuilt, but was back at Larkhill within a week. *Flight* considered it had established its manufacturer 'once and for all in the front rank of the British industry'. Later, Parke became only the second British pilot to recover his aircraft from a spin.

Even worse was to come during military manoeuvres involving machines from both RFC wings. On 6 September Captain Patrick Hamilton was flying a Deperdussin monoplane above Graveley near Hitchen with Lieutenant Wyness-Stuart as his passenger when the machine was seen to break up in the air. Both occupants were killed. Four days later, Lieutenant Edward Hotchkiss, who had been chief instructor at the Bristol company's flying school at Brooklands, and Lieutenant Charles Bettington, died when their Bristol-Coanda monoplane crashed near Oxford while flying from Larkhill to Cambridge.

Subsequent investigation revealed that the machine had come apart in the air. The immediate result was a ban imposed by Colonel Seely on the operation of monoplanes by the Military Wing. The Admiralty did not follow suit, leading to the strange situation where pilots of the Naval Wing were able to continue to fly monoplanes while their military counterparts could not. The official ban continued until February 1913 but its influence continued to be felt, setting monoplane development back by decades.

Following the RFC's formation, the War Office commissioned the building of an airfield to the north-east of Larkhill on the eastern side of the Avon valley. The Netheravon site near Choulston Farm was selected towards the end of 1912 and was initially called Choulston Camp. Until it was ready, service personnel were housed in tents or at the former cavalry school at Netheravon House, south of Netheravon village. Standardised building designs and prefabricated methods helped construction to proceed quickly and No 3 Squadron RFC moved there in June 1913, followed soon after by No 4 Squadron.

In June 1914 the whole of the military wing was gathered at Netheravon to test mobilisation of the corps for a month of training. This involved 70 aircraft, over 100 flying officers and 650 mechanics. It was an impressive showing but not good enough for *Flight*, which grumbled that Germany and France could probably have assembled a greater show of force. That same month the Bristol Company and its Flying School moved from Larkhill to Brooklands.

Two months later Britain was at war. For most of the coming conflict, Netheravon would be an operational base for the RFC and later the RAF. Between 1963 and 2012 it was an Army Air Corps base. Remarkably, the hangars at Larkhill still survive, as do many of the buildings at Upavon and Netheravon, which has retained the layout of its flying field together with officers' and airmen's accommodation and associated messes.

The site contains a number of memorials to mark the death of pioneer airmen who flew from Larkhill. At Wood Road off The Packway, a metal plaque attached to a stone pedestal commemorates the start of military flying on the site, together with the establishment of the BCAC flying school and the military air trials of 1912.

AIRCRAFT ENTERED FOR THE 1912 MILITARY TRIALS

Hanriot monoplane (100 hp Gnome, flown by J. Bielovucic)
Hanriot monoplane (100 hp Gnome, Sydney Sippe)
Vickers No 6 monoplane (70 hp Viale, Leslie F. MacDonald)
Blériot XI-2 monoplane (70 hp Gnome, Edmond Perreyon)
Blériot XXI monoplane (70 hp Gnome, Edmond Perreyon)
Avro Type G biplane (60 hp Green, R.L. Charteris)*
Avro Type G cabin biplane (60 hp Green, Lieutenant W. Parke RN)
Breguet U2 biplane (110 hp Canton-Unne, René Moineau)

Breguet U2 biplane (110 hp Canton-Unne, W.B. Rhodes-Moorhouse)
Coventry Ordnance Works biplane (100 hp Gnome, T.O.M. Sopwith)*
Coventry Ordnance Works biplane (110 hp Chenu, T.O.M. Sopwith)*
Bristol G E 2 biplane (100 hp Gnome, Gordon England)
Bristol G E 2 biplane (70 hp Daimler-Mercedes, Howard Pixton)
Bristol-Coanda monoplane (80 hp Gnome, Harry Busteed)
Bristol-Coanda monoplane (80 hp Gnome, James Valentine and
   Howard Pixton)
Flanders biplane (100 hp ABC, Frederick Raynham)*
Martin-Handasyde monoplane (75 hp Chenu, Gordon Bell)
Aerial Wheel pusher monoplane (50 hp NEC, Cecil Pashley)*
Mersey monoplane (45 hp Isaacson, Robert Fenwick)**
Deperdussin monoplane (100 hp Anzani, Lieutenant John Porte RN)
Deperdussin monoplane (100 hp Gnome, Jules Védrines)
Maurice Farman biplane (70 hp Renault, Pierre Verrier)
DFW Mars monoplane (100 Mercedes, Lieutenant H. Bier)*
Lohner biplane (120 hp Austro-Daimler, Lieutenant von Blaschke)*
Harper monoplane (60 hp Green)*
Deperdussin monoplane (100 hp Gnome, Maurice Prévost)
Handley Page Type F monoplane (70 hp Gnome, Henry Petre)*
Piggott biplane (35 hp Anzani, S.C. Parr)*
Cody IV monoplane (120 hp Austro-Daimler)*
Cody V 'Cathedral' biplane (120 hp Austro-Daimler, Samuel Cody)
Borel monoplane (80 hp Gnome, Chambenois)*
* Did not take part; ** crashed during trials, pilot killed.

Overall awards
  1. Cody biplane (Cody)
  2. Deperdussin monoplane (Prévost)
  3. Hanriot monoplane (Bielovucic) and Maurice Farman biplane
     (Verrier)
  5. Blériot two-seater (Perreyon) and Hanriot monoplane (Sippe)
  7. Deperdussin monoplane (Gordon Bell), Bristol monoplane
     (Busteed) and Bristol monoplane (Pixton)
 10. Blériot (Perreyon).

Chapter 14

The Factory

It sounds like the kind of caper that the readers of the *Boys' Own Paper* would have appreciated: a group of clever young scientists, eager to push back the frontiers of knowledge, systematically deceiving their stuffy London-based bosses to bypass their fossilised thinking.

But then, perhaps, naming their place of work the Army Aircraft Factory (later the Royal Aircraft Factory) when it was not supposed to be building aircraft for the army or, indeed, anyone else, was asking for trouble.

The fact was that the successor to the Balloon Factory at Farnborough was definitely not supposed to be designing aircraft, let alone making them, and its staff used every piece of subterfuge they could think of to conceal from the War Office that that was exactly what they were doing. The result, though, in true story-book fashion, was to lay the foundations for one of the world's most respected aeronautical research establishments.

Initially, the deception enabled factory personnel to work on new aircraft even though they did not have official permission to do so. In fact, the ban continued even after it was renamed the Royal Aircraft Factory on 11 April 1912. Official permission to design new aircraft was not received until 14 November 1913, less than a year before the outbreak of the First World War.

The story began in October 1909 with the appointment as superintendent of what was still known as the Army Balloon Factory of a highly talented Brighton-born engineer of Irish heritage who brought with him some definite ideas about the science of aeronautics. The approach to the job by the 38-year-old Mervyn Joseph Pius O'Gorman was certainly in contrast to his predecessor, Colonel James Capper.

O'Gorman was also something of an eccentric, with his flamboyant gold-rimmed monocle and taste for Turkish cigarettes whose distinctive odour, it was said, enabled his location in the factory to be pin-pointed by his staff. To start with his appointment was part-time, at a salary of £950 a year. He reported directly to the Master-General of Ordnance, an arrangement which was intended to bypass the military traditionalists, many of whom still failed to see any military value in aircraft of any kind.

In October 1910 the War Office announced that the scope of the Balloon Factory was to be enlarged to include aeroplanes. But that did not mean it would be allowed to design or build them: instead its remit would extend no further than conducting experiments on machines obtained from private industry in conjunction with the National Physical Laboratory at Teddington.

Even so, Frederick M. Green was recruited from the Daimler car company as engineer in charge of design. Green, in turn, recruited as designer and test pilot a talented young engineer who was later to make a name for himself as one of the pillars of the British aircraft industry. Geoffrey de Havilland had just built his second aeroplane and was not quite sure what to do with it. The factory resolved his dilemma by acquiring the machine for £400 and subsequently using it for research.

These appointments would suggest that from the outset the factory's senior management had no intention of remaining within the War Office remit. 'There was nothing to stop us repairing or reconstructing damaged [machines],' de Havilland later recalled in his autobiography, 'and we quietly got around this ruling by making use of odd pieces of crashed machines and reconstructing them – adding our own ideas here and there – into entirely new 'planes.'

The skulduggery was maintained by use of a complex aircraft designation system which provided an additional smokescreen to cover the true extent of what was actually going on at Farnborough. This system was evolved from a paper O'Gorman presented to the Institute of Automobile Engineers entitled 'Problems Relating to Aircraft Design', which was also published in *Flight* in March 1911. In it O'Gorman defined the three major aircraft configurations then in use.

Class S (for Santos Dumont) covered machines whose main wings were preceded by a horizontal plane with the engine located behind the pilot and driving a pusher propeller with a rudder behind it. Class B (for Blériot) defined the conventional tractor machine with the fuselage culminating in a tail with vertical and horizontal surfaces. Class F (for Farman) was also a pusher but with a conventional tail mounted on booms behind the engine and a tail plus small horizontal plane mounted ahead of the wings.

O'Gorman was keen to experiment with these configurations but his terms of reference precluded this. He therefore set about trying to find ways round them. The remains of a wrecked Blériot XII previously operated by the Balloon School had been taken to the factory even though it was thought to be beyond repair. Permission was sought from the War Office to 'reconstruct' the wreck, but the real intention was to transform it into a Class S machine under the designation SE1 (E for experimental). Meanwhile, de Havilland's machine became the FE1, while a wrecked Voisin donated to the army by the Duke of Westminster was also about to play its part as the BE1.

The letter to the War Office from the factory's works superintendent, Theodore Ridge, sought permission to reconstruct the Voisin. In cataloguing its defects, Ridge said that the control system was out of date and that the wings' wooden structure and canvas covering needed replacing. Fortunately though, Ridge just happened to have in stock spare wings and struts and could modify the control system to make it similar to Farman's. 'I am in a position,' he added, 'to effect these alterations quickly and economically and it would be equal to a good Farman machine.' Most of this was completely untrue but the War Office approved Ridge's proposal.

Meanwhile, the transformation of the wrecked Blériot was proving to be anything but straightforward. The only component retained in the reconstruction was the 60 hp water-cooled ENV engine, which was installed at the front of the tapering fuselage with a horizontal tail at the other. But a pair of vertical rudders was mounted ahead of the wings and the propeller. It was an odd-looking device.

During testing, the position of the wheels had to be changed several times before it could be persuaded into the air with de Havilland at the controls. It was subjected to continual modification through the summer of 1911. Even so, it remained tricky to manage but Ridge, who had only recently learned to fly, insisted on taking it up despite advice to the contrary. During his second flight, on 18 August, Ridge lost control while attempting a turn and spun into the ground. He received serious injuries from which he died later the same day. The machine was not rebuilt and the canard layout was abandoned. Later, S. Heckstall-Smith was appointed to succeed Ridge.

Geoffrey de Havilland, meanwhile, began design work on the conversion of the third machine, which would become the BE1, on the basis of a design brief formulated by O'Gorman. Power was to be provided by the 60 hp water-cooled Wolseley V8 engine donated by the Duke of Westminster's Voisin. The machine itself was to be a two-bay two-seat tractor biplane with lateral control effected by wing warping.

The long slender fuselage was constructed of cross-braced timber, formed in two sections joined by fishplates just behind the rear cockpit. There was no top decking between the seats. A large radiator was mounted vertically in front of the forward centre section struts in a position which severely restricted the pilot's view directly ahead. The horizontal tail was mounted on top of the fuselage and constructed of steel tubing with fabric covering, as was the rudder.

The long exhaust pipes running along the lower fuselage as far as the rear cockpit earned the machine the nickname of the 'silent aeroplane' bestowed on it by *The Times* reporter. In those days, journalists visited Farnborough on the off-chance of catching a glimpse of something new and it was soon clear to them that here was a machine which represented a considerable advance in aircraft design. To *Flight*'s representative it was one of 'singular interest'. He added:

> The detail construction also gives evidence of extreme care, and the application of the streamline form together with the complete absence of visible rigging wires in the tail are both points worthy of comment.

The machine made its maiden flight on 4 December 1911 with de Havilland at the controls. He covered just three miles but it was long enough to show that the Wolseley engine's speed could not be varied.

The carburettor was therefore replaced, enabling de Havilland to report a considerable improvement by the end of the month. Stability was good but the wheels needed moving further rearwards and the elevator control required gearing down.

These and other improvements had been made by mid-January. The propeller tips had been cropped to increase engine revolutions. More fundamentally, the machine was re-rigged to provide one degree of dihedral on each plane. Later in the year the Wolseley engine was replaced by an air-cooled Renault which solved the problem of the radiator obscuring forward visibility. It also improved performance.

The deception continued with the production of the BE2, a designation which had been chosen to foster the impression that it was merely the second machine in the BE series. Actually, it was virtually identical to its predecessor except that the upper and lower wings were of equal span and it was powered from the start by a Renault V8. This unit had been taken from a Breguet biplane which had been 'reconstructed'. The BE2 also incorporated the improvements made to the BE1.

The machine's first flight was made on 1 February 1912 with de Havilland at the controls. Its more sprightly performance was soon apparent and no changes were required. By early March de Havilland was sufficiently confident to make long distance flights: 40 miles, then 200 a few days later. The machine was subsequently equipped with a wireless set for experiments in directing artillery shoots. New test instruments were added and in May the machine was tried with floats.

On the 17th it was demonstrated to the King and Queen when they visited Farnborough and in June de Havilland even found time to take his wife for a ride. There were further developments of the BE line some of which were powered by rotary engines, but it was the BE2a which entered production even though it was ineligible for participation in the War Office competition to select a suitable aeroplane for military use at Larkhill.

Then, in a demonstration of the machine's ability on 12 August 1912, Geoffrey de Havilland made a spectacular early morning record-breaking flight. Accompanied by Major Frederick Sykes, de Havilland took 45 minutes to reach an altitude of 10,560 ft, which not only bettered the previous record for an aircraft carrying a passenger but also the mark for one flown solo.

The War Office was clearly impressed with the machine's capability. It ordered four examples to be built by Vickers, which was already an established government contractor. When Samuel Cody's entry in the competition was adjudged the winner, even the War Office could see that it was unsuitable for Army use and instead ordered further BE2as powered by 70 hp Renault engines.

The result was that by early 1913 BE2s built by Vickers and also Bristol were in service with the RFC. As the War Office believed it would encourage the growth of the nascent aircraft industry by spreading its business among as many different companies as possible, further orders were placed with Sir W.G. Armstrong Whitworth and Co and Coventry Ordnance Works. Handley Page and Hewlett & Blondeau also built a number of BE2s but they were subsequently transferred to the navy.

The first Bristol-built machine was accepted by the RFC in January 1913 and joined the sole BE1 with No 2 Squadron at Farnborough the following month. The BE2 series, particularly the BE2c, was built in considerable numbers for the RFC. Around 3,500 were eventually turned out, but by 1916 the aircraft which had seemed so advanced in 1911 was thoroughly outdated. Indeed, its lack of manoeuvrability and performance had made it easy meat for the new breed of fighter aircraft epitomised by the Fokker Eindekker. It was the inherent stability of the machine which the War Office initially believed would make the type so suitable for military use that made it so vulnerable. Pilots, it was assumed, would be too busy with their primary task of reconnaissance to want to bother with constant control inputs. As a result, the staff at Farnborough had worked hard to endow the machine with natural stability. This was achieved at the expense of heavy controls which made rapid changes of direction difficult. The observer occupied the front seat from which he had a limited field of fire for his Lewis gun, but to compensate for the BE's lack of performance, observers were often not carried.

No-one at Farnborough had worked harder than Edward Busk to ensure the BE's inherent stability. The factory had been determined to achieve this through aerodynamic means as Dunne had been doing with his tail-less designs at Eastchurch; Busk, a Cambridge graduate, had been engaged for that express purpose. By late 1913 his research into stability had created the world's first inherently stable aeroplane, the RE1. It was intended to automatically correct for the effects of any bump or gust without input from the pilot. Busk, who had learned to fly at Hendon in 1912, flew the RE1 'hands off' in winds gusting up to 38 mph. He frequently carried high-ranking officers as passengers and demonstrated the machine to the King and Queen.

Two prototypes were built in the Farnborough workshops but the RE1 was never adopted for production. Instead, Busk incorporated many of its principal design features into a revised version of the BE, the BE2c. The prototype was created by modifying a BE2a with staggered wings having pronounced dihedral. It was equipped with ailerons for lateral control, which allowed the introduction of a new and deeper aerofoil since there was now no need for the flexibility to permit warping. There was also a new tail-plane but engine and undercarriage remained unaltered. This new variant made its maiden flight in May 1914.

Busk's favourite trick was to take the BE2 to a great height, lower the nose straight down and release the controls. Each time the aircraft righted itself, but he was well aware of the risks he was taking. 'It is a pity,' Busk wrote to his mother in 1914, 'that everything that is the most interesting is also the most dangerous.'

Further proof, if it was needed, that the RFC now had the stable observation platform it thought it wanted, came in June when Major William Sefton Brancker, the officer in charge of RFC supplies, flew the BE2c from Farnborough to Netheravon. Sefton Brancker was later appointed as the Air Ministry's Director of Civil Aviation and was lost with the R101 airship in 1930. So stable did he find the BE2c that, having taken off, climbed to 2,000 ft and set course for Netheravon, he was able to write notes about his flight without touching the controls again until he prepared to land.

Later the aircraft was flown regularly by service pilots and earned itself the nickname *Stability Jane*. A second prototype differed from the first by its use of the factory's newly-developed engine, the RAF 1. This unit was similar to the Renault which powered the prototype but offered an additional 20 hp. The engine was later put into production by Daimler and others as the RAF 1a and became the standard power plant for the BE2c.

It was in this aircraft that Edward Busk met his death. In November 1914 a leaking fuel tank caused the machine to catch fire over Laffan's Plain and it crashed in flames. *Flight* called him 'the practical scientific man.' But the journal's obituary added,

> he was no mere theorist, for the results of his researches in the realms of practical science, notably in regard to the stability of aeroplanes, have achieved world-wide renown…

Mervyn O'Gorman wrote to Busk's mother that 'he did the most magnificent things without announcing any intention and without applauding audience…He was a genius.'

Meanwhile, de Havilland was busy developing the FE1 which was, in turn, based on the machine sold to the army. Initially it was found to be unstable but extensions to the upper wings and a bigger rudder improved its characteristics to de Havilland's satisfaction. The front elevator was then removed with consequent adjustments made to the rigging of the wings. It was in this form that the machine was flown by Theodore Ridge.

After his accident the machine was comprehensively rebuilt. It featured a nacelle housing the crew of two with the pilot in the rear cockpit and power provided by a 50 hp Gnome rotary. The machine now became known as the FE2. The first flights showed that it needed adjustments and de Havilland flew it again on 30 August 1911. Later tests showed the machine to have a top speed of 46 mph. Before the year was out the FE2 had shown itself capable of flying over 100 miles in 2.75hr and climbing to over 1,900 ft.

In the summer of 1912 the FE2 was fitted experimentally with a belt-fed Maxim machine gun mounted in the nose. It is not recorded if the gun was tested in flight but the aircraft was present at Larkhill with the gun in place during the military aeroplane competition in August. It did not take part.

In 1913 a second FE2 made its appearance. It was claimed to be a reconstruction but was really a new design with a revised nacelle and air-cooled V8 Renault engine developing 70 hp and driving a four-bladed propeller. However, the machine crashed during stalling trials in March 1914. The pilot, Roland Kemp, survived with a broken leg, but his passenger, Ewart Haynes was killed.

A further development attempt resulted in the FE3, which was intended to mount a Coventry Ordnance Works one-pounder cannon in the nose. It was powered by a 100 hp Chenu engine mounted ahead of the pilot. This unconventional layout used a shaft passing under the pilot's seat and chains to drive the pusher propeller. A circular aperture in the nose admitted cooling air for the engine.

Testing revealed shortcomings including a lack of rigidity which meant that factory staff had to return it to the original FE2 specification. This machine was also intended to mount a COW gun but it eventually appeared with a single Lewis in the nose. The nacelle was constructed of steel tubing with alloy sheet cladding. The pilot's cockpit was behind and above the gunner's to give him an unobstructed field of fire ahead. Power came from a closely-cowled in-line six-cylinder 100 hp Green engine with the radiator positioned ahead of it and fed air via scoops on either side of the nacelle. The machine went into production as the FE2a. A developed variant, the FE2b with 120 hp Beardmore engine, entered service with the RFC in 1916. Later versions had 160 hp Beardmore engines and even 250 hp V-12 Rolls-Royce Eagles.

During the war the FE2 equipped a number of RFC squadrons and acted as a makeshift fighter. In the interim period before the British followed the Germans in developing a synchronising gear enabling aircraft to have fixed forward-firing guns, the FE2 was better than nothing. Former gunner James T. McCudden, who was to become the second highest scoring British fighter pilot of the war, called the Rolls-Royce powered FE2d 'a very good and powerful machine,' which the 'enemy very much respected'.

By mid-1916 the past was beginning to catch up with the Royal Aircraft Factory. Heavy losses to German fighters, particularly during what became known as the 'Fokker Scourge', resulted in fierce public debate about the quality of the RFC's equipment, particularly the lumbering BE2.

During a Parliamentary debate, Noel Pemberton-Billing, MP for East Hertfordshire, claimed that due to 'colossal blunders', many RFC airmen had been 'rather murdered than killed.' Pemberton-Billing was supported by C.G. Grey, editor of *The Aeroplane*, already a critic of the factory. The upshot was the appointment of a committee of inquiry into the management of the Royal Aircraft Factory. It was chaired by Richard Burbridge, general manager of the Harrods department store.

The report of the Burbridge Committee, published as a White Paper, was muted in its criticism, although it noted that 'the War Office has laid it down that the Royal Aircraft Factory should be devoted to experimental rather than manufacturing purposes.' It found that some departments were overstaffed. The factory was certainly not a commercial undertaking but rather a 'very large experimental laboratory, probably the largest in the United Kingdom where experiments are carried out to full scale, therefore expenses must necessarily be high'. The committee found that while private industry had built over 2,000 machines, the factory had turned out 77 and consequently it thought that the factory could be reorganised to produce more machines.

Flight thought that most of the criticism of the factory had 'sprung from the feeling which has unquestionably obtained that, in the background, there was the ever-present shadow of a firm intention to build up a huge government aircraft arsenal to the glorification of those who might be 'in possession...'

Meanwhile, a parallel inquiry by the Air Board contradicted much of the Burbridge report. But the constant abuse heaped on the factory meant that many key staff had decided to leave. The BE2c soldiered on pending its eventual replacement by newer and more capable aircraft but the War Office agreed that aeroplane design at the factory should be discontinued, although this took some time to happen, mainly because of a need to complete on-going projects.

These included the SE5, which would become one of the war's finest fighters and the mount of aces like Major Edward Mannock VC and Major James McCudden VC. No further designs reached production after the SE 5. O'Gorman was not found to be at fault but his contract, which was due to expire in October, was not renewed. In 1918 the factory was renamed the Royal Aircraft Establishment, which at last defined its true role as research.

Farnborough airfield was declared surplus to military requirements in 1991 and the government decided it should be redeveloped as a business aviation centre. Following a competitive process, TAG Aviation won the bid to operate it. The company took full control under a 99-year lease in 2003 and bought the freehold four years later. The Farnborough international air show, first staged in 1948, continues to be held every two years.

GEOFFREY DE HAVILLAND

The fact that the designer of the aircraft which became the backbone of the Royal Flying Corps was the same man whose company built the world's first jet airliner was a tribute not only to the skill and ability of Geoffrey de Havilland but also a measure of the way aeronautical technology had evolved in half a century.

By that time the company he founded had built 46,000 aircraft, 9,000 jet engines and 115,000 propellers. Among its best-known creations were the Mosquito, considered to be among the most versatile combat aircraft ever built, the Vampire, one of the world's first jet fighters, and, of course, the epoch-making Comet.

De Havilland was born in 1882 the second son of the Rev Charles de Havilland and his first wife. Although destined to follow his father into the church, he opted instead to study engineering and between 1900 and 1903 attended Crystal Palace engineering school. One of his first engineering accomplishments was the design and construction of a motor cycle on which he commuted between the school and his home in Hampshire.

He started work in the motor industry but, bored with being a draughtsman for the Wolseley company, he left after six months and joined the Motor Omnibus Construction company. He was, however, inspired by the achievements of the Wright Brothers and by Louis Blériot and borrowed money from his grandmother to build his first aircraft.

It was unsuccessful and so too was de Havilland's second machine yet he was able to sell it to the government balloon factory at Farnborough. The establishment, which was later to become the Royal Aircraft Factory, also hired him as a designer and test pilot and renamed his aircraft the FE1. For the next three years de Havilland designed several other types but was unhappy when in 1913 he was appointed an inspector of aircraft in the Aeronautical Inspection Department because it took him away from his drawing board.

In May 1914 he left the Royal Aircraft Factory to become chief designer at the Aircraft Manufacturing Company, which had been formed by George Holt Thomas. Airco turned out around 4,000 aircraft, many of which were designed by de Havilland and used his initials in their designation. Large numbers of machines such as the DH2 fighter and the DH4 and DH9 bombers were used by the Royal Flying Corps and later the Royal Air Force. The DH4 was also built in the USA.

After the war Airco suffered for its reliance on military aircraft and was bought out by Birmingham Small Arms (BSA) which had no interest in aircraft manufacture. De Havilland raised £20,000 to buy the Airco assets he needed and in 1920 the de Havilland Aircraft Company was established at Stag Lane aerodrome, Edgware. It was there that de Havilland assembled a talented team which included engine designer Frank Halford and Ronald Bishop who later became chief designer.

The new company's products included the Moth family of popular light aircraft designed for the private owner, as well as airliners like the DH34 and the three-engined DH66 Hercules used by Imperial Airways. Other highly successful designs were the Dragon, Dragon Rapide and Dragonfly light transports.

In 1933 the company moved to Hatfield aerodrome and the following year its DH88 Comet twin-engined long-distance racing aircraft won the prestigious Mildenhall to Melbourne air race. Its wooden construction foreshadowed the elegant Albatross four-engined airliner which was noted for its purity of line and aerodynamic efficiency. The company also built the all-metal DH95 Flamingo.

On the outbreak of the Second World War de Havilland pledged to concentrate on supporting Britain's war effort, which was notably achieved with the astonishing, mainly wooden-built Mosquito, 8,000 of which were completed in bomber, fighter and reconnaissance variants.

De Havilland was an early convert to the advantages of jet propulsion, and the company's twin-boom Vampire, powered by the Halford-designed Goblin, was Britain's second operational jet fighter. It sold in large numbers and many were exported. A developed version, the Venom, used the more powerful Ghost engine which also powered the first Comets.

De Havilland had three sons, two of whom died in test flying crashes. He was also affected by the loss of two BOAC Comets in 1954 which resulted in the grounding of the airliner and a lengthy investigation into the cause of the accidents. 'There is no denying that we had been through a period of what might be called "technical depression" during which difficulties loomed greater than they really were,' he declared in his autobiography *Sky Fever*. 'Uncertainty and waiting can be mentally devastating.'

Knighted in 1944, de Havilland retired from active involvement in his company's affairs in 1955 although he remained its president. He continued flying up to the age of 70 and died of a cerebral haemorrhage in 1965.

He had lived long enough to see the rationalisation of the British aircraft industry in 1960 when de Havilland's company was merged into Hawker Siddeley. In 1977 there was a further consolidation in a merger with the rival British Aircraft Corporation to form the nationalised British Aerospace.

MERVYN O'GORMAN

Described as one of Britain's greatest aeronautical engineers, and as a charming and humorous man with enormous physical and mental energy, Mervyn O'Gorman seems to have been almost universally liked and admired. His obituary in *The Times* summed him up as 'a man of agile mind and Hibernian eloquence'.

He was born in December 1871 to Edmund Gorman and his third wife Margaret. In later life he added the O' prefix to his surname which had been dropped by his great grandfather after he moved from Ireland in the mid-eighteenth century. O'Gorman read classics and science at University College, Dublin before obtaining a City and Guilds diploma in electrical engineering. He proved his ability in a succession of jobs which involved several significant promotions. In 1898 he co-founded a London-based consultancy which continued in business for ten years until the departure of his partner in the enterprise.

The following year, Secretary of State for War Richard Haldane selected O'Gorman to be the first civilian superintendent of the army's Balloon Factory at Farnborough. Haldane's aim was to remove the establishment from military control and place it under civilian scientific administration.

Although the controversy which enveloped the renamed Royal Aircraft Factory in 1916 did not result in any blame being attached to O'Gorman, it did result in his departure from the factory, although he was appointed as a consulting engineer to the Director-General of Military Aeronautics. He joined the Aircraft Manufacturing Company (Airco) where Geoffrey de Havilland was chief designer, but the company was acquired by BSA in 1920 and there was no place for aeronautical engineers.

In the 1920s O'Gorman returned to one of his first loves, motoring – in 1904 he wrote *O'Gorman's Motoring Pocket Book* as well as articles for *The Times* – and he was vice-chairman of the Royal Automobile Club from 1928 to 1931 and president in 1952. In 1930, in response to the recently passed Road Traffic Act, he was instrumental in the RAC's publication of a simple guide for all road users, an idea later taken up by the government as the Highway Code.

O'Gorman was chairman of the Royal Aeronautical Society in 1921–22. He died in March 1958 at the age of 86.

Chapter 15

Heading for Glory

On 11 November 1918 Britain had the world's largest and most powerful air arm.

The day the First World War ended, the Royal Air Force, which had been formed little more than six months earlier, was operating 22,000 aircraft with an establishment of 291,175 officers and men.

Its Sopwith Camels, SE5As, Bristol Fighters and DH4s were acknowledged to be among the world's finest and most advanced military aircraft. Much of the RAF's power was derived from the support it received from the world's largest aircraft industry. Its strength was amply demonstrated by its ability to make good the RAF's aircraft losses in the latter stages of the conflict: between 1 August and 11 November the service lost 2,692 aircraft, more than double the Royal Flying Corp's total strength on the Western Front at the time of the final German offensive on 21 March 1918.

It had been an almost unbelievable change over a decade. In those pioneering days British aviation was dominated by foreign-built aircraft and overseas aviators. The first powered aeroplane flight in Britain was made by an American citizen even if he was naturalised soon afterwards. But within a few years the aeroplane was beginning to be taken seriously. No longer was it merely the 'fascinating plaything' of 1909/10 when it was seen as fit only for crowds of spectators to goggle at.

And despite the earlier head-in-the-sand attitude of the military and naval authorities, it was now obvious to the War Office and the Admiralty that the aeroplane had potential for a more serious purpose. It was therefore inevitable that building aeroplanes would quickly be seen as a worthwhile commercial enterprise.

It was during this period that some of the entrepreneurs and visionaries who would not only lay the foundations of a great industry but also dominate it for the next half century began to emerge, such as Armstrong-Whitworth, Avro, Blackburn, Bristol, Handley Page, Short and Vickers.

There were plenty of others too. But companies like Blériot, Caudron, Coventry Ordnance Works, Hewlett and Blondeau, H.T. and W. Wright, to name just a few, failed to survive the First World War while some perished in the harsh post-war economic climate.

To that list might be added the Royal Aircraft Factory. But then it had never been intended that the successor to the Balloon Factory should do more than conduct experiments upon machines it had obtained from private industry. The military aircraft trials of August 1912 probably represented the turning point. The trials at Salisbury Plain had been eagerly awaited by both British and foreign aircraft constructors and would represent the most searching test to which flying machines had been subjected either in Britain or anywhere else.

Despite the superiority of foreign-built aircraft and engines, one of Avro's two entries provided a glimpse of the future. The intriguing cabin biplane represented a notable advance in design and construction. Particularly noteworthy was the cleanliness of its lines and the depth of the fuselage needed to allow the occupants to sit protected from the airstream. Dual controls were fitted, enabling the machine to be flown from either of the two cockpits. The first successful such machine built in Britain was powered by a 60 hp Green engine. The machine was one of three ordered from Avro by the government for the RFC in advance of the trials.

The Bristol Aeroplane Company, formerly British and Colonial, was also expanding, having doubled its working capital. During 1911 Bristol had turned out over 100 machines. In January a sales trip to Spain had resulted in a substantial order for both monoplanes and biplanes. A two-seat monoplane was later taken to Berlin where it was demonstrated to senior officers of the German Aviation Corps. A Bristol machine was used by the first pilot to gain a Royal Aero Club pilot certificate in Australia.

While many of the founders of major aircraft companies had been pioneer aviators, Sir George White was very different. He never flew nor did he become directly involved with aircraft. Born in 1854, he was also considerably older than men like Roe and Sopwith. A self-made businessman, White was the son of a painter and decorator and a former domestic servant. He joined a Bristol law firm as a junior clerk and worked his way up to become secretary of the Bristol Tramways Company. After setting up his own stockbroking and accountancy firm he began investing in ailing businesses in the transport sector.

In 1909, by now a wealthy man, White was in Pau for his health. There he saw Wilbur Wright flying and realised that this could signal the start of a new industry. As the *Daily Mail*'s Harry Harper put it: '...the possibilities it [speed in the air] offered made the future of flying almost illimitable, as far as he could see. And there was the immense and more immediate scope in military and naval operations.'

On his return home in early 1910, White startled shareholders of the Bristol Tramways and Carriage Company, of which he was now chairman, with ambitious plans for the development of an aviation industry based in Bristol. He did point out that it would benefit the tramways company by generating new traffic.

In February, White established the British and Colonial Aeroplane Company with capital of £25,000 subscribed by himself and his family. It would operate from premises leased from the tramways company at Filton, four miles from the centre of Bristol. Some of the company's skilled wood and metal workers were also transferred to the new enterprise.

Initially White's intention was not to build aircraft from original designs but to act as agents for established (foreign) manufacturers, particularly Farman. The next step was to produce an updated version of the French-made biplane and to establish a flying school at Brooklands in September 1910.

Earlier that year the War Office had leased White a site at Larkhill on Salisbury Plain with permission to fly over military land. By July the first of the Farmans modified with 50 hp Gnome engines was flying at Larkhill; by November they were being turned out from the Filton factory at the rate of two per month. Later these aircraft would come to be known as Bristol Boxkites.

Examples were sold to the Russian government and the company embarked on a sales tour of India and Australia. By the end of 1910 seven pupils had passed their flying tests at Bristol schools and sixteen aircraft had been built.

New monoplane and biplane designs appeared at the 1911 Olympia exhibition where British and Colonial had the biggest stand. A two-seat version of the Boxkite joined the existing variants to facilitate more advanced flying instruction at Bristol schools. White's offers to the War Office and Admiralty to provide training for army and naval officers were rejected but despite the establishment of the RFC's Central Flying School at Upavon, the Bristol schools continued to expand. Indeed, new ones were set up in Germany, Italy and Spain.

White also recruited talented new designers to push the company forward. From Romania came Henri Coanda who set about improving the original monoplane designs of Pierre Prier. Frank Barnwell became White's assistant and Lieutenant Charles Burney RN was recruited to work on a series of aircraft for naval operations.

The ban on the RFC's use of monoplanes led to the company being contracted to build BE2a biplanes. Meanwhile, Barnwell's work led to the highly-regarded Bristol Scout of which the War Office ordered 12 in 1914 and the Admiralty 24. This aircraft became the major product of a new factory at Brislington. Development of the Scout led to the F2B Bristol Fighter, which was ordered in large numbers by the RFC. By the time of the Armistice the RAF operated 1,583 examples and the type remained in service until the early 1930s. George White, however, did not live to see this success. He died in 1916, by which time the enterprise he established had become the Bristol Aeroplane Company.

In 1913 the War Office asked the engineering conglomerate Sir W.G. Armstrong Whitworth and Company to build aeroplanes and aircraft engines for the army. In response, the company established an aircraft department with the Dutchman Frederick Koolhoven, formerly chief engineer of British Deperdussin, as chief designer.

Koolhoven's first design for his new employer was a small, single-seat single-bay tractor biplane intended as a scout aircraft. The Sissit or FK1 was fitted with balanced elevators and no fixed tail plane. It was intended to be powered by an 80 hp Gnome rotary engine but only a 50 hp unit was available. It was with this power plant that the aircraft made its maiden flight in September 1914 with Koolhoven at the controls. Not unexpectedly, it proved underpowered and was later modified with a fixed tail plane and enlarged ailerons.

But, as greatly superior single seat scout aircraft like the Sopwith Tabloid and Bristol Scout were already available, no further development of the Sissit was undertaken. The Armstrong Whitworth FK3 scout was more successful, and the FK8, which served on the European front as well as in the Middle and Far East, did even better with over 1,700 ordered.

Avro, meanwhile, was going through hard times as it sought additional financial backing. Approaches to major companies like Armstrong Whitworth and Vickers proved negative but a member of a prominent local brewing family did invest in the operation which resulted in Avro becoming a limited company. In April 1913 it moved out of the workshops at Brownsfield Road, Ancoats and into new premises at Clifton Street, Miles Platting, Manchester.

But the imminence of war and the success of the 504 meant that a further move was required. In October 1914 larger premises were acquired at Newton Heath with Clifton Street remaining as the woodworking department. With the prospect of orders for naval aircraft, the company decided to establish a new factory at Hamble on the south coast. But plans for large-scale production there were shelved and it became an experimental shop.

The company was kept afloat through the lean post-war years by continuing orders for the 504. In 1924 Avro moved again, this time to farmland seven miles north of Macclesfield, Cheshire, which would be known as Woodford aerodrome. Four years later, Roe, the visionary pioneer, sold his interest in the company to Sir John Siddeley, head of Armstrong Whitworth. Humphrey had already sold his shareholding in 1917 when he joined the RFC.

On the other side of the Pennines Robert Blackburn was laying the foundations of a rival company. His first Blackburn Monoplane had a high-mounted wing with the engine and pilot's seat located on a three-wheeled platform. A cruciform tail was carried on an uncovered boom extending from the wing. The 8 ft 6 in propeller was mounted just below the wing's leading edge and driven by a chain from the 35 hp Green engine below.

Designed during a stay in Paris, construction of the first machine began at Thomas Green & Sons engineering works at Leeds, where Blackburn's father was general manager. It was later relocated to workshop space in a small clothing factory. When complete, it was transported to the beach between Saltburn and Marske for testing from April 1909. In that year, only taxying trials with the occasional hop were made. The machine made its only flight on 24 May 1910. It lasted for around a minute and ended in a crash which damaged the aircraft beyond repair. Blackburn later recalled the incident:

> After racing along the sands at what seemed a dizzy speed, the machine certainly did take off and then started a series of wobbles due to deviating from the straight and the low centre of gravity which I fear took charge.... I had probably been in the air for a minute only, but it seemed ages when I eventually pulled myself together and looked at the wreckage. Thus terminated my first attempt at flight, with no personal injuries other than bruises and cuts but with the total wreckage of months of laborious work.

Blackburn operated from a 70 ft wooden hangar which had previously been used by William Tranmer's Flying School. G. Stuart Leslie of Scalby near Scarborough told the *Filey and Hunmanby Mercury* in 2011:

> The hangar was built on the Flat Cliffs for Tranmer's Northern Automobile company and was used for the overhaul and assembly of Blériot monoplanes until it was joined by Robert Blackburn who took over the premises to house a machine built in Leeds. The aircraft were winched down to the sands via a concrete slipway and parts of that could still be seen a few years ago.

Blackburn's next design, known logically enough as the Second Monoplane, was very different. It resembled Léon Levavasseur's

Antoinette which Blackburn had seen on a visit to France. The wing was rectangular and had a constant chord, significant dihedral and square tips together with a thin aerofoil section cambered on the underside, as was usual at the time. Lateral control was by wing warping.

The wing was wire braced with a king post passing through the fuselage, extending above and below it. The fuselage, like the wings, comprised a wooden structure covered with fabric. It was triangular in section and tapered towards the tail. There was a finely tapered fin and tail plane like the *Antoinette*'s, the rudder being divided into two triangular sections above and below the elevator.

The pilot's seat was located at the trailing edge of the wing and contained Blackburn's 'triple steering column' which was moved up and down for elevator control, from side to side to warp the wings and rotated to move the rudders. This system had been used on the First Monoplane. The main axle of the undercarriage was carried at the bottom end of the king post with wheels at either end and skids made of ash. During development and taxying trials, this structure was braced and sprung in different ways before the undercarriage was considered satisfactory. The aircraft was powered by a new and untried engine, a seven-cylinder radial designed by R.J. Issacson of the Hunslet Engine company of Leeds. It drove a wooden two-blade propeller via a 2:1 reduction gear.

The aircraft was taken to the North Yorkshire resort of Filey for testing on the extensive flat sandy beach with Benny Hucks at the controls. On 8 March 1911, after taxying for several miles, he made the first take-off. He flew successfully for a while at about 30 ft and 50 mph, but he side-slipped into the sands when attempting his first turn. The machine was repaired and performed well at Filey as an instructional aircraft, bringing publicity to Blackburn's name and later machines.

After the first flight in March 1911, Blackburn continued to design aircraft and founded the Blackburn Aircraft Company, building the hangar and a bungalow for staff between Primrose Valley and Hunmanby Gap. Factories were later established at Olympia, Leeds, Sherburn-in-Elmet, Brough (East Yorkshire) and Dumbarton, Scotland. In the early days, Blackburn himself flew aircraft from the beaches at Marske and Filey. Before production shifted to Sherburn-in-Elmet and Brough, aircraft were flown in and out of the Olympia works via an adjacent airstrip in Roundhay Park.

In 1913 a Blackburn aircraft won a match race with Lancashire rival Avro. The so-called Wars of the Roses race with Avro's 504 was organised by a local newspaper (see box on page 232). The company later became well-known for a series of naval aircraft culminating in the Buccaneer which was operated by both the Royal Navy and the RAF. By that time Blackburn had joined its old rival Avro in the Hawker Siddeley group on its way to becoming British Aerospace and later BAe Systems. Blackburn's original hangar, which latterly stood in a Hunmanby engineering yard, was later transferred to the Yorkshire Air Museum in Elvington to protect its legacy and links to Britain's aviation history.

Meanwhile, the nation's first publicly traded aircraft manufacturing company had been established in a shed at Barking near the Thames Estuary in Essex in 1909. For decades the port had boasted one of the country's biggest fishing fleets and during the days of Henry VIII was a centre for the repair of ships of the royal fleet. It was Frederick Handley Page who began its association with aviation. Born in Cheltenham in 1885, he was the second son of Frederick Joseph Page, a furniture maker and member of the Plymouth Brethren. He was educated at Cheltenham Grammar School, and in 1902, against his parents' wishes, moved to London to study electrical engineering at Finsbury Technical College.

On qualifying in 1906 he was appointed head designer at Johnson & Phillips Ltd, an electrical engineering company based in Charlton, south-east London. While still working with Johnson & Phillips, Handley Page let his enthusiasm for aviation run away with him and started conducting experiments at his place of work that had nothing to do with the task at hand. He was sacked.

In 1907 he joined the Royal Aeronautical Society where he met expatriate French artist and aviation pioneer José Weiss who was experimenting with gliders using an inherently stable wing design which he was to patent in 1908. Handley Page joined Weiss and the colourful Noel Pemberton Billing at South Fambridge, Essex.

Later he moved to Barking where he erected a shed and leased a small stretch of marshland. Contemporary photographs showed a flat, scrubby piece of land with several sheds, the biggest of which displayed the legend 'Handley Page Limited' along the side in large letters. At first he was carving wooden propellers and other fittings for aircraft. One of his customers was Welsh aeronaut Ernest Willows.

Handley Page soon had his first commission to build an aircraft for a customer. It was a canard configuration glider with a tricycle undercarriage. Its wing was based on the Weiss pattern following an agreement which enabled him to use José Weiss's patents in exchange for making an improved wing for the Frenchman's next glider. It was also decided to take a stand at the 1909 Aero Exhibition at Olympia.

On 17 June 1909 Handley Page established his business as a limited liability company, with an authorised capital of £10,000. His early monoplane designs were characterised by their swept-back wing shape with curved leading edges. The *Bluebird*, so called because of its blue-grey rubberised fabric covering, was exhibited at the 1910 Aero exhibition after which Handley Page set about learning to fly it. A brief, straight flight was achieved on 26 May 1910 but his first attempt at a turn ended in a crash. The machine was rebuilt with a slightly more powerful engine and wing-warping for lateral control, but it proved no more successful and was abandoned.

A larger monoplane nick-named *The Yellow Peril* because of the colour of its wings followed the *Bluebird*. This 50 hp machine proved to be inherently stable and its most noteworthy flight took it over London from Barking to Brooklands flown by Edward Petre. A Type F monoplane with its 70 hp Gnome engine and side-by-side seating was intended to participate in the 1912 military trials but was withdrawn.

Bigger premises were needed and Handley Page moved to Cricklewood in North London. Initially he occupied 110 Cricklewood Lane, before moving to Claremont Road where he built a succession of aircraft. In May 1914 a Handley Page biplane powered by a 100 hp Anzani engine crossed the English Channel in fifteen minutes. Flown by Rowland Ding, accompanied by Princess Ludwig of Lowenstein-Wertheim, it actually started from Hendon but fog obliged Ding to land at Eastbourne before moving on to Dover for the cross-channel flight to Calais, which he completed in record time.

With the outbreak of war in August 1914, Handley Page approached the Admiralty and offered to provide aircraft for the Navy. A senior official took him up on his offer and asked him to create 'a bloody paralyzer of an aeroplane' able to carry a large offensive load of bombs. This led to the development of the twin-engine Type O which was the largest aircraft yet built in the UK. The O/100 first flew late in 1915 and led to the O/400 of which about 400 were built before the end of the war. The aircraft were used by the Independent Air Force commanded by Major General Hugh Trenchard for night attacks on targets in German-occupied France and Belgium and for strategic bombing of industrial and transport targets in the Rhineland.

One of the company's greatest contributions to aircraft development was the slotted wing. This device increased the lift of a wing and increased the safe speed range of aircraft, enabling them to be controlled at low flying speeds without the risk of spinning. In 1928 the Air Ministry ordered Handley Page slots to be fitted to all British service aircraft.

Aircraft built at Cricklewood were flown from the adjacent airfield which became known as Cricklewood aerodrome. After the war it was used by Handley Page Transport, one of Britain's first airlines, which subsequently merged with two others to create Imperial Airways, ancestor of British Airways. The factory was later sold off and converted into Britain's largest film studios. New premises were acquired at Radlett but Handley Page's association with Cricklewood continued until 1964.

The company specialised in building large airliners and heavy bombers, notably the Second World War Halifax and Victor jet which served the RAF until 1993. But Handley Page declined to become involved in the mergers which transformed the industry in the early 1960s. The company went into voluntary liquidation and ceased to exist in 1970.

In 1928 Vickers-Armstrong acquired Supermarine and renamed it Supermarine Aviation Works (Vickers) Ltd. In 1938 all Vickers-Armstrong's aviation interests were reorganised to become Vickers-Armstrong (Aircraft) Ltd, although Supermarine continued to design, build and trade under its own name. It was during this period that Supermarine produced one of the most successful and revered aircraft of all time, the Spitfire single-seat fighter.

Despite its position as the site of Britain's first aircraft factory, Eastchurch did not continue as a manufacturing centre after the departure of Shorts. In 1913 the expansion of Short's seaplane work for the Admiralty meant that it had outgrown the Eastchurch premises. A new factory was built at the Esplanade, Rochester, on the right bank of the Medway. Oswald Short took charge of seaplane production there.

Today, this area of the Kent cathedral town is occupied by elegant riverside houses with the only reminder of the area's association with the manufacture of aircraft being the slipways down which waterborne aircraft were launched into the River Medway. The Esplanade runs from Corporation Street, past the castle and the cathedral, thought to be the location of Charles Dickens's great unfinished novel *The Mystery of Edwin Drood*, to meet Shorts Way at its western end.

After the outbreak of war many other firms, mainly in the wood-working and light engineering industries, were awarded Admiralty contracts to build Short-designed seaplanes. They included Fairey, Mann Egerton, Parnall, Phoenix Dynamo (later English Electric), Sage, Saunders, Supermarine (Pemberton Billing), Westland and J. Samuel White. All established their own design teams and some survived into the second half of the century.

During the war Shorts were contracted to build two rigid airships for the Admiralty. The deal also included a £10,000 loan for the company to buy land on which to erect a 700 ft airship shed and associated buildings at Cardington, Bedfordshire. Cardington was later nationalised by the government under the Defence of the Realm Act and renamed the Royal Airship Works. Even though Shorts severed its connection with Cardington, the area continued to be known as Shortstown.

In 1913 Gordon Bell had become Shorts' first professional test pilot. He was succeeded the following year by Ronald Kemp, but such was the amount of work being generated that he was unable to handle the volume of flight testing and development alone so that by 1916 other pilots were employed on a freelance basis. One of them was John Lankester Parker, who in 1918 succeeded Kemp as chief test pilot, a post he was to occupy for the next twenty-seven years. Of all the prominent sites in Britain used by pioneer aviators, only Brooklands emerged as a major manufacturing centre. Around twenty individuals and companies had been building aircraft at the Surrey facility since 1908 but it was Sopwith, Martinsyde and Vickers which put it on the manufacturing map.

In October 1912 at the age of 24, T.O.M. Sopwith made the fateful decision to become an aircraft constructor. His flying school at Brooklands was gradually run down and mechanic Fred Sigrist concentrated on building machines designed by Sopwith. Harry Hawker was to be test and demonstration pilot. The foundations of one of Britain's greatest aeronautical concerns had been laid.

Sopwith had built aircraft in association with other constructors, particularly Howard Wright, but in November 1912 he made his first sale of an aircraft of totally original design to the Admiralty. The tractor biplane's delivery flight from Brooklands to Eastchurch turned out to be both hazardous and protracted. Hawker, accompanied by fellow Australian Harry Kauper, got lost in fog and had to land until it cleared. The remaining 25 miles of the flight was accomplished in 30 minutes the following day. A second machine was delivered later in the year.

With the proceeds of these sales, Sopwith was able to take possession of a disused skating rink near the station at Canbury Park Road, Kingston-on-Thames. This would be his production centre while Brooklands was retained for testing and experimental work. The new firm was registered as the Sopwith Aviation Company, which advertised itself as prepared to undertake 'aeroplane construction in any branch'.

Collaboration with the S.E. Saunders boatyard of East Cowes on the Isle of Wight produced the Bat Boat of 1913. A flying boat with a laminated hull, it could operate on sea or land. The Admiralty, meanwhile, became interested in an improved version of its first Sopwith aircraft. This was the Three-Seat Tractor Biplane, also known as the 80 hp Biplane, the D1, or just the Tractor Biplane.

The aircraft was flown on 7 February 1913 before being displayed at the International Aero Show at Olympia the following month. It had two-bay wings, with lateral control by wing warping and power provided by an 80 hp Gnome Lambda rotary engine. It had two cockpits, the pilot sitting aft with the passengers sitting side by side in a separate one ahead. Three transparent celluloid windows were placed in each side of the fuselage to give good downward vision.

A second aircraft was retained by Sopwith as a demonstrator. Between June and July 1913 it set a number of British altitude records. A further two examples were built for the RNAS, being delivered in August and September 1913, with the original hybrid rebuilt to a similar standard. Following tests of a Tractor Biplane fitted with ailerons instead of wing warping for lateral control, a further nine examples were ordered for the RFC in September 1913.

But it was the Tabloid which really put Sopwith on the map. The original machine was first flown by Harry Hawker on 27 November 1913. It was a neat and compact two-seater single-bay biplane with side-by-side seating, which was unusual at the time. The equal-span wings were slightly staggered and warping was used for lateral control. The rectangular-section fuselage was a conventional wire-braced wooden structure with the forward section covered in aluminium and the remainder, aft of the cockpit, covered in fabric. The control surfaces were of fabric-covered steel tubing and the undercarriage featured a pair of forward-projecting skids ahead of the wheels. The most distinctive feature, however, was the metal cowling which almost entirely enclosed the engine, cooling air being admitted through two small slots at the front.

With its 80 hp Gnome Lambda rotary engine, the aircraft reached 92 mph in trials at Farnborough. It took just a minute to reach 1,200 ft while carrying a passenger and had enough fuel for 2.5 flying hours. A production order from the War Office was placed early in 1914 and forty were built to this specification.

It was also clear that the aircraft's speed made it an obvious candidate for the Schneider Trophy competition for waterborne aircraft. Accordingly a floatplane adaptation was prepared, to be powered by a 100 hp Gnome Monosoupape rotary. The aircraft was initially fitted with a single central float but during its early taxying trials with Howard Pixton at the controls the aircraft turned over as soon as the engine was run up. It remained in the water for some hours before it could be retrieved. Because there was no time to make a new set of floats, the existing one was simply sawn in half down the middle and converted into a pair. After a satisfactory test flight on 7 April the aircraft was shipped to Monaco where the competition was to take place.

Pixton won the contest easily. He completed his first circuit in around two-thirds of the time taken by the faster of the aircraft which had taken off before him. In fact, the Tabloid's superiority was so obvious that some of the later competitors did not even bother to take off. After completing the required twenty-eight circuits at an average speed of 86.75 mph, Pixton completed two more laps at a speed of 92 mph, setting a new world record for seaplanes in the process.

The first order, for twelve replicas of the Schneider aircraft, differing in only minor detail, was placed in November 1914. Later production aircraft were fitted with ailerons in place of wing-warping, had an enlarged fin and a Lewis machine gun firing upwards through an opening in the wing centre-section. Single-seat variants went into production in 1914 and thirty-six eventually entered service with the RFC and RNAS. Deployed to France on the outbreak of war, Tabloids were used as fast scouts. In all 160 were built. No original Tabloids or Schneiders survive today but full-size replicas of each are displayed at the RAF Museum at Hendon and the Brooklands Museum.

Later came the One and a Half Strutter, the Pup and the immortal Camel. During the war Sopwith built more than 16,000 aircraft with many more turned out by sub-contractors like Fairey and William Beardmore. At the beginning of the conflict the company employed 200 people; by the time of the Armistice this had increased to 6,000. After the war the company was dissolved and reformed as Hawker Aircraft to avoid a crippling tax liability – and win further fame.

The second of the successful Brooklands manufacturers was Martinsyde, which was formed in 1908 as a partnership between H.P. Martin and George Handasyde. This partnership was originally known as Martin & Handasyde. Their first monoplane was built at Hendon in 1908/09 and succeeded in lifting off the ground before being wrecked in a gale. A move to Brooklands followed together with a succession of mostly monoplane designs. It was, however, a biplane, the S1 of 1914, that transformed the operation into an established aircraft manufacturer.

In 1915 the company became Martinsyde Ltd. During the First World War it was Britain's third largest aircraft manufacturer with flight sheds at Brooklands and a large factory at nearby Woking. Martinsyde built sixty S1s which saw about six months' operational use by the RFC on the Western Front before being relegated to the training role. Other successful designs included the Elephant and the Buzzard. After the war Martinsyde built an aircraft specifically designed to win the *Daily Mail* £10,000 prize for the first non-stop Atlantic crossing. Known as the *Raymor*, a contraction of the surnames of its crew Raynham and Morgan, it was damaged on its first attempt to take off from St John's, Newfoundland, and wrecked on its second. In the post-war slump the company turned to motor cycle manufacture but this could not save it.

The third of the Brooklands triumvirate – and as it turned out the longest surviving – was Vickers. It was just after the start of the twentieth century that the major armaments firm of Vickers, Sons and Maxim became interested in the military potential of aircraft. In 1908 Vickers was contracted by the Admiralty to build a dirigible, called somewhat whimsically the *Mayfly*. It was not a success, suffering structural failure during its trials.

Undaunted by this failure, Vickers established an aviation department in 1911 to design and build aeroplanes and also established a flying school at Brooklands. Part of the Vickers works at Erith, Kent, was allocated to aircraft construction and a drawing office was established at Vickers House, Broadway, Westminster.

The company acquired a licence to build French-designed R E P aeroplanes and engines and its first machine was essentially a development of the R E P monoplane schemed by Archibald R. Low. The design team also included George Challenger and also Leslie McDonald, a pilot recruited from British and Colonial. They were later joined by Howard Flanders who had been constructing machines of his own design at Brooklands.

This team proved prolific in terms of its ability to produce new designs, including a pusher biplane with Lewis gun mounted in the nose. This led to the FB5 Gunbus, the first aircraft purpose-built for air-to-air combat to see service. But the most noteworthy Vickers design of the period was the Vimy twin-engined bomber. Years later Captain Peter Acland, general manager of Vickers' aviation department, would recall: 'The designing, building and flying of the machine in a period of four months was, to my mind, one of the highest spots of cooperative effort I have come across in many years in the industry.'

The Vimy was too late for the war, but the type was to win undying fame in June 1919 as the first aeroplane to cross the Atlantic non-stop flown by Sir John Alcock and Sir Arthur Whitten Brown. In fact, the three aircraft whose crews actually attempted the crossing all originated from Brooklands. Had the Vimy not buried its nose in an Irish bog, it is likely that it would have ended its historic journey in triumph at Brooklands.

Sopwith's first customer aircraft had left the site in October 1912, while the last Vickers VC10 four-jet airliner was flown out of Brooklands on 16 February 1970. The final complete aircraft to be built there was a BAC One-Eleven airliner which departed on 19 December 1979, bringing to an end more than sixty years of aircraft manufacture. During that time Brooklands had turned out over 18,500 aircraft of 258 types by more than 20 different manufacturers. During the First World War over 4,300 aircraft were assembled on the site with many more flight tested there. Components for Concorde, Hawk trainers and Airbus continued to be built at Brooklands until April 1979.

Even today Brooklands is probably better known as a motor racing track, yet the site's greatest significance to Britain was as one of its key aircraft manufacturing centres. Arguably, aviation was the cuckoo in the Brooklands nest; motor racing stopped there in 1939 and never resumed, while aircraft manufacture, which was already expanding, continued for another forty years.

It was barely a decade before the Armistice that Britain had stumbled into the era of powered flight. Those magnificent, heroic men – and indeed, women – who had risked their lives in their determination to fly had laid the foundations of a great industry. And they had done so at airfields around the country many of which are still recognised as the pioneering places of British aviation.

YORKSHIRE v LANCASHIRE

It was inevitable that a contest involving participants from Yorkshire and Lancashire would be seen as a rerun of the Wars of the Roses but the idea that a match between aircraft manufactured in the two counties would become an annual event was stifled by the outbreak of a real war.

In October 1913 two of Britain's fledgling aircraft manufacturers, A.V. Roe and Co of Manchester and the Blackburn Aeroplane Company of Leeds were challenged by the *Yorkshire Evening News* to a 100-mile race starting and finishing at the Yorkshire Aerodrome at Moortown, Leeds. Check points would be at York, Doncaster, Sheffield and Barnsley.

Avro entered its prototype 504 which, a few weeks earlier, had taken fourth place in the Aerial Derby, a 95-mile race around London. The aircraft, powered by an 80 hp Gnome rotary engine, was to be handled by Avro's test pilot, 20-year-old Fred Raynham. Despite his youth Raynham had received the Royal Aero Club's pilot certificate No 85 in May 1911. His passenger in the 504, seated ahead of the pilot, would be Humphrey Verdon Roe, co-founder of A.V. Roe & Co, with his younger brother, Alliott.

In the white (rose) corner was the Type I monoplane designed by Robert Blackburn and powered by an 80 hp Gnome. Harold Blackburn (no relation) was to be its pilot with Dr Malcolm Christie, the aircraft's owner, as his passenger also sitting in the front seat.

A crowd variously estimated at 20,000 and 60,000 gathered to watch the start of the race. Although Raynham had a small advantage at York, he was three seconds down on Blackburn at Doncaster. The weather was bad with mist making it difficult for the participants to sight landmarks and keep to the course. 'Blackburn scored over his opponent as he was more familiar with the country,' *Flight* reported.

By the time Raynham reached Sheffield the mist was so bad that he could not locate the check point and had to make several descents before he was able to do so. He had the same trouble at Barnsley where he flew past the control and arrived instead at Dewsbury some miles away. 'As it was then hopeless to try and put matters right,' *Flight* reported, 'he flew direct to Leeds and arrived some time before Blackburn.'

So it was that the Yorkshire crew received the handsome cup donated by the *Yorkshire Evening News*. They had taken 5hr 48min to complete the course. Plans to make the race an annual event were frustrated by the outbreak of the First World War in August 1914.

Bibliography

Books

Andrews, C F and Morgan E B, *Vickers Aircraft Since 1908*, Putnam, London 1969/1988.

Barnes, C H, *Shorts Aircraft since 1900*, Putnam, London 1967.

Lord Brabazon of Tara, *The Brabazon Story*, William Heineman, London, 1956.

Brett, R Dallas, *History of British Aviation 1908-1914* Volume I, The Aviation Book Club, London.

Brett, R Dallas, *History of British Aviation 1908-1914* Volume II, The Aviation Book Club, London.

Brown, Timothy C, *Flying with the Larks, The Early Aviation Pioneers of Lark Hill*, The History Press, Stroud, 2013.

Croydon, Air Commodore Bill, *Early Birds, A short history of how flight came to Sheppey*, Sheppey Heritage Trust.

Donne, Michael, *Flying into the Future, A pictorial history of Shorts*, Good Books, Wiltshire, 1993.

Gardner, Charles (ed), *Fifty Years of Brooklands*, Heinemann, London, 1956.

Gibbs-Smith, Charles, *Early Flying Machines, 1799-1909*.

Handley Page Limited, *Forty Years on, 1909-1949*, Fonthill Media, 2012.

Hare, Paul R, *Aeroplanes of the Royal Aircraft Factory*, The Crowood Press, Marlborough, 1999.

Hughes, David T, *Flying Past, A history of Sheppey aviation*, The History Press, Stroud, 2009.

Jackson, A J, *Avro Aircraft since 1908*, Putnam, London, 1965.

Jarrett, Philip, *Trials, Troubles and Triplanes, Alliott Verdon Roe's Fight to Fly*, Ad Hoc Publications, Suffolk, 2007.

Loobey, Patrick, *Flights of Fancy, Early aviation in Battersea and Wandsworth*, Wandsworth Borough Council, 1981.

Mackersey, Ian, *The Wright Brothers, the Remarkable Story of the Aviation Pioneers who Changed the World*, Little, Brown, London 2003.

Oliver, David, *Hendon Aerodrome – A History*, Airlife, Shrewsbury, 1994.

Pembery, Malcolm, *Colonel Templer and the Birth of Aviation at Farnborough*, the Royal Aeronautical Society, 2000 and 2007.

Priddle, Rod, *Wings over Wiltshire, An Aeronautical History of Wiltshire*, ALD Design and Print, Sheffield, 2003.

Reese, Peter, *The Flying Cowboy, Samuel Cody, Britain's First Airman*, The History Press, Stroud, 2006.

Reese, Peter, *The Men who Gave us Wings, Britain and the Aeroplane 1796-1914*, Pen & Sword, Barnsley 2014.

Smith, Graham, *Taking to the Skies, The Story of British Aviation 1903-1939*, Countryside Books, Newbury, 2003.

Venables, David, *Brooklands, The Official Centenary History*, Haynes Publishing, 2007.

Walker, Elizabeth M, *Three Brilliant Brothers*, self-published, 2017.

Walker, Elizabeth M, *A 'Short' Story, The lives and works of the Short Brothers*, self-published, 2018.

Periodicals
Flight
Aeroplane

Websites
www.flightglobal.com
www.rafmuseum.org.uk
www.eastchurchaviationmuseum.org.uk
www.brooklandsmuseum.com

Index